SOCIAL CHANGE AND HISTORY

Social Change and History

Aspects of the Western Theory of Development

•••

ROBERT A. NISBET

OXFORD UNIVERSITY PRESS

LONDON   OXFORD   NEW YORK

OXFORD UNIVERSITY PRESS
Oxford   London   Glasgow   New York
Toronto   Melbourne   Wellington   Cape Town
Ibadan   Nairobi   Dar es Salaam   Lusaka   Addis Ababa
Kuala Lumpur   Singapore   Jakarta   Hong Kong   Tokyo
Delhi   Bombay   Calcutta   Madras   Karachi

Printed in the United States of America

To Frederick J. Teggart, 1870–1946,
whose book it is

PREFACE

The primary purpose of this book is to set forth the essential sources and contexts of the Western idea of social development. The book is in large part historical, in smaller part analytical and critical. In the rather long final chapter I explore some of the difficulties which seem to me to arise in the study of social change when this study is made subject to the fundamental concepts of developmentalism. But although this final chapter is closely related to the chapters which precede, it must nonetheless be kept distinct from the central and guiding aim of the book, which is well within the realm of the history of ideas. Developmentalism is one of the oldest and most powerful of all Western ideas; very little in the Western study of social change, from the early Greeks down to our own day, falls outside the perspective of developmentalism; this perspective, together with its constitutive assumptions and its consequences to the study of society, is the essential subject of this book.

So far as I am aware, nothing novel in the way of argument exists in any of the book's individual sections, save possibly in the final chapter. I have tried scrupulously to avoid such novelty, for I have wanted the substance of each of these sections to correspond as closely as possible with the accepted understandings of modern scholarship. Wherever possible, therefore, I have relied heavily on the testimony of those for whom the subject matter of each of these sections has been the substance of their own more specialized investigations. Even so, I have not hesitated to stay as closely as possible to my own reading of the primary works as these are to be found in the original or in standard translation.

Whatever novelty or originality may lie in the book comes from my having brought into single perspective ideas and themes which are ordinarily considered in separation from one another. We do not lack for excellent treatments of the Greek idea of *physis*, of the classical doctrine of cycles, of the Augustinian epic, the idea of progress, the theory of natural history, the theory of social evolution, the Comparative Method, and the whole theory of functionalism in the contemporary social sciences. Rarely, however, are even two or three of these brought together in common focus. Nowhere to my knowledge are all of them united within a single frame of reference that is formed by their common assumptions in the history of Western social thought. This I have tried to do.

Generally, my obligations to the scholarship of others are sufficiently acknowledged, I think, in the Notes. There is, however, one signal exception to this. It is very difficult for me to imagine much of this book's content apart from the remarkable work of the late Frederick J. Teggart, for many years Professor of Social Institutions at the University of California, Berkeley. Occasionally I make reference to one or other of his books, chiefly his *Theory of History*, one of the profoundest and most original works of this century, but such references can barely even suggest the full measure of his influence on what is contained in this volume. Those who also know the work of this man will know the extent of my indebtedness to him. All others I refer to the dedicatory words.

I wish to thank the University of California, Riverside, for financial support of much of the work involved in preparation of the manuscript.

R. A. N.

Riverside, California
October 1968

CONTENTS

SOCIAL CHANGE AND HISTORY

INTRODUCTION

1. HISTORY AND METAPHOR

No one has ever seen a civilization die, and it is unimaginable, short of cosmic disaster or thermonuclear holocaust, that anyone ever will. Nor has anyone ever seen a civilization—or culture or institution—in literal process of decay and degeneration, though there is a rich profusion of these words and their synonyms in Western thought from Hesiod to Spengler. Nor, finally, has anyone ever seen—actually, empirically seen, as we see these things in the world of plants and animals—growth and development in civilizations and societies and cultures, with all that is clearly implied by these words: change proceeding gradually, cumulatively, and irreversibly, through a kind of unfolding of internal potentiality, the whole moving toward some end that is presumably contained in the process from the start. We see none of these in culture: death, degeneration, development, birth.

All that we see are the mingled facts of persistence and change. We see migrations and wars, dynasties toppled, governments overthrown, economic systems made affluent or poor; revolutions in power, privilege and wealth. We see human beings born, mating, child-rearing, working, worshipping, playing, educating, writing, philosophizing, governing. We see generation succeeding generation, each new one accepting, modifying, rejecting in different proportions the works of preceding generations. We see, depending upon our moral or esthetic disposition, good and evil, greatness and meanness, tragedy, comedy, and bathos, nobility and baseness, success and failure. We see men's creative energies turned now to peace, now to war, now to business and trade, now to arts and letters, now to theology and philosophy, now to science and technology. We see all of this and much more.

But we do not see "death," "decadence," "degeneration," or "sickness." We do not see "genesis," "growth," "unfolding," or "development." Not in cultures and societies. All of these words

3

have immediate and unchallengeable relevance to the organic world, to the life-cycles of plants and organisms. There they are literal and empirical in meaning. But applied to social and cultural phenomena these words are not literal. They are metaphoric.

What is a metaphor? Much more than a simple grammatical construction or figure of speech. Metaphor is a way of knowing— one of the oldest, most deeply embedded, even indispensable ways of knowing in the history of human consciousness. It is, at its simplest, a way of proceeding from the known to the unknown. It is a way of cognition in which the identifying qualities of one thing are transferred in an instantaneous, almost unconscious, flash of insight to some other thing that is, by remoteness or complexity, unknown to us. The test of essential metaphor, Philip Wheelwright has written, "is not any rule of grammatical form, but rather the quality of semantic transformation that is brought about." Wallace Stevens writes of "the symbolic language of metamorphosis," thus reminding us that the relation between metaphor and metamorphosis is, in the world of knowledge and meaning, more than merely etymological.[1]

"Metaphor," writes Sir Herbert Read, "is the synthesis of several complex units into one commanding image; it is the expression of a complex idea, not by analysis, nor by direct statement, but by sudden perception of an objective relation." [2] Metaphoric knowledge, in short, is the very opposite of the type of knowledge that comes to us through mere additive experience, through patient dissection of observations, through elaboration, deductive or inductive, of meanings already contained in a proposition, through either analysis or synthesis as these terms are best known. Metaphor is none of these. Metaphor is our means of effecting instantaneous fusion of two separated realms of experience into one illuminating, iconic, encapsulating image.

Language without metaphor is inconceivable. How better to describe one type of anger than as "hot," another as "cold," a passion as "burning," a silence as "heavy," a resolve as "iron," a mood as "cloudy"? Is not each of these expressive of a reality that all of us have experienced and know to be as valid as anything that might be stated in the symbols of analytical psychology? Strip from language its metaphors and we should be removing a great deal of what we "know." Much of what Michael Polanyi has called, in his recent volume, "tacit knowledge" is expressible—insofar as it is expressible at all—in metaphor.[3]

Metaphor is not only the consequence of experience, it is often the prerequisite. Thus to refer to God as a "mighty fortress" may be, as it doubtless was to Luther, a summarization of past, felt experience. But to countless others since, the words "a mighty fortress is our God" have served to create the experience, to add dimensions of religious feeling not previously known. Metaphor can be, in short, not merely anterior to personal experience but the cause of it.

It is easy to dismiss metaphor as "unscientific" or "nonrational," a mere substitute for the hard analysis that rigorous thought requires. Metaphor, we say, belongs to poetry, to religion, and to other more or less "enchanted" areas of thought. So it does. But metaphor also belongs to philosophy and even to science. It is clear from many studies of the cognitive process generally, and particularly of creative thought, that the act of thought in its more intense phases is often inseparable from metaphor—from that intuitive, iconic, encapsulating grasp of a new entity or process in the ways that Sir Herbert Read described above.

Imagination could hardly do without metaphor, for imagination is, literally, the moving around in one's mind of images, and such images tend commonly to be metaphoric. Creative minds, as we know, are rich in images and metaphors, and this is true in science and art alike. The difference between scientist and artist has little to do with the ways of creative imagination; everything to do with the manner of demonstration and verification of what has been seen or imagined.

Complex philosophic systems can proceed from premises that are either directly metaphoric or metaphoric in their origin. Such, obviously, is the case with Freudianism. Divest classical psychoanalytic theory of its metaphors—Oedipus complex, etc.—and there would not be a great deal of substance left. Much the same is true of the Marxian view of history with its envisagement of social orders forming embryonically in the wombs of preceding orders, with each transition akin to birth, and requiring the assistance of the midwife, revolution.

Metaphor allies itself well with proposals for social action. Most of the millennialist visions of revolution that we find in the Western tradition spring from diagnoses of society that are at bottom metaphoric. If one believes that the society around him is a "sick" society, dying of poisons generated in its own being, or ridden with "cancers," "tumors," "gangrenous" substances (I am drawing from a literature that is as recent as it is old), what else but total action can remove the alien bodies or poisons? The metaphors of sickness and health, applied to society, are doubtless responsible for as much redemptive action as the labels of evil and good.

Metaphors can be lasting as well as powerful. Generations, even centuries and millennia, may be required to liberate the mind from ways of thinking which began in analogy and metaphor. What we think of as revolutions in thought are quite often no more than the mutational replacement, at certain critical points in history, of one foundation-metaphor for another in man's contemplation of universe, society, and self. Metaphoric likening of the universe to an organism in its structure will yield one set of derivations; derivations which become propositions in complex systems of philosophy. But when, as happened in the seventeenth century, the universe is likened instead to a machine, not merely physical science but whole areas of moral philosophy and human psychology are affected.

To repeat, metaphor is indispensable—indispensable in language, poetry, philosophy, and even science. But, clearly, metaphor is also dangerous. It is dangerous when from the initial encapsulating and iconic vision of something distant, or unknowable in standard terms of analysis, there begin to be drawn corollaries of ever more literal and empirical signification. To look at the whole universe and say it is like a machine or organism is one thing: forgivable in proper time and place. But to seek to build rigorous propositions of scientific analysis upon either metaphor, mistaking attributes of analogy for attributes of reality, can be, as the history of science teaches us, profoundly limiting and distorting. And this, all too often in the social sciences, is the fate of some of the more powerful metaphors in human consciousness. Nowhere is this more evident than in the study of social change.

2. THE METAPHOR OF GROWTH

Of all metaphors in Western thought on mankind and culture, the oldest, most powerful and encompassing is the metaphor of growth. When we say that a culture or institution or nation "grows" or "develops," we have reference to change in time, but to change of a rather special and distinctive type. We are not referring to random and adventitious changes, to changes induced by some external deity or other being. We are referring to change that is intrinsic to the entity, to change that is held to be as much a part of the entity's nature as any purely structural element. Such change may require activation and nourishment from external agencies, just as does the growth in a plant or organism. But what is fundamental and guiding is nonetheless drawn from within the institution or culture.

When we speak of growth we have reference to certain other attributes as well: to directionality; by which we mean that growth, unlike random changes, has trend or longitudinal shape; it moves, we say, from one point in time to another. Further, in such directional movement it is cumulative; what is to be seen at any given moment is the cumulative result of all that has gone before in its life. Developmental change is something we also like to think of as irreversible, just as is growth in the biological being. Development has stages, and these have genetic as well as merely sequential relation to one another. Finally, growth or development has purpose. We may argue in the social world about just what the precise purpose is of a given development. The Marxist may see the purpose of human development as the final achievement of the classless society, with everything that has gone before to be seen as developmental, cumulative preparation. The Christian, following St. Augustine, may see the purpose of the human drama in trans-historical terms. No doubt there are as many purposes as there are religious, moral, and social philosophies. But the belief that there *is* a purpose in cultural, political, economic, or social development is one more legacy of the metaphor of growth.

Closely related to the metaphor of growth, supporting it indeed, is an analogy: the analogy of cultural and social change to the growth manifested in the organism. This analogy can be seen as part of that wider one in which society as a whole, its structure and processes, is declared to be organismic. But my concern here is solely with the analogy of the life-cycle, one of the oldest analogies in the history of human thought. In its most succinct form the analogy tells us, and has told us for at least twenty-five hundred years in Western history, that civilization (or mankind or society or the nation, as the case may be) "passes through the age-phases of the individual man. It has its childhood, youth, manhood, and old age."

The quoted words happened to be from Oswald Spengler's *The Decline of the West.* But without leaving the confines of a rather limited personal library, I can find the identical analogy in a long succession of philosophers, historians, and social scientists in the West: among them Heraclitus, Aristotle, Polybius, Lucretius, Seneca, Florus, St. Cyprian, St. Augustine, Francis Bacon, Pascal, Fontenelle, Turgot, Hume, Condorcet, Hegel, Comte, Spencer, and, in our own day giving company to Spengler and his theory of cycles, such otherwise dissimilar figures as Toynbee, Berdyaev, Reinhold Niebuhr, Sorokin, and the late Robert H. Lowie. In all of these writers, representing a span of at least two and a half millennia, it is possible to find the express analogy of human society, or one or other of its institutions, to the phases of growth so plainly to be seen in the plant or organism.

If the analogy were no more than the figure of speech it so plainly is, if it were simply a rhetorical device, a play on words to enliven discourse, we could leave it at that. It would surely be worth no more than a footnote, an antiquarian essay at best. After all, philosophers and historians, like the rest of us, are entitled to images and metaphors.

It is, however, the principal argument of this book that the metaphor of growth and the analogy I have just cited are much more than adornments of thought and language. They are, as the following chapters will make evident, quite inseparable from some of the profoundest currents in Western thought on society and change. They were inseparable in ancient Greek thought and in the thought of the centuries which followed the Greeks; and they remain closely involved in premises and preconceptions regarding the nature of change which we find in contemporary social theory.

One may liken the metaphor of growth to the axiom in a geometrical demonstration, which we may conceive for our purposes as strung out over some twenty-five hundred years. In the beginning was the axiom: society's likeness, its sameness indeed, to the organism and its cycle of growth. To the Greeks and Romans there was nothing metaphoric about the "axiom"; it was literal. That society and each of its institutions possessed organismic nature, participated in the entire realm of organismic reality, was, of course, fundamental in Greek and, then, Roman thought.

From this fundamental acceptance, this "axiom," proceeded corollaries and derivations. Some of them were drawn by the Greeks themselves; by no one more systematically and enthusiastically than by Aristotle, although the sources of Aristotle's influential philosophy of growth are plain in such pre-Socratics as Heraclitus. Among the derivations drawn very early from the analogy of society to the life-cycle of the organism was that most powerful of Greek scientific concepts: *physis*. *Physis* was defined by the Greeks as "way of growth," mistranslated by the Romans as "nature," and destined to become perhaps the single most influential of all the derivations of the analogy.

But there were others: the whole cyclical conception of cosmic and social development, the framework of investigation of society and its changes, a framework built around such crucial concepts as origins, stages of growth, immanent cause, purpose, and the like.

Above all, there was the whole characteristically Greek and Roman
conviction that reality, whether social, physical, or biological was
to be conceived in terms of incessant, ongoing change; change that
was deemed to be as natural a part of society as any element of
structure.

These were some of the derivations from the analogy, corollaries
to an axiom. In time there were others. The rise of Christianity
within the Roman Empire did not dislodge the centrality of the
metaphor of growth; it merely brought it within the whole realm
of the sacred, of God's will deemed to have unfolded itself from
the time of the Creation—Creation itself, as St. Augustine insisted, only the first manifestation of a process that was at first
latent and that required several millennia to become fully evident.
Between the Christian theory of sacred development and the
Greek metaphor of growth, albeit a modified metaphor, there is
close and profound relation.

Nor did the metaphor and the analogy disappear from thought
with the onset of the Renaissance, the Age of Reason, the Enlightenment, or the nineteenth century, when the foundations of
the modern social sciences were formed. Nor are they absent from
the thought of our own day and policies and actions based on
thought. There is as close a relation between the analogy, although
once again an analogy modified, and the modern idea of progress
as between the analogy and the earlier theories of the cycle and
the Christian epic. Likewise is there a vital relation between the
analogy and those theories of the eighteenth and nineteenth centuries which are so closely related to the idea of progress: the theory of social evolution, the theory of natural history, and the whole
conception of change that we term developmental or, more recently, functionalist.

It can hardly be claimed that the analogy holds the same direct
relation to contemporary, even eighteenth and nineteenth century,
thought that it held to Greek and Roman. Who today believes,
really believes, that society or one of its institutions is an organism,
actually obeys the principle of the life-cycle of growth? Probably
no one. It is not certain how many believed it in the two centuries

before our own, although Herbert Spencer is far from being alone in his belief that the principle of differentiation of growth that is the essence of the organism is also the essence of social change. It does not really matter. For one of the most frequent of all phenomena in the history of ideas is this one: that long after a principle or "axiom" has been forgotten, or ignored, or transmuted into metaphor alone, principles that are themselves rigorously drawn from the initial principle remain intact, remain relevant, and are the sources of countless hypotheses in the study of human experience.

True, the validity of a principle is not dependent, we are fond of saying, upon the specific origin of the principle. That the theory of development arose in the first instance from what is today metaphor alone does not offset its possibility of being a correct body of theory for the understanding of social change. I concede readily that such does not offset the *possibility*. But as the final chapter will, I hope, make clear, it is very hard to concede the *probability*.

PART I

CIVILIZATION AS GROWTH IN TIME:

THE BIOGRAPHY OF A METAPHOR

ONE

THE GREEKS

For that which encompasses us will be enough
for the student of how things grow; seeing it
is reasonable and intelligent.

Heraclitus

It follows that the coming-to-be of anything,
if it is absolutely necessary, must be cyclical—
i.e., must return upon itself.

Aristotle

For time changes the nature of the whole world
and all things must pass on from one condition
to another, and nothing continues like to itself;
all things quit their bounds; all things nature
changes and compels to alter.

Lucretius

Whether the world is a soul, or a body under
government of nature, like trees and crops, it
embraces in its constitution all that it is destined
to experience actively or passively from its
beginning right on to its end; it resembles a
human being, all whose capacities are wrapped
up in the embryo before birth. Ere the child
has seen light, the principle of beard and grey
hairs is innate.

Seneca

1. BEING AS BECOMING

"What sort of being must being be when being becomes?" This
question, which we are told was an obsessive one to much Greek
philosophy and science, is at the very heart of what concerns us in

this book: ideas of growth and development applied to human society and institutions.

The Greeks, above any people known to us in antiquity, were fascinated by change, its sources, properties, directions, and its relation to the principles of organic growth. Aristotle built an entire system of philosophy around the principle of growth. So, long before him, were the early physical philosophers of Miletus equally preoccupied by change. "All is change." This is a lasting theme in Greek thought from beginning to end, and it transferred itself to Rome and then to all subsequent Western intellectual inquiry. True, there were Greeks, as there have been individuals in all ages, our own included, who turned their backs on change, so to speak, and who in the interests of seeking refuge in the abiding and the permanent, declared change to be mere appearance, not reality. From early to late in Greek thought this theme may be found; and, as I say, so may it be found in our own day. But to conclude, as some have, that Greeks were fearful of change, blind to change, ignorant of growth and development in time, is one of the rankest calumnies ever hurled at a civilized people. The Greeks not only knew, accepted, and even liked change, they were the first in history, so far as we know, to make a science of the study of change. When the first Greek declared that change is a part of the nature of each living thing and that it has its own laws of cause, mechanism, and purpose, he began, in an almost literal sense, a scientific pursuit that is one of the principal glories of Western intellectual history.

Change, the Greeks were fascinated by; growth, they virtually adored. From the model of growth in the organic world around them they drew some of the deepest and most far-reaching ideas in Western philosophy. High among these is the idea of *physis*; I shall come back to this in a moment. Suffice it to say here that this word—meaning quite literally *growth*—signifies the key concept in all of Greek science. From it the Romans, and then the Latinized West, derived their equally crucial concept of *nature*. We shall have to look most carefully at this word and its meanings.

It is hardly strange that the Greeks should have become early fascinated by growth and its myriad manifestations of genesis and decay. As John Linton Myres has emphasized, in his vastly illuminating essay "The Background of Greek Science," [1] behind all the physical and organic theories that abounded in Greece from early times lay direct exposure to a kind of natural theater of geographical, biological, and vegetative contrasts perhaps more vivid than anywhere else in the ancient world. As Myres notes, there were in this part of the world the evocative contrasts of *wet* and *dry*, *hot* and *cold*, *light* and *darkness*, *hard* and *soft*, *sweet* and *bitter*, contrasts all of which, as we know, loom large in Greek myth, literature, and also science.

But rising above any of these contrasts in importance is that between *growth* and *decay* which is to be seen so strikingly in a type of climate in which the seasonal cycle of plant life is made brief by the concentration of rains in one part of the year and in which aridity and drought are only too well known. We can scarcely even guess what subtle processes of thought were first involved, how long a time must have elapsed, before the Greeks and, before them, other peoples, many peoples, transferred what they saw in the plant and animal world to representations of reality. It must have been very early, once man discovered the uses of the seed-plant, once agriculture and human settlement began to replace what had previously been an existence of incessant wandering in search of food supply. Given the life-assuring dependence of the early human community upon the precious seed, it is easily imagined that the seed and plant would early become objects of man's wonder, adoration, and myth. For what more precious and also awe-inspiring elements were there in his environment?

Even today in our information-cluttered, science-saturated, and disenchanted age, it is hard to resist the mystery and drama of what is involved in the seed and its transfiguration in time.

There is first the seed itself: hard, dry, seemingly as lifeless as any pebble. We commit it to the earth, and thereby begin, with the aid of sun and moisture, a truly amazing succession of changes, changes that in their entirety compose what we call its life-cycle. For days no change is visible, then slowly and inexorably the process of genesis and growth becomes manifest—manifest in the tiny green shoots which for all their fragility push through the crust of the earth. There follow in fixed order the successive phases of the plant's growth, reaching at climax the full being of the plant, with its life-giving bounty for man. And then comes, with the same relentless regularity that had marked its growth, the decline, decay, gradual loss of life, culminating in the death of the plant, with only the sere and yellow to remind man of what had preceded it. But death is only an interlude, for now comes the most awe-inspiring of all the seed's transfigurations: the dead becomes, once again, the living. What had appeared to be death and termination turns out to have been but a cloak covering an inner reality that is eternal in its capacity for life. Once again genesis occurs, and once again the wonderful cycle of genesis and growth and decay and death.

In primitive consciousness nothing, of course, happens naturally. It was no doubt inevitable therefore that the arcane processes of genesis and decay would become the elements of religious myth. Nothing so vital to man as food supply could be taken for granted; it had to be made the object of thanksgiving, of supplication, and of rites designed to ward off malign interferences that, all too often, could result in drought or pestilence with famine as the consequence to man. There are, as Frazer has told us in opulent detail in his *The Golden Bough*, numerous gods and goddesses of the seed and the plant to be found throughout the earliest manifestations of man's religious belief. Where and when worship of the seed began in man's history we cannot even guess accurately. All we know is that by the time Western civilization makes its beginning in the areas surrounding the Mediterranean, rites and ceremonies pertaining to the seed are in full abundance. Osiris, Tammuz, Adonis, Dionysis are but a few of the better known of the sacred representations of a fascination with the seed that must have begun long before the times of even the earliest of the peoples who lie in our records.

So far as Western thought is concerned, the most famous and, by all odds, most influential of the seed-deities was Demeter. And the reason for this is the relation of Demeter to the Greeks, especially the Athenians whose own worship of her is almost indistinguishable from the beginnings of Greek sacred and, then, philosophical thought. Of all the gods and goddesses, Demeter was closest to Athenian hearts, and it is entirely fitting that the Athenians should have, at a fairly early time, annexed Eleusis, scene of the awesome Eleusinian mysteries, themselves the representation of Demeter's relation to mankind. The story of Demeter is told in the beautiful *Hymn to Demeter*, written in the seventh century B.C.[2]

Persephone, lovely daughter of Demeter, was one day playing in a field, alone, gathering crocuses, roses, lilies, and violets, when suddenly the earth burst open and Pluto, Lord of the Dead, ruler of the lower world, appeared, to carry off Persephone to live with him, as he intended, forever. Demeter, grief-stricken upon learning of her daughter's abduction, "caused a most dreadful and cruel year for mankind over the all-flourishing earth: the ground would not make the seed sprout, for rich-crowned Demeter kept it hid." This was, of course, the most terrible punishment that could have befallen man—as it is the most terrible that could befall the human race today—and every possible form of expiation was employed, we learn, to seek to undo the curse that Demeter had placed upon the world. But nothing availed. Such was Demeter's sorrow at the loss of her daughter that she would have allowed the whole human race to become destroyed by famine had not the mighty Zeus himself come at last to man's rescue. He commanded Pluto to return Persephone to her mother, the only way by which mankind could be redeemed from the curse placed by Demeter upon it. Pluto was forced to obey, but, loving Persephone deeply and irremediably, he released her to her mother only after he had given her a pomegranate seed to eat in which he had instilled an elixir, one that would, by the spell cast, force her to return to him for at least a third of each year.

Demeter, now appeased, hurried down from the peaks of Olympus to the plain of Rharus, "once a rich and fertile corn-land but now in nowise fruitful, for it lay hidden by design of trim-ankled

Demeter. But afterwards, as springtime, it was soon to be waving with long ears of corn, and its rich furrows to be loaded with grain in upon the ground, while others would already be bound in sheaves."

Then, having given back to the people the fertility of their ground with promise of life once again, Demeter showed them "the conduct of her rites and taught them all her mysteries, awful mysteries which no one may in any way transgress or pry into or utter, for deep awe of the gods checks the voice."

Thus the mythic origin of the cycle of seasons, of the commitment of mankind to a winter as well as a spring. Thus too the origin of the Greeks' worship of Demeter, whose symbolization of the life-giving plant and its arcane wonders of growth and decay, of death and rebirth, seemed to Athenians even more sacred than the fire-giving feat of Prometheus. Veneration of Demeter in Athens would continue well into the age of Greek rationalism.

If we look closely at the myth of Demeter, all of the essential elements of conceptualization of growth are to be seen immediately: fecundity and sterility, of course, but also cyclical development and recurrence, potentiality, immanence, and telic purpose. Above all, Sir James Frazer has written, "the thought of the seed buried in the earth in order to spring up to new and higher life readily suggested a comparison to human destiny." [3] If—as it was for long in Greece, and indeed ever after in one formulation or other, including Christianity—human destiny was conceived in religious terms of transmundane fulfillment, this was assuredly not its only possible formulation. A great deal of Greek rational philosophy and specifically Greek philosophy of civilization and its development was also suggested by the seed buried in the earth, unfolding, developing, and reaching its purpose before the cycle ended, with a new cycle then to commence.

"There is no sudden transition," Professor Guthrie reminds us, "from a mythical to a rational mentality. Mythical thinking does not die a sudden death, if indeed it ever dies at all. . . ." There are, surely, abundant evidences of this in our own time when, as Guthrie suggests, we find physicians solemnly referring to diseases as entities acting in certain predetermined ways—instead of to sick people—and the scholarly and lay alike treating "nature" as though they were deferring to an arbiter. In how many instances, asks Guthrie, have we not simply given up the language of mythology and overlaid its figures with the terminology of reason? "In Greece too one can find the concepts of myth dressed up in rational terms and living on in the guise of rational ideas." [4]

Born of religious awe and thanksgiving, the metaphor of the seed, of growth, of becoming acquired transcending importance very early in Greek philosophy and science. From representation of the divine and supernatural, the metaphor became the basis of an entire world view. On this point, which is so essential to our understanding of the Greek perspective of historical change, I cannot do better than quote the erudite Professor Sambursky:

> The Greek remained closely attached to the cosmos as the result of his viewing the cosmos as a living organism, a body that can be understood and comprehended in its entirety. The Greek had a profound awareness which was characterized by his biological approach to the world of matter. The teleological principle is essentially biological and anthropomorphic, so that the first basis for the conception of order in the universe was found in the system of the world of living things. [5]

This basis, considered as concept, was what the Greeks called *physis*, one of the profoundest and most far-reaching of all ideas in classical thought. Although the word and its meanings are well known to classicists and have been fully explored by such classical scholars as John Linton Myres and Francis Cornford, it remains a fact both extraordinary and lamentable that this word and its meanings are nearly absent from treatments of the social and political thought of the Greeks.

In part this neglect is the result of the translation—mistranslation—that the Romans gave to the word *physis*. They used the word *natura*, from which, of course, our own word *nature* derives. The Romans, however, generally meant by *natura* the physical world, including the physical aspects of man and society. Unwit-

tingly, they set in existence that fateful dualism between the physical, or between the "natural," and the social that has plagued
Western thought ever since. Of the number and diversity of
meanings Western thought has assigned to the word *nature* there
is no end.

But for the Greeks—and this is true as early as Heraclitus—
physis is at once *less* than and *more* than the meaning the Romans
gave to *natura*. *Physis* is more than that "inner essence" or "residual being" that is the most frequently encountered philosophical
meaning of *nature*; and it means much less than the sum total of
all that is physical in the universe, which is the more popular
meaning of the word nature. *Physis* was no doubt each of these in
some degree, but what the word meant most tellingly to the Greek
mind was *growth*. Originally, according to Cornford, *physis* meant
"to give birth to"; this of course at a time when "the mythical
imagery of sex—the marriage of Father Heaven and Mother
Earth and the genealogical scheme of cosmogony"—was still regnant in the Greek consciousness. *Physis* thus referred to the principle of generation or, more precisely, the generative power in the
world, which was conceived in the manner of sexual generation.
Hesiod's *Theogony* is rich in this kind of mythic sexuality.[6]

But by the time of the rise of Greek scientific rationalism *physis*
had taken on the related but more encompassing meaning of
growth: growth in general and in the sense of each element. "The
Greek word φύσιζ," writes Myres, "is simply the verbal substantive
from φύειν, 'to grow'; but it can share the causative meaning of
the aorist-stem φύσαι, 'to make grow.' In phrases from the Ionian
physicists, however, it seems always to be used intransitively; and
also to be used always in its strict verbal sense." [7] If the nature of a
thing, then, is how it grows, and if everything in the universe,
physical and social alike, has a *physis* of its own, a distinctive way
of growing, a life-cycle, then the task of the philosopher or scientist is clear. It is to find out what the *physis* is of each thing: to
learn its original condition, its successive stages of development,
the external factors such as water, light, and heat, that affect it,

and, finally, what its "end" is; that is, its final form, the form which may be said to be the ultimate "cause" of it all.

An interest in the *physis* of things—quite literally their "physiology"—is, then, the point of departure of Greek science and rational philosophy. Whether the object of inquiry was a tree, dog, man himself, the state, or the cosmos, the point was to discover through whatever means were indicated—analysis, comparison of types, deduction—its "way of growth," the way of being and becoming that was unique to it and its type.

Heraclitus—by all odds the most powerful scientific mind among philosophers of nature prior to Aristotle—wrote three treatises, we are told, on the *physis* of things: one about the universe, one on society, and one explaining God's relation to the world. One of the titles within the Heraclitean corpus is "A Judgment of Behavior." Another, and Professor Myres believes in all probability the title of the entire corpus, was "On the Way Things Grow." [8] Heraclitus's procedure, Myres writes, was to examine and distinguish things according to the way they grew or, as we should say, developed. To this end he gathered—even as Aristotle was to do later—as many specimens of things as he could, and he by no means limited himself to the merely physical and organic, for he was interested in a comparison of social customs and codes as well as the other.

Heraclitus, himself apparently something of a veteran in political matters, may well have been the first to give *physis* that sense of moral or ideal norm that this word, and the cognate word *nature*, was to carry throughout the subsequent history of Western thought—down indeed to this very moment. For in moral and psychological matters, and also political and economic, it is still held to be important to adapt circumstances so far as possible to what we conceive the "nature" of a thing to be: whether this thing is the human personality, the state, or the economy. Heraclitus compared "the way things grow" to a "moral police," implying strongly that if things do manage to deviate from what is the *physis* of each, retribution will be swift. We must observe, compare, and study what is around us and in us, Heraclitus adjured, "for that which encompasses us will be enough for the student of how things grow; seeing it is reasonable and intelligent." One could describe a very great deal of subsequent Greek, and then Western, philosophy as a series of footnotes on this pregnant observation. From the notion of *physis* as "moral police," as "the judgment which steers all things through all" (the words are from Heraclitus), it is an easy step to the notion of *physis* as the ideal-type on which to build schemes of social reform and even revolution—a matter to which I shall return later.

How deeply the concept *physis*, conceived as "growth," was embedded in Greek thought may be inferred from the fact that Aristotle, in his *Metaphysics*, where he is defining the key terms of philosophical and scientific discourse, puts the first three meanings of the concept in precisely the terms of growth or generation. The first meaning of *physis*, Aristotle writes, is "the generation of growing objects." The second meaning is closely related: it is "the first constituent from which a growing object grows." The third is "the source from which motion first begins in each natural thing, and which belongs to that thing *qua* that thing."

It is characteristic of Aristotle himself and of Greek thought generally that he should elaborate on the above by writing: "Objects are said to grow if they increase by means of something else by contact and also by growing together or by adhering together by nature (*physis*), as in the case of embryos. A growing together differs from contact; for in the latter case nothing else besides touching is necessary, but in things growing together there is something, one and the same in both, which, instead of touching, makes them grow together and is one with respect to continuity and quantity, but not with respect to quality." [9]

I can think of no better way of illustrating the doctrine of *physis* in Greek usage than by citing Aristotle's celebrated account of the nature—that is, the *physis*—of the state. We find this at the beginning of his *Politics*.[10] "He who considers things in their first growth and origin, whether the state or anything else, will obtain the clearest view of them." This is a declaration that would have found as much favor with Heraclitus earlier as it would have, two millennia later, with a Comte or Spencer. So would what follows.

Since the state must be comprehended in terms of its full growth, it is imperative that attention be given its origin in time. For, in the origin of a thing that grows are to be found all of the potentialities of the actual pattern of growth. Hence Aristotle's concern with the family. The family is, he reminds us, a self-sustaining form of social organization in which many peoples still live, without benefit of more elaborate institutions. But, despite its autonomy as a "species," the family is also the origin of the state. From it proceed over time two more complex forms of social organization: the village and the state itself.

The village, then, is the second stage of development. "The most natural form of the village appears to be that of a colony from the family, composed of children and grandchildren, who are said to be 'suckled with the same milk.'" Here Aristotle quotes from revered Homer the account of the Cyclopes: "Each one gives law to his children and wives." The village, plainly, represents change from the family that is not merely additive but cumulative; it is sequential in the biological sense of genetic sequence.

The state, which is the next stage of development, is an emergent of the village in precisely the same way that the village is an emergent of the family. When several villages are brought together into a single community, the state, properly so called, comes into existence. It is new, but only in the sense that the full-grown organism is new as we compare it with its preceding stages of growth. On this point Aristotle is emphatic. "If the earlier forms of society are natural, so is the state, for it is the end of them, and the completed nature is the end. *For what each thing is when fully developed, we call its nature, whether we are speaking of a man, a horse, or a family.*" (Italics added.)

And then we come to the famous sentence in which Aristotle deals with what in modern thought we call the "final cause." As I shall emphasize in a moment it is not "cause" at all, not in any sense that has usefulness, and it derives, like "nature," from Roman mistranslation. But first the passage itself. "Thus," Aristotle concludes, "the state is by nature clearly prior to the family and to the individual, since the whole is of necessity prior to the part. . . ." Aristotle says that the proof of this is that "the individual, when isolated, is not self-sufficing; and therefore he is like a part in relation to the whole." But in fact Aristotle's "proof" is more encompassing than this. Given the teleological developmentalism of his treatment, a treatment drawn plainly from the model of growth in plant or organism, the state is by nature prior to the family in the genetic sense that the seed, though first in manifest time, is itself a derivative of, a mere first stage in the growth of, the completed whole which is, so to speak, the *imago*.

Now, I would suggest that in the foregoing treatment of the state we have all the essential elements of the perspective of developmentalism, truly one of the master-ideas of the Western tradition. It is often said, however, that in Aristotle's view (and I shall quote here a representative example of the charge against Aristotle) "the process of development was regarded as strictly confined within the limits of the individual life. . . . In other words, the boundaries between *species* are fixed and ultimate; there can be no beginning in time of the existence of a new species, and therefore no origination of new species by development from other types. As Aristotle epigrammatically puts it, 'it takes a man to beget a man.' " [11]

That this statement reflects Aristotle's conception of organic evolution, of the problem of speciation in biology, is true enough, and it would be folly to pretend otherwise. But if we consider Aristotle as sociologist instead of biologist, it is also true that he had a very clear sense of what might be called social speciation: the emergence of one type of society from another. There is every reason for regarding family, village, and state as different social species. And, as we have seen, Aristotle has a very clear awareness of the genetic relation among these three types. We may conclude from this a point that I shall come back to again: that in Western thought a theory of social developmentalism long preceded biological evolution in having respectability in philosophy. (Though I am aware that during Aristotle's time, as well as before and after, there were other philosophers who had fewer doubts than did Aristotle about biological speciation as an ongoing process in nature. We need merely look at Aristotle's predecessor, Empedocles.)

Before leaving Aristotle, one other observation seems to me important. I said a moment ago that "final cause," as a phrase, does less than justice to what Aristotle meant by the relation of the completely developed state to the seed-origin, the family. The word "cause," with all its complex and forever ambiguous associations, is something we owe to Roman preoccupation with the legal actor and, then, to Christian preoccupation with divine volition. To Aristotle—and to the Greeks generally, I believe—something different is involved, something that is somewhat less "cause" in our inherited sense of the word than it is a point of reference in a self-contained, developmental process. This is clear if we look briefly at the so-called doctrine of four causes.

If we assume, as all Greeks did, that being is in fact *becoming*, then it is plain that the process of becoming may be considered from any and all of four points of view; four checkpoints, as it were. There is, first, the material—the raw, undeveloped substance of the entity undergoing the development—and this is best to be observed in the original condition, the seed. This, by now accustomed, usage we are prone to call the "material cause," though it is not, as I say, cause at all. Second, there is the form ("formal cause") or pattern of development revealed from beginning to end. And this is at bottom simply the life-cycle of the entity considered as a whole. There is, third, what is translated in Aristotle as the "efficient cause" or "motor cause," and here our attention is directed to the mechanism—conflict?, strife?, cooperation?, love?; the number of proffered mechanisms is great in Greek and all subsequent Western thought—by which the process of development is kept going. Such "causes" compare with the action of sun and water in the growth of the plant. Fourth, and perhaps most famous, is the "final cause." But this is no more a cause than any of the others. It is cause only in the distorted sense that in any being which is subject to true growth the final state is, so to speak, contained in the process of growth from the very beginning. When we plant a petunia seed we get invariably—*unless accident or chance has entered*, and this is a vital point in the theory of development —a full petunia; not a rose or daffodil. And so with the state. It is natural, Aristotle tells us in effect, that kinship organization will normally develop over long periods of time, given propitious circumstances, first into the village, then into the state—the latter being, in growth-terms, the *imago*. The so-called four causes of Aristotle are not, in sum, causes at all; they are points of reference in the understanding of the *physis* of anything. Admittedly, each of the four causes could be and was used—by Aristotle and by others—in a sense that did not directly apply to the process of growth and development. There are many discussions of the causes that make this fact plain. All that I am emphasizing here is simply that like so much in Aristotle's thought, the doctrine of the four causes was suggested to him in the first instance by a conception of reality in which development and becoming were prime attributes. We need but note in his *Metaphysics*, when he is defining "cause," the heavy reliance upon the concept of "generation." Generative power was, beyond any question, the principal referent in the Greek mind of the notion of cause—the generative power best illustrated in the act of reproduction. Between *physis* and "cause" there is, in Aristotle, a very close, even unbreakable, relation; and, as we observed above, one need but read the opening lines of Aristotle's treatment of *physis* in his *Metaphysics* to be reminded that for him, as for Heraclitus several centuries earlier, the model of growth and generation is foremost in his mind.

We can, I think, go farther with what has been said here about the "four causes." Far from being restricted to Aristotle in their significance, they may properly be regarded as categories of inquiry in Greek thought as a whole, physical and social. And, after that, of Roman thought. Nor would one wish to suggest that they have not played a strategic role in Western thought since the Greeks and Romans. I limit myself here for good reason to social thought alone. A very great deal of Western social thought can be arranged, its ideas and inquiries classified, in the categories of inquiry into society that are furnished by the so-called four causes:

the *origins* of things, the pattern or *form of the development* of things, the *motor cause* (internal or external) of this development, and, finally, the *purpose* or final cause of the whole process of development. From Heraclitus through Aristotle and then Lucretius, from Augustine down to Comte, Hegel, Marx, and Spencer, this pattern of inquiry, this framework of the investigation of human society, has been powerful and widespread. It is perhaps the single greatest consequence of the Greek concept of *physis*.

Now let us turn to still another, though closely related, consequence of the idea of *physis*: the classical doctrine of recurrent cycles of development in time.

2. CYCLES OF GENESIS AND DECAY

Geometrically speaking [writes Gomperz,] the cosmic process might be compared with either a trajectory or with a cycle. As the first, it would be a journey to an unknown goal; as the other, it would be a circular course of phenomenon, always returning to its starting point. And with these alternatives before him, the Greek could not hesitate which to choose. There was no decisive analogy to impel him to the first. In favor of the cyclical theory he could quote the spectacle of decay and resurrection which constantly renewed itself in the life of the plants.[12]

In short, from the self-same analogy that produced the momentous Greek concept of *physis*, "the way things grow," came, logically enough, a conception of life-cycle, in the literal sense, to which the flux of physical and social change in time could be referred for understanding.

This by itself may seem too simple an explanation. There were assuredly other aspects of nature—the rise and fall of the sun, the rhythmic oscillation of day and night, the annual cycle of the seasons—that must also have suggested a cyclical model of change in cosmos and society. In intellectual terms there was Greek contact with old idea-systems, Egyptian, Persian, Babylonian, among others, in which a cyclical conception of change had long been present. There can be little doubt a variety of influences bore upon the Greek notion of the cultural cycle.[13]

And yet, with all recognition of these, it was, I believe, the analogy of the plant and organism, together with the whole metaphoric conception of reality-in-becoming that was drawn from the analogy, that, above anything else, predisposed the Greek to a cyclical view of change in time. *Physis*, as a framework of investigating reality, would alone have suggested a cyclical pattern of change. For, a thing in growth has not only its genesis and development, but also its decay and, eventually, its termination: to be followed then by another cycle of genesis and decay, *ad infinitum*.

Here I want to make what I believe to be a crucial point with respect to the famous Greek doctrine of cycles. These cycles, as we find them intermittently in the literature, are cycles *not of history but of development*. The difference here may seem tenuous, but it is not, and it is a part of a larger difference in interpretation of the past that remains characteristic of Western thought to this day. Admittedly, we are free to use the words "history" and "development" interchangeably, and most of us do so commonly. But this said, there is nevertheless strong reason for distinguishing between treatment of the past as *historians* tend to see this past—in a tradition that extends from Herodotus and Thucydides through the medieval chroniclers, down to the Gibbons, Rankes, Mommsens, and Motleys of the modern era—and, on the other hand, treatment of the past as developmentalists—in a line reaching from Aristotle to Herbert Spencer—tend to see it. One past there may indeed be, in the ultimate sense, but there are assuredly different perspectives for seeing it, and the two that I have mentioned are fundamentally different.[14]

In the first, in what I have called the historian's past, the past is conceived as a kind of genealogy of events, acts, happenings, and persons, each a point in recorded time that is theoretically specifiable, even datable. The very essence of the matter is time: time conceived in terms of moments, days, years, given dramatic exemplification by signal personages and events. In the lineage of historians I mentioned above should surely be placed those ancient Hebrews who composed the Old Testament, for this work is nothing if not historiographic in its rendering of the past in the terms of events, persons, motives, and the like. The emphasis in the historiographic perspective is upon exactness of time and place and relationship. In the nineteenth century, Leopold von Ranke gave memorable definition to this type of pursuit of the past when he said the task of the historian is to tell it *wie es eigentlich gewesen ist,* exactly how it actually or uniquely happened.

In the second great perspective, the developmental or evolutionary, the emphasis is not upon the past conceived as a genealogy of happenings and persons, but upon more or less timeless sequences of emergent *changes.* If *event* is the key to the historiographic perspective, *change* is the key concept in the developmental perspective. Time in the very broad sense matters, of course, but the developmentalist, whether social or biological, is far more interested in arriving at correct before-and-after relationships in his changes and types than in the probably futile search for dates as to when exactly a certain change occurred. How, in any event, could change conceived as growth be dated? At what hour of the day, what day in the month, does the organism pass from one stage to another? How does one date, except in the broadest terms of centuries or millennia, the alleged passage of peoples from one stage of culture to another, from one phase of the development of an institution to the next?

Aristotle in his *Politics* and Thucydides in his *The History of the Peloponnesian War* exemplify perfectly for our present purposes the difference between the two traditions. When Aristotle, social developmentalist *par excellence,* traced the succession of forms of the *polis* from kinship through the community to the final, emergent state itself he was dealing, not with strings of events and personages, each theoretically datable in time, but with genetic emergences of change of type, with the growth of an institution from one stage to another, and it would have seemed to him (and been in fact) as absurd to put this sequence of types and stages in a time-order composed of days and months and years as to seek to do this with the growth of a plant or individual human being. What Aristotle was interested in was, not the *history* of the state, but, if we may use here a term that becomes of immense importance in the eighteenth century, the *natural history* of the state: the manifestation or actualization of conditions there are regarded as inherent, as potential, in the institution from the start.

How very different is the approach to "the state" that we find in Thucydides' famous history of the Athenian war with Sparta. Except only in the first few paragraphs when he delves more or less randomly in the earliest past of Hellas, Thucydides confines himself literally to the specific events and happenings, the identifiable persons and acts, that seemed to him to be of decisive importance in explaining exactly what had happened in the several decades leading up to the Peloponnesian War. For Thucydides, the Greek *polis* is best to be presented, and explained, not in terms of timeless emergences of conditions, but in terms of concrete events and political figures.

Now the point regarding the Greek and Roman doctrine of the cycle that I wish to emphasize here is that it pertains to the developmental perspective, not the historiographic. It was cycles of change in a given entity—be it the *polis*, civilization, or the cosmos —that classical philosophers had in mind, not cycles of exactly-to-be-repeated events and individuals in time. The cycle was a model used by the developmentalist, not primarily by the historian.

It is this fact, I believe, that explains why we do not come up with a clear picture of cycles when we scan the works of the Greek and Roman historians—as so many scholars, in pursuit of the doctrine of the cycle, have done. Two apparent exceptions to this may come to mind: Thucydides and Polybius, both among the greatest of classical historians. But the exceptions are only apparent, not real.

Thus in Thucydides there is a brief passage that has often been cited to imply the possible existence in his mind of cyclical pattern for the events he describes. He tells us that he has written his history in order to help "whoever might wish to have a clear view both of the events which have happened and of those which will someday, in all probability, happen again in the same or similar way." [15] At first sight this is indeed cyclical in implication, and the noted classicist, J. H. Finley, among others has so taken it. But I would myself espouse the view taken by other students of Thucydides that this passage, far from implying anything so complex and grandiose as a cycle, implies rather the familiar conviction in the history of thought—a conviction nowhere more resoundingly stated than by historians in all ages, even those who have never heard of cycles—that from generation to generation, century to century, types of events and acts tend to repeat themselves. This is why, it is said in ageless refrain, we can "learn from history."

It is surely unlikely that Thucydides thought that the details of Athenian history, which he explored so relentlessly and objectively, would ever repeat themselves. It is even more unlikely that this eminently sophisticated mind, even assuming he believed in the cultural cycles of genesis and decay that we shall come to in a moment, thought that his own text would somehow survive the catastrophe that, for all the philosophers of the cycle, marked the end of a cycle of civilization. What is much more likely is that Thucydides thought, much as any historian today might think, that since invasions, wars, defeats, demagogues, and noble men are the recurrent stuff of history, any later Greek might well be able to profit, in the understanding of what was going on in *his* time, from a reading of the happenings that Thucydides set down in such vivid and detailed fashion for his own.

Bear in mind that I am not declaring Thucydides to be devoid of belief in cyclical change. As a Greek he almost certainly did so believe when his mind roamed to the larger matters of whole civilizations, from their beginning to their end. The fact that today, in any good history of the American Civil War we cannot come up with evidence of the historian's view one way or other on the evolution or progressive development of mankind, or even of American civilization, does not argue this historian's disbelief in evolution or progress. It is a matter of contextual relevance, of appositeness of perspective.

Parenthetically, we might note here still another statement often asserted to be evidence of Greek belief in cycles of exactly repeated events and persons. This is the remark of Eudemus, pupil of Aristotle, who one day lecturing to his students on the

doctrines of Pythagoras said: "If we are to believe the Pythagoreans, I shall once more gossip among you with this little staff in my
hand, and again as now will you be sitting before me, and likewise
will it be with all the rest." [16] But this charming remark with its
implicit picture of an endless succession of teachers named Eudemus sitting staff in hand, would seem to me to have more in common with the Pythagorean doctrine of transmigration of souls (in
or out of cyclical context) than it would to a very serious theory of
development that for Greek scientists like Aristotle was cast in
terms of cycles of genesis and decay.

Far more telling, it seems to me, is the appearance of the theory
of cycles in the sixth book of Polybius' *Histories*.[17] Here Polybius
does indeed present the cycle, and Polybius was indeed a historian,
one of the very best. In an intermittent succession of paragraphs
Polybius tells us that political societies—such as those of the Romans and Carthaginians, which he is writing about in his *Histories*
—undergo cycles of genesis, growth, and decay, each returning finally to the point from which it started. He tells us further that in
the beginning political societies are rude and primitive, that they
have long, slow ascents to maturity, and equally long, slow de-
scents to old age and feebleness. And Polybius even tells us of "the
destruction of the human race, as tradition tells us has more than
once happened, and as we must believe will often happen again,
all arts and crafts perishing at the same time, then in the course of
time, when springing from the survivors as from seeds men have
again increased in numbers . . ." with the human race then once
again in process of development.

All of this is indeed to be found in the historian Polybius, but it
is in what he specifically and clearly offers as the *context* of these
ruminations on the human race and political societies that Polybius
is to be seen as no more an exception, than was Thucydides, to the
proposition that the theory of cycles was never designed for specific events in time. For what Polybius tells us at the very outset of
his passages on the cycle is that they are only a digression and form
but "a short summary" of theories that, he tells us plainly, belong
to Plato and "certain other philosophers." More, he says, he is

offering this theory of the philosophers for such help as it may provide to larger understanding of peoples in history. In Polybius' own words: "I will attempt to give a short summary of the theory *as far as I consider it to apply to the actual history of facts and to appeal to the common intelligence of mankind.*" (Italics added.) At no point does Polybius intimate that in his view the complex genealogy of events he is describing, along with personages, acts, and utterances, will repeat itself in the future, or that it has happened before in some remote preceding cycle. All that he is doing is to borrow—as historians to this day borrow in their contextual perspectives from the philosopher or sociologist—a philosophical theory or model for the illumination he thinks it might offer as to *why* the great Carthage was beaten by Roman troops. Carthage, we are told repeatedly, was "well contrived" in its constitution, its government, leaders, and other "distinctive points." Why, then, did Carthage lose the war? Here is where Polybius sees fit to borrow the wisdom of the philosopher and scientist. "As every body or state or action has its natural periods of first growth, then of prime, then finally of decay, and as everything in them is at its best when they are in their prime, it was for this reason that the difference between the two states manifested itself at this time." Thus the union of sociological theory and historiography. This, however, is a far cry from any notion of the multitudinous events and actions that went into the history of Rome and its relations with foreign powers ever repeating themselves in a fantasy of ever-recurrent Hannibals, Scipios, and crossings of the Alps with elephants.

The classical theory of cycles was a theory of broad, developmental changes of *things*—ranging from insects to nations, the human race, and the cosmos. It was not a theory of recurrent specific events and persons; not, certainly, in its serious and profound statement, the kind of statement of the cycle we get in a Plato or Aristotle or Lucretius or Seneca, for whom it was a theory that served precisely the same synthesizing function regarding change that the idea of unilinear development served in the nineteenth century. No doubt there were Greeks and Romans who did indeed believe in recurrent cycles of the specific history of events of an

Attica or Rome; no doubt there are such individuals who believe this today. Suffice it here to say, however, that I can find no statements along this line in the classical texts that survive.

I have dealt at some length with the theoretical context of the idea of the cycle, and with the distinction between two contrasting envisagements of the past, historiographic and developmental, simply because this distinction remains a vital one in Western thought. It has manifestations that we shall be concerned with in later sections of this book. It is fundamental to Greek and Roman thought—certainly in the age of rationalism—and it is only by stressing this profound distinction that we are able to see at one and the same time the actual character of the doctrine of cycles and the relation of this doctrine to the larger classical philosophy of growth and development.

The doctrine of cycles is to be found, in short, precisely among those thinkers who gave us, and who then elaborated, the momentous idea of *physis*. Everything—that is, everything substantive and living—has its normal mode of growth, declared Heraclitus, and so, *ex hypothesi*, does it have its *cycle*. For all living things manifestly undergo cycles of genesis and decay, of life and death. This was a view that informed classical cosmology as well as classical sociology and anthropology.

I do not wish to imply that the idea of developmental cycles was limited solely to scientists such as Heraclitus and his successors. Like everything else in Greek thought it has its mythological sources. We saw earlier the cyclical character of the seed worshipped by votaries of Demeter; or rather, the cyclical implications of the myth of Demeter. Hesiod, who lived well before Heraclitus, and whose thought is steeped in religious and mythical elements, gives a clear vision of belief in recurrent cycles. In his *Works and Days* Hesiod tells us of the sequence of "races" of men that have inhabited the earth: Golden, Silver, Bronze, and, finally, Iron.[18] It is the race or age of Iron that Hesiod lives in, and a truly dismal age he believes it to be; one of evil, baseness, hardship, and incessant strife; an age in which the crops can be made to grow only by ever greater and more exhausting labor; an age in which everywhere there seems to be a running-out of vitality—moral and spiritual as well as physical. I shall have more to say about Hesiod's races or ages in the next section, for they set a pattern of thought that continues down to the present. For the moment, however, I want only to bring out the cyclical cast of his thought, which is in the following words: "I would, then, that I had not lived among the fifth race of men, *but had either died before or been born afterward.*" In Western thought this is the first, but it is far from being the last, expression of confidence that the cycle of man's happiness on earth will once again turn to its starting point, a Golden Age in which human goodness and felicity will have been restored and granted to those fortunate enough to be born in it. From Hesiod's words it is difficult to doubt that in his mind his own age of Iron had come close to its nether point, leaving little alternative to the prospect of its final decline and, then, the beginning anew of the world's great age.

Now let us turn to the two greatest of classical thinkers, Plato and Aristotle. In the works of both the cycle is a model of change to express not merely the small and empirically immediate, but the vast and temporally remote. Plato believed in the existence of great cosmic cycles, lasting for tens of thousands of years, and within them smaller and more or less concentric cycles for this or that sphere of existence. In *The Statesman* Plato writes: "There is a time when God himself guides and helps to roll the world on its course; and there is a time, on the completion of a certain cycle, when he lets go, and the world, being a living creature, having originally received intelligence from its author and creator, turns about and by an inherent necessity revolves in the opposite direction." [19]

Of greatest interest here are the cycles which Plato conceives for mankind, for civilization. For him eternity is but an endless succession of these. Invariably one of these cycles is held to terminate in some great catastrophe, usually a flood—which is, as we know, one of the oldest and most nearly universal of myths—with but a handful of individuals left alive to commence the next cycle of civilization. In both *The Statesman* and *The Laws* [20] Plato speculates on the possibility of a "few shepherds, high in the hills" surviving the flood that has wiped out the rest of mankind and all its institutions. From these few simple, unlettered, and good individuals, Plato tells us, a new cycle of civilization begins; for they are the "seeds," and from them and their primitive ways will gradually, slowly, and cumulatively develop all that will compose the new cycle of civilization. Like its numberless predecessors and successors this cycle will move from primitive simplicity to gathering complexity to, finally, its own dissolution in some great catastrophe. There is, of course, much more to all this than the mould of the cycle in which it is cast, but I prefer to reserve discussion until we deal with classical thought as a whole on matters of cultural progress and its supposed relation to moral degeneration.

There is, so far as I can myself conclude, no single, overarching, and consistent theory of the cycle in Plato. Let us say that it was a profoundly held perspective within which he did much speculating, not always consistent, as to relationships of great cycles to lesser ones, cosmic cycles to cultural cycles, cycles of civilization to cycles of political affairs, and so on. To observe this is not to cavil. How consistent, after all, are any of the great cosmic philosophers of history, including those of our own day, Spengler, Toynbee, Sorokin, et al.? How consistent is the modern idea of progress in, say, the works of a Comte or Marx? We can hardly expect consistency and fine articulation of details in such matters. Suffice it to say that for Plato the cycle was as natural and obvious a perspective within which to examine physical and cultural reality as the idea of unilinear progress was to be for a Condorcet or Comte. In each instance we are looking at combined synthesis and prophecy.

Aristotle was no less convinced of the cyclical character of existence, and he makes cyclical recurrence the very essence of reality. And for him, as for all other Greeks, it was the model of the organic life-cycle that served larger purposes. "To say that the universe alternately combines and dissolves is no more paradoxical than to make it eternal but varying in shape. *It is as if one were to think there was now destruction and now existence when from a child a man is generated, and from a man a child.*" [21] (Italics added.) Aristotle, in the passage just quoted, is, to be sure, citing the views of a school of philosophers, and there are assuredly elements of his own physical thought that appear to be in disaccord with this, but taking it generally there is no conflict with the cyclical theme that runs through much of Aristotle's thought.

In his *Genesis and Decay* (*De Generatione et Corruptione*) Aristotle writes that the coming-to-be of anything, if it is absolutely *necessary*, that is, moving in the way it is so constituted to move, "must be cyclical." The following words may appear circular in rhetoric as well as argument: "It is in circular movement, therefore, and in cyclical coming-to-be that the 'absolutely necessary' is to be found. In other words, if the coming-to-be of any things is cyclical, it is 'necessary' that each of them is coming-to-be: and if the coming-to-be of any things is 'necessary,' their coming-to-be is cyclical." [22] But rhetorical circularity is only apparent here. Beneath the words lies Aristotle's powerful and constitutive principle of, first, distinction between the necessary and natural, on the one hand, and the merely accidental or random on the other; and, second, his conviction that all that is natural and necessary in the world is organic, is in a constant process of genesis and decay and, hence, cyclical change.

Aristotle's distinction between the "necessary" and the "accidental," found in his *Metaphysics*,[23] bears closely on the distinction I made above between the developmental and the merely historical. Thus, from Aristotle's point of view, a plant has a development, which consists of the determinable sequence of changes proceeding from its very structure and which is as "necessary" to its being as any other intrinsic attribute. The same plant may also, however, have a "history" in the sense of its subjection to either benign or malign forces from the outside: for example, the "accident" of either unusually good or unusually bad weather conditions in a given year, or unusually diligent or unusually slovenly care by its human tenders. Or, through some fatal "accident" the plant may be destroyed altogether—by a hail storm in July or by a clumsy foot. Hence Aristotle's insistence that "a science of the accidental is not possible," that "science is of that which is always or for the most part"—that is, regular, normal, necessary. The necessary or natural course of anything is cyclical in time, though, plainly, accidents may deflect or even destroy a thing and its natural course of change. Above anyone else it was Aristotle in Greek thought who gave systematic expression to the distinction between development or *natural* history on the one hand, and history in the sense of narrative of the unique or accidental on the other. The first was, for him, the stuff of science; the latter of art only. Hence Aristotle's placing of history—in the narrative sense of a Thucydides—in the realm of, not science, but art.

Aristotle deals with the cycle in many contexts: in the sociology of knowledge, when he tells us that "the same opinions appear in cycles among men not once or twice, but infinitely often." [24] In his masterful treatment of the political state and its regular—that is, "natural" and "necessary"—mutations from monocracy through aristocracy, oligarchy, republic, democracy, and back to monocracy.[25] In such matters he is not, let us emphasize, doing as Thucydides did, simply observing the tendency of types of event and action to repeat themselves more or less in a measurable period of time; not musing, in the fashion of the Book of Ecclesiastes, on the fact that there is nothing new under the sun, that all things have their seasons and, like the seasons, come again and again. There may be a hint of the cycle in the latter, but it is no more than that. In Aristotle, however, the cycle is the very model, the framework of methodology, by which he investigates reality. Whether he is writing as political scientist, sociologist, or geologist, the cycle is his framework of observation and conclusion. Thus, describing the mutations of terrain and climate, he tells us that "we must suppose these changes to follow some order and cycle. The principle and cause of these changes is that the interior of the earth grows and decays, *like the bodies of plants and animals*." [26] So also as anthropologist. There comes a time in the life of any people when "the land is unable to maintain any inhabitants at all. So a long period of time is likely to elapse from the first departure to the last, and no one remembers and the lapse of time destroys all record even before the last inhabitants have disappeared. In the same way a nation must be supposed to lose account of the time when it first settled in a land that was changing from a marshy and watery state and becoming dry. Here, too, the change is gradual and lasts a long time and men do not remember who came first, or when, or what the land was like when they came. . . ." [27]

"The change is gradual and lasts a long time. . . ." These words form virtually a *leitmotif* in the Western contemplation of historical change, of the evolution of civilizations and institutions. They were old when Aristotle uttered them. I can think of no single misapprehension greater than that which says the Greeks were lacking in a sense of distant past and future, of slow, gradual, and cumulative change in time.

The model of the cycle was Roman as well as Greek. This is hardly strange, for there is very little in Roman philosophical and scientific thought that is not the direct and lineal continuation of Greek ideas—brought to Rome for the most part after Rome had conquered Greece militarily and politically, then to be conquered in turn by even more powerful ideas of Greek rhetoric and philosophy.

Lucretius' *On the Nature of Things* (*De Rerum Natura*) [28] is, perhaps over all extant works from the classical age, matchless in its union of the several spheres of reality—astronomy, geology, biology, anthropology, *et al.*—by the single concept, *physis*; translated, as I noted above, into the Latin *natura*, a translation, however, in Lucretius' case, that is nearly identical to Greek root-meaning: *growth*.

We discover repeatedly that what has youth must have old age, what has genesis must have death.

> Wherefore, again and again, rightly has the earth won, rightly does she keep the name of mother, since she herself formed the race of man, and almost at a fixed time brought forth every animal which ranged madly everywhere on the mighty mountains, and with them the fowls of the air with their diverse forms. But because she must needs come to some end of child-bearing, she ceased like a woman worn with the lapse of age. For time changes

the nature of the whole world, and one state after another must needs overtake all things, nor does anything abide like itself: all things change their abode, nature alters all things and constrains them to turn. For one thing rots away and grows faint and feeble with age, thereon another grows up and issues from its place of scorn. So then time changes the nature of the whole world, and one state after another overtakes the earth, so that it cannot bear what it did, but can bear what it did not of old.[29]

It is such a sentence as the last one that is responsible for the conviction in so much modern writing about the classical philosophers that for them "time was the enemy of world and man." But time, let us not forget, was also friend for the classical philosopher, for it was only over long periods of time that the slow, gradual, and continuous progress of man, the "step by step, little by little" advancement, as Lucretius called it, could have taken place. It is not, in any event, time that is at the crux of the matter; it is development.

For Lucretius, as for his masters Democritus and Epicurus, a developmental view of the world did not bespeak pessimism or melancholy. Nature, Lucretius tells us, is made up of "everlasting seeds," and whatever the rearrangements of matter that growth and decay, formation and dissolution, involve, nature herself is indestructible. "Moreover, if time utterly destroys whatsoever through age it takes from sight, and devours all its substance, how is it that Venus brings back the race of living things after their kind into the light of life, or when she has, how does earth, the quaint artificer, nurse and increase them, furnishing food for them after their kind?"[30] The cycle, by its nature, brings birth as well as decay, and in our knowledge of this, Lucretius declares, man can find a true serenity of spirit, one based upon knowledge of "how things grow."

But, of course, degeneration is a fact. Even though, Lucretius assures us, "our whole world is in its youth, and quite new is the nature of the firmament, nor long ago did it receive its first-beginnings,"[31] still, by this same logic, old age for the world lies ahead. It would be hard to find a lovelier and more profoundly moving statement of this than in the final lines of the second book of *On the Nature of Things*:

> Thus even the walls of the wide world all round will be stormed and fall into decay and crumbling ruin. . . . For it was no golden rope, I trow, which let down the races of living things from heaven above on to the fields, nor did the sea or the waves, that lash the rocks, create them, but the same earth conceived them, which now nourishes them of her substance. Moreover, at first by herself of her own accord she created for mortals the smiling crops and glad vine-plants, herself brought forth sweet fruits and glad pastures; which now scarce wax great, though aided by our toil: we wear out our oxen and the strength of our husbandmen: we exhaust the iron ploughshare, though scarce supplied by the fields so do they grudge their produce and increase our toil. And now the aged ploughman shaking his head sighs ever and again that the toil of his hands has perished all for naught, and when he matches the present days against the days of the past, he often praises the fortunes of his father. So too gloomily the planter of the wornout, wrinkled vine rails at the trend of the times, and wearies heaven, and grumbles to think how the generations of old, rich in piety, easily supported life on a narrow plot, since aforetime the limit of land was far less to each man. Nor does he grasp that all things waste away little by little and pass to the grave foredone by age and lapse of life.[32]

Vergil, in his "Messianic" eclogue (so called by later, Christian writers struck by the likeness between Vergil's vision and what Isaiah had written), gives us a glowing vision of restoration, of the cycle beginning anew with the inauguration of Augustan peace in the empire. But this would appear to be a cycle within a cycle.

> Now is come the last age of Cumaean prophecy: the great cycle of periods is born anew. Now returns the Maid, returns the reign of Saturn: now from high heaven a new generation comes down. Yet do thou at that boy's birth, in whom the Iron race shall begin to cease, and the golden to arise over all the world, holy Lucina, be gracious; now thine own Apollo reigns.[33]

But it is not Vergil who speaks most surely here for the Roman mind; it is Seneca, writing perhaps a century later. What is free of the risk of change, asks this wise philosopher? "All things move in accord with their appointed times; they are destined to be born, to grow, and to be destroyed." [34] The stars, the seemingly immovable earth, everything, will in time cease to exist. "There is nothing that does not have its old age; the intervals are merely unequal at which Nature sends forth all these things towards the same goal. Whatever is will cease to be, and yet it will not perish, but will be resolved into its elements. . . ." [35]

All of this has been foredestined from the beginning.

> Whether the world is a soul, or a body under the government of nature, like trees and crops, it embraces in its constitution all that it is destined to experience passively from its beginning right on to its end; it resembles a human being, all whose capacities are wrapped up in the embryo before birth. Ere the child has seen light, the principle of beard and grey hairs is innate. Albeit small and hidden, all the features of the whole body and of every succeeding period of life are there.[36]

Such is the classical doctrine of the recurrent cycle of genesis and decay in time. Did "all" Greeks and Romans believe in recurrent cycles? Who can say? Do all Moderns believe in the idea of Progress that has supposedly governed the main line of Western thought since the late seventeenth century? Certainly not—not, at least in the sense of the constant and inevitable amelioration of man's moral lot on earth; perhaps not even in respect of knowledge and culture. There may well have been Greeks and Romans who scoffed at cycles as there were, surely, minds in the Christian Middle Ages which scoffed at the idea of the Trinity—or of God.

3. PROGRESS AND DEGENERATION (1)

At first thought it might seem that the question of the origin of things, and the related question of what has happened to man and his estate since it all began, are both natural to human consciousness. But such, a moment's reflection tells us, is not at all the case. It would be at least as likely, perhaps even more likely, that early man, once he began reflecting at all on such matters, would have assumed the world to be fixed; with no history or development, no beginning in time, no ending ahead, no genealogical succession of events and changes connecting past and present, no difference between present and past; only fixity and eternality. What is has always been and will always be.

For what, on the evidence of the senses, could seem more massively stationary than the physical world around man, and what more permanent and unchanging than the social customs and codes by which his life was governed and protected from birth to death?

To be sure, there was motion everywhere. But motion is not necessarily change, least of all growth and development. The regular mutations of the sun and moon, the rhythmic alternation of light and dark, the measured succession of the seasons, the endless rushing of rivers and streams, the fury of storms: all of these suggested, or might have suggested, a world in motion, even in some degree change. But they could, in themselves, hardly have suggested the subtle and complex idea of development, of change proceeding lineally, cumulatively, and purposively over long periods of time. No more could they have suggested the question that has, from its inception, never ceased to haunt Western consciousness: the goodness or badness of this development, its "progressive" or "degenerative" character.

What did suggest the problem of progress and degeneration to the Greek mind—and with it the developmental or evolutionary relation of present to past—was, of course, the idea of *physis*. Plainly, if everything in the universe has its *physis*—its inherent pattern of growth, its fixed succession of stages, its purpose—then so does mankind, so does culture, within whatever dimensions of time and space these abstract entities may be regarded.

More concretely, if the cycle is the normal pattern of change for each and every thing in the world, certain questions are virtually automatic to human reflection. How did it all begin? What was man's original condition? What has been the course of change in the long periods which have intervened between this original con-

dition and the present? And what is likely to be the future consequence of this course of change? Questions such as these followed
rigorously from a view of reality conceived in the cyclical terms of
genesis and decay, of rise and fall—of, in short, *growth*.

To say, as many writers have, that the Greeks and Romans
lacked any sense of progressive development in culture is, it would
appear evident, insupportable. Here, for example, is the usually
knowledgeable Logan Pearsall Smith: The order "which the ancients found in the universe was a fixed and unchangeable one.
. . . The belief in progressive change, in evolution, is modern, and
forms, perhaps, the most essential difference between our view of
the world and that of the Greeks and Romans." [37] And here is
J. B. Bury: "We can see how it was that the speculative Greek
minds never hit upon the idea of Progress. In the first place their
limited historical experience did not easily suggest such a synthesis;
and in the second place, the axioms of their thought, their suspi-
ciousness of change, their theories of Moira, of degeneration and
cycles, suggested a view of the world which was the very antithesis
of progressive change." [38]

I think it would be hard to combine in one statement more
errors and misconceptions than are contained in this one. In the
first place, Greek historical experience was far from limited. What
is more to the point is that their *consciousness* of a long past, a
past extending back into a remote point of origin, was a vivid consciousness; as vivid as any since, including our own. Second, synthesis of this experience was, as has been repeatedly made evident
here, a preoccupation of the Greek historical and philosophical
mind from earliest times. Third, the Greeks were anything but
suspicious of change. It was, after all, the Greek physical philosophers who first made change—omnipresent, universal change—a
constituent principle of reality. And, among the Greeks, it was
the Athenians who, through Solonian and Cleisthenean reforms,
not to emphasize the dazzling succession of changes and reforms
of the great fifth century B.C., made the idea of a created, *planned*
society the image of political achievement that it has been ever since
in the West. The period that began about the year 600 B.C. and

lasted for two centuries (I omit altogether the earlier Homeric age as being perhaps beyond the realm of evidence here) is one of the greatest ages of change, of creative achievement, in history. It is more than a little difficult to conceive this age in terms of a people deemed to be suspicious of change. True, there must have been Greeks who feared change of one sort or another. There are many such today in our own society; there must have been then. But this hardly affects a question that has to be decided on the basis of relative achievement—political and economic, as well as literary and philosophical.

But the major source of Bury's error (and Logan Pearsall Smith's also) has to do with what is an extremely parochial conception of the idea of progress on the one hand and, on the other, a misconception of the cycle. Bury's crowning error consists in having taken a single conception of the idea of progress—a conception that, as we shall see, flourished in the European eighteenth and nineteenth centuries—and, in effect, declaring this to be *the* idea of progress. This idea, as we find it in such writers as Condorcet, Comte, Spencer, and a few others in that age, argued that civilization has progressed, is now progressing, *and will continue to progress forever*. Given this historically limited yardstick, it is assuredly possible to find the Greeks and Romans—along with most other people in history, including ourselves—lacking in "the idea of progress." So be it.

But if, taking a somewhat less parochial view of a major idea, the idea of progress may be understood as containing a view of human cultural and intellectual advancement over a very long period of time, then it would be a rash soul who denied the idea in Greek and Roman thought. For, as we have seen, there was, from earliest times, a clear notion among the Greeks, and then among the Romans, of a long past characterized by what Lucretius was to call step-by-step advancement (*pedetemtim progredientis*), an advancement caused by man's own faculties, leading to a present that, in cultural and technological terms, was clearly and incontestably superior to anything that had been known in remote antiquity.

True, there was one line of classical thought, beginning with Hesiod, which, while not denying the fact of advance in knowledge and technology, saw in this advance the condition of a falling-away from the simple goodness and happiness that, it was said, had existed in the beginning. There is no question about this. But two points must be noted immediately or, in light of what I have already written, emphasized again. First, the sense of a decline from an original golden age of primal simplicity and happiness did not prevent those who held this view from being aware of the advance of knowledge and culture. On the contrary. It was this advance that, according to the view, *caused* the diminution of human justice, goodness, and felicity. But this, as is only too apparent, is a timeless view of the matter; one as often to be found indeed in the supposedly progress-intoxicated eighteenth and nineteenth centuries as among the Greeks and Romans.

Second, and more important, this conception of decline from a golden age of the human spirit was not by any means universal. It does not appear to have been the view of Aeschylus, of Sophocles, of Protagoras. It was hardly the view of Aristotle. And it was emphatically not the view of Lucretius. The idea of continuous degeneration from some original point in the past was no more a universally Greek and Roman idea than it is a universal idea in our own day. By almost all ancients there was a clearcut vision of the progress of knowledge and the arts from the original condition of man. And by a good number, including some of the greatest names of the classical world, there went with this a conception of spiritual progress—of progress from the fear, uncertainty, and misery that had, according to quite a few, been the actual primitive condition of man's spirit.

Let us look at the matter in more detail, and try to see how, given the basic premises of classical thought on the subject of change, *both* an idea of progress and an idea of degeneration might necessarily be contained in Greek and Roman thought. Let us begin, however, with a few general observations on the two broadly different ways men have taken in specifying the character of the original condition of mankind. Both ways are as evident in contemporary thought as they were in Greek and Roman and indeed have been ever since the classical age.

The first of the two ways is *psychological*. Here the origin of things is portrayed in terms of imagined states of mind or feeling in primitive man: his happiness or misery, his security or insecurity, his confidence or fear. The second of the two ways is *cultural*. And here the emphasis is on, not affective states of consciousness as these might be presumed to have existed, but on actual traits of culture—material and immaterial, physical and social—as *these* might be presumed to have existed in the earliest condition of mankind. Both ways of dealing with origins are to be found among the Greeks and Romans and within each way contrasting conclusions are to be found also.

We can best begin, I think, by taking Hesiod's account, contained in his *Works and Days*, composed sometime in the eighth century B.C. If we look carefully in this work of quasi-mythological proto-ethnology we shall find both ways of describing man's earliest condition on earth. First, the psychological or affective condition: it was, in Hesiod's notable word, golden. A golden race of mortal men were the first to inhabit the earth, after the deathless gods; and their life, Hesiod tells us with obvious wistfulness, was one "apart from evil and grievous toil and sore diseases that bring the fates of death to men." These men, like the gods themselves, were spared sorrow and also toil and travail. All good things were theirs; they lived in peace and quiet, they were not subject to the weaknesses and pains of old age, only to its joys. "And they died as overcome by sleep." Hunger and want were alien to these men. "The bounteous earth bare fruit for them of her own will, in plenty and without stint." [39]

But let us turn now to what I have called the second of the two ways of envisaging mankind's earliest condition: the cultural. Here attention is drawn not to states of feeling but to states of technology, institutions, beliefs, and other aspects of culture. What do we find regarding these in Hesiod's account? What we find may be summarized in a word: *simplicity*. Precisely paralleling the psychological innocence and felicity of the first account is the asserted primitivism in the second account. In the beginning men did not need the complex techniques and forms of association now to be seen around us, Hesiod implies, for "the bounteous earth bare fruit for them of her own will, in plenty and without stint." Government and laws were unnecessary because, as we have seen, men were just and lived in peace and quiet.

There is, however, more than mere parallel between the two conditions, happiness and ignorance; there is, we are justified in concluding, causal relation. In knowledge lies the beginning of the fall from felicity. Hesiod tells us of Pandora who, like Eve, could not resist drawing from what she had been specifically forbidden to touch. In the myth of Pandora it is not the tree of knowledge but a box of secrets that is involved. Unable to resist the pull of that curiosity which in so many literatures is held to be essentially feminine, Pandora opens the box, thus releasing the miseries—cupidity, avarice, strife, ambition, jealousy, etc.—to which mankind has been heir ever since. The primal condition of felicity and spontaneous justice is now ended. Henceforth man is condemned to work for these states of mind as best he can, never wholly achieving them, left with the haunting memory of the Golden Age.

But note carefully! While the release of man's miseries is the most obvious point of Hesiod's tale, it is not the only point. For, just as, in the Old Testament, eating from the tree of knowledge is the cause of expulsion from the Garden but carries with it the necessary fact of *having eaten from the tree of knowledge,* thus setting in motion what Augustine and the Christians were to call the "education of the human race," so in Hesiod there is the implication that the same womanly curiosity that caused the release of miseries caused also the beginnings of human knowledge and culture. In another section of *Works and Days* we are given indeed the story of Prometheus, bringer of fire and, hence, the arts of culture to man.[40]

The relation between ignorance and innocence, between knowledge and corruption or unhappiness, that Hesiod presents to us remained a lasting one, not only in Greek and Roman thought but in all the centuries that have elapsed since. From Hesiod's *Works and Days* it is an easy journey to Plato's *The Laws*. There, describing the earliest life of mankind on earth as it must have been, Plato tells us that there could not have been faction and war then, for the very desolation of what lay around primitive man would have created in him nothing but feelings of affection and good will toward his fellows. Men were good because, Plato writes, they were simple in habits and tastes. No one had the wit to suspect another of falsehood. There were no organized governments or institutions because men, being naturally good, trusting, and affectionate, did not require them for the maintenance of order.[41] And, just as Hesiod had implied so strongly, through his two myths of Pandora and Prometheus, that with the rise of knowledge innocence suffers, so does Plato. The gradual advancement of knowledge, and of all the arts and institutions which compose civilization, accompanied a gradual decline in men's happiness and their goodness.

Centuries later, in Rome, the poet Ovid recaptured the Hesiodic theme: "Golden was that first age, which, with no one to compel, without a law, of its own will, kept faith and did the right. There was no fear of punishment, no threatening words were to be read on brazen tablets; no suppliant throng gazed fearfully upon its judge's face; but without judges lived secure." And all of this, predictably, had ignorance for its companion. Men knew none of the metallurgical or agricultural arts, had no writing, no learning. None of these were necessary. "The earth herself, without compulsion, untouched by hoe or plowshare, of herself gave all things needful. And men, content with food which came with no one's seeking, gathered the arbute fruit, strawberries from the mountainsides, cornel-cherries, berries hanging thick upon the prickly bramble, and acorns fallen from the spreading tree of Jove." [42]

Thus the lovely, haunting myth of the Golden Age. Far from being confined to Greek and Roman thought, it is, as we know, a recurrent theme in European writing. In the eighteenth century Rousseau, first in his *Discourse on the Arts and Sciences*, then in his extraordinary pre-ethnological essay, the *Discourse on the Ori-*

gin of Inequality, paid his respects to the greater nobility of character, the greater decorum and happiness too, that lie among those, be they simple tillers of the soil or man's ancient forebears just out of the state of nature, who have not yet been corrupted by the fruits of success, by culture. And in our own day the lasting popularity of such a work as Freud's *Civilization and Its Discontents* is reminder perhaps of the timelessness, the universality, of the myth of the Golden Age, of the affinity between innocence and ignorance that, we tend to think, young cultures, like human infants, manifest in a way that mature civilizations cannot know.

But it would be a great error to suppose that all classical thought revolved about the theme of primal happiness *cum* ignorance. Judging from the literature extant, I would guess that there were as many Greeks and Romans, throughout the whole of the classical period, who took a view the very opposite of that we have just noted in Hesiod, Plato, and Ovid. We are prone to think today that it was not until the appearance in the seventeenth century of the "modern" idea of progress that it was possible for men to think of the earliest state of mankind as being other than a Golden Age, as one characterized by fear, insecurity, and misery, with the absence of knowledge paralleled by an absence, too, of felicity and goodness. But, in clear fact, *both* contemplations of mankind's primal beginnings are to be found in Greek and Roman thought just as they are to be found in modern European literature and philosophy. On the evidence, there was, in the classical age, for every Hesiod or Ovid, an Aeschylus or Lucretius who saw primal ignorance associated with fear and misery.

Here, for example, is Aeschylus, in his magnificent *Prometheus Bound:* "What is my crime that I am tortured for?" asks Prometheus in the agonies of his eternal torment. "Zeus had no sooner seized his father's throne than he was giving to each god a post and ordering his kingdom, but mortals in their misery he took no thought for. His wish was they should perish and he would then beget another race." [43]

There follows, in matchless cadence, Prometheus's account of all that he had given to mortals in order to rescue them from the misery that was their lot as the result of Zeus's callousness. He taught them to see the wonders of the world and to hear its harmonies, to build houses and thus be able to depart "the sunless crannies deep down in the earth," to learn the signs that bespeak the coming of the seasons, thus to plant and tend their crops, to learn to read the stars in their movements, and all the other signs of the natural world that could, by their learning, benefit man. He taught the wretched mortals their numbers, how to write. "I gave to them the mother of all arts, hard working memory." So too did Prometheus give mankind its first knowledge of the use of beasts of burden, of means of transportation, including navigation of the seas. "None else but I first found the seaman's car, sail-winged, sea-driven." He showed them "the gift of healing," for want of which men "wasted to a shadow," and he showed them how to avoid the terrors of strife, through council, through love and understanding. "All arts, all goods, have come to men from me." [44]

So spoke Prometheus. So wrote the incomparable Aeschylus in the early fifth century B.C. in Athens. How can we miss the affinity in Aeschylus' mind between happiness and, *not ignorance*, but knowledge? Only through knowledge was mankind liberated from fear.

Now let us turn to the important matter of *stages* of progress. As early as Hesiod we have the clear intimation of stages of development. True, these are cast in myth with reliance upon the gods, whose existence Hesiod never failed to honor. But they are fixed and regular stages nonetheless: in his telling, they are the successive races of men. There was first, as we will recall, the golden race, and this was at the infancy of mankind, a time of felicity and cultural primitivism. Then comes the second great age, that formed by the silver race; times were still good, but not as good as in the preceding age. But men knew more; the arts of learning were growing and spreading. Third is the bronze race or age, a time of greater unhappiness, though by no means the worst, but of still expanding culture. Then Hesiod intercalates an age of heroes, one in which, at least among some men, ancient virtues seemingly had

been reborn. But this age was not to last. Fifth and last was the
iron age, Hesiod's own time. This, he tells us, is the worst of all
times, for toil grows more oppressive, strife ncreases constantly.
"Now verily is a race of iron. Neither by day shall they ever cease
from weariness and woe, neither in the night from wasting, and
sore cares shall the gods give them." [45] It is here that Hesiod ut-
ters that most quoted of all his lines: "I would then that I lived
not among the fifth race of men, but either had died before or had
been born afterward." [46]

Actually, the developmental perspective is to be seen even earlier than Hesiod, in the two greatest epic poems ever written, the
Iliad and the *Odyssey*. As Guthrie writes: the Greek attitude to
these poems was very different from ours. "Where we see only two
magnificent epic poems, in which the didactic element is at a
minimum, they looked for instruction on an astonishing variety of
subjects, from religion to military science or even boatbuilding.
. . . Behind the fairy-tale of the Cyclopes in the *Odyssey*, as Mr.
Moses Finley has said, 'there lay a distinct view of social evolution.' " [47]

To the Greeks, even as late in their history as the age of Plato
and Aristotle, what Homer had to say about the Cyclopes and
their rude, rural existence, their kinship social organization, their
lack of agriculture and dependence upon what the earth gave naturally, all of this was cited seriously—by Thucydides in his brief
treatment of earliest Hellas, by Plato, and by Aristotle—as part of
the comparative evidence by which the earliest stages of human
culture were reconstructed.

By the fifth century B.C. the developmental view of culture was
taken for granted. One sees it in the speech of Prometheus in
Aeschylus' *Prometheus Bound* to which I have already referred.
Part of Prometheus' noble brief in his own behalf, after telling the
privations and miseries of earliest man, is an account, one of the
most moving in all Greek literature, of all the cultural benefits that
have accrued to mankind—fire, agriculture, commerce, navigation,
laws, philosophy—as the result of his original act of daring, for
which he now is condemned to eternal punishment. Behind the

being and words of Prometheus lies the pride Aeschylus took in being a Greek and in being a man as he surveyed the development and progress of human culture.

The same pride and same sense of human development are to be seen in the magnificent Chorus of Sophocles' *Antigone* which begins: "Many a wonder lives and moves, but the wonder of all is man." Here too, and without allegorical veil, lies a vision of mankind's slow development, through man's own "engine of wit," his own "wind-swift thought and city-moulding mind," from cultural primitivism to the immense riches and mastery of environment that every Greek could look about on.[48]

We turn from drama to history and then philosophy. Observe Thucydides in the early sections of his detailed history of the Peloponnesian War. These are, we would say today, not so much history in the conventional sense as ethnology. His reason for going back to beginnings is simply that he wishes to make clear to his readers that the Peloponnesian War, far from being merely *a* war, was the greatest, the most demanding of men and resources, in human history. A war so great demands, as Thucydides realized, a society great in terms of both civil and military resources. Nothing like it could have taken place, he argues, in earlier times when there was no settled population, when people lived in wandering tribes rather than in communities and cities, when there was no commerce, when technology and capital did not exist, when migration, war, and even piracy were constant elements.

When we come to Plato we find an even more detailed picture of cultural development. Here a word of clarification should be interjected about the idea of development in Plato's works. It is so often stated, categorically, that Plato had no conception of change, that for him reality was unchanging or, equally common, that everything represented a falling-away from a primordial Golden Age, that modern readers may be forgiven their misunderstanding. The fact is, as Cornford has pointed out in his *Plato's Cosmology*, there were, for Plato, *two* orders of existence or reality. The first and higher is indeed the realm of the unchanging and eternal Forms. But there is a second realm for Plato, admittedly lesser, approachable through the senses rather than eternal reason, but a realm nevertheless. More to the point here, this second realm is one of incessant development. "The lower realm," Cornford writes, "contains 'that which is always becoming,' passing into existence, changing, and perishing. . . ." [49] That this world does not have, in Plato's view, eternality, and is not possessed of divine essence, connotes nothing more than the type of distinction that all religious believers, including many twentieth century scientists, make between two orders of reality. It assuredly does *not* mean that Plato was, as he is so often charged with being, insensitive to the manifest facts of change and development.

Consider the famous third book of *The Laws*. Here we are treated to a fairly detailed account of man's cultural progress through the ages. Plato's account begins with total absence of culture, as we have seen, but this is associated with an absence also of the strife, ambition, avarice, and hate that, he feels, characterize much of civilization. But out of this primal condition has "sprung all that we now are and have: cities and governments, and arts and laws, and a great deal of vice and a great deal of virtue."

The earliest mode of culture is pastoral; from their cattle the primitive inhabitants drew their milk and meat, supplementing, Plato suggests, with the flesh of other animals, killed in the chase. Such men, it pleases Plato to believe, would have been possessed of "the plastic and weaving arts," their potentiality endowed in man by the Creator, and, over a long period of time, man would have learned from these arts to clothe and shelter himself. From these rude beginnings, in most ancient times, there would gradually develop ever more complex arts and skills. Drawing from Homer's account of the Cyclopes, Plato declares that primitive man lived within the ties alone of kinship. "They could hardly have wanted lawgivers, as yet; nothing of that sort was likely to have existed in their days, for even letters are wanting to those born at this time in the cycle of ages; they live by habit and the customs of their ancestors, as they are called." [50]

Gradually, Plato tells us, there came into existence more complex forms of social organization—settled communities which for the first time permitted discovery and utilization of the agricultural arts. Pasturage and tillage were at first done communally; for individual enterprise did not make its appearance until rather late. So believed and declared Plato, as other philosophers had before him and as many more were to believe and declare after him, all the way down to modern anthropology. Slowly the institutions of government came into being and with them the marks of civilization proper.

The account I have given does not stand alone. In the *Statesman* and also the *Protagoras*, not to emphasize the most familiar of his accounts, *The Republic*, there are repeated references to the primitive state of mankind, its probable types of culture, and the order in which more complex forms of civilization developed. We are prone to call *The Republic* a "utopia," and this it is, but much of its genius lies in its correspondence to the kind of anthropology that is best seen in some of Plato's other works. It was out of the materials known to Plato the anthropologist that Plato the sociologist and political scientist constructed his model state—for good or bad in the long history of the Western mind.

I will not multiply examples of classical developmentalism, but it would be unfair to conclude this section without reference once again to that remarkable work in physical and social science, Lucretius' *On the Nature of Things*. The same balanced rationality that we observed in his treatment of the earliest state of mankind is to be seen in his perceptive account of mankind's development.

It is Lucretius who is responsible for the phrase *pedetemtim progredientis*—literally, "step-by-step advancement" [51]—that comes the closest of any phrase in classical thought to summarizing the Greek and Roman view of the nature of human development. Development was slow, gradual, and continuous, and, although in the judgments of some (not Lucretius) the entire process may have been started by divine force, the real essence of the matter lay in the self-propelling character of development, once begun, and the fact that what happened over time was but an unfolding of capacities that lay inherent in man from the beginning.

Nowhere is this more vivid than in Lucretius. In the paragraphs that follow I literally do no more than paraphrase an account that fills some fifty pages of the Cyril Bailey translation.[52] What man is he has made himself in his long history, without intervention of the gods. For, Lucretius tells us, it is no sacrilege to deny that the world and all within it are divine, whatever may be the life of the gods in another sphere. The world as we know it was fashioned by the operations of chance. "For so many first-beginnings of things in many ways, driven on by blows from time everlasting until now, and moved by their own weight, have been wont to be borne on, and to unite in every way, and essay everything that they might create, meeting with one another. . . ." The world was not made by design but by chance, and for this a very long time was necessary. Seas, mountains, and plains, all are the products of natural causes, as indeed are the motions of the stars, the winds, and the seasons. First, after the earth was formed and made solid, appeared the plants and only then the animals and birds and insects. All of these sprang from the mother earth herself, not from external intervention. There were, Lucretius tells us, almost in the words of Darwin, more representatives of life than the earth could easily support, and many perished.

Observe the theory of natural selection: "And it must needs be that many races of living things then perished and could not beget and propagate their offspring. For whatever animals you see feeding on the breath of life, either their craft or bravery, aye or their swiftness has protected and preserved their kind from the beginning of their being." Many qualities—fierceness but also shrewdness, strength but also subtlety, swiftness but also cunning— proved necessary in the preservation of types.

Lucretius scoffs at theories which people the earth in its beginning with exotic and fantastic monsters. Such beings were no more possible then than now. And he stresses a point that was to become the very core of Darwinian theory: the uniformity of the processes throughout the history of the world by which the fauna and flora have been brought into being. So important is this point in the whole history of developmentalism that I quote it in full.

For because there were many seeds of things in the earth at the time when first the land brought forth animals, yet that is no proof that beasts of mingled breed could have been born, or the limbs of living creatures put together in one; because the races of herbage and the crops and fruitful trees, which even now spring forth abundantly from the earth, yet cannot be created intertwined one with another, but each of these things comes forth after its own manner, and all preserve their separate marks by a fixed law of nature.[53]

Then, in time, man appears; at first scarcely different from other forms of animal life. He lived from the direct fruits of the earth, its nuts and berries, its smaller animals, its streams and lakes, and was without fire or housing or even clothing. Gradually, *pedetemtim progredientis*, he acquired these things, literally fashioning them out of a combination of inventiveness and necessity. Men, "after they got themselves huts and skins and fire, and man and woman yoked, retired to a single dwelling; the laws of marriage were learnt, and they saw children sprung from their own union." Fire came to man from the lightning that struck trees; language grew up spontaneously from the gestures and cries that were natural to man from the beginning; in this, man was but improving upon precisely the same elemental modes of communication that existed among animals. Cooking began from chance observation of the effects of the sun's rays on food that lay around.

Then, slowly but remorselessly, ambitions to power began to seize men. Kings appeared, men stronger than their fellows, and with them the notion of property, for the kings parcelled out the land and gave flocks to their favorites. In time monarchy was overthrown, anarchy existed temporarily, and men were now led to "appoint magistrates and establish laws" that they might be freed from the terror and violence of the blood feud. The appearance of gold and silver and other precious metals and stones only increased the necessity of laws and secure government.

Religion arose, the consequence of men's awe and fear of the unknown. Gods were but the shapes of the phantoms men first learned of in their dreams, according to Lucretius, and to the gods, cast in the likeness of the more exceptional of the human beings in their midst, were assigned majesty that went beyond anything in the hands of princes and magistrates. "And they placed the abodes and quarters of the gods in the sky, because through the sky night and the moon are seen to roll on their way, moon, day and night, and the stern signs of night, and the torches of heaven that rove through the night, and the flying flames, clouds, sunlight, rain, snow, winds, lightning, hail, and the rapid roar and the mighty murmurings of heaven's threats." [54] Rationalist that Lucretius is to the depths of his being, he can only deplore the misery that he sees as the consequence of such beliefs, and rejoice in the serenity of mind that true piety, which is understanding, can confer.

The arts of cultivation in agriculture, weaving, stonemasonry, roadbuilding, appeared, as did the fine arts of music (gained from listening to birds and the wind in the hollows of reeds), the dance, and painting. A love of novelty and of luxury is acquired; the old ways are despised, and, in the ceaseless quest for wealth, the seeds of war begin to burgeon. The following could have been written by any of the great moral prophets of civilization: "And so the race of men toils fruitlessly and in vain for ever, and wastes its life in idle cares, because, we may be sure, it has not learned what are the limits of possession, nor at all how far true pleasure can increase. *And this, little by little, has advanced life to its high plane, and has stirred up from the lowest depths the great seething tide of war.*"(Italics added.)

From Hesiod through Lucretius to Mandeville and Rousseau in the eighteenth century the theme embodied in Lucretius' final words ("private vices, public benefits" was Mandeville's terse way of putting it in his *The Fable of the Bees* in 1729) has been a persistent one in Western thought.

Did Lucretius have a clear-cut idea of progress? The following passage is a sufficient answer to this question:

Ships and the tilling of the land, walls, laws, weapons, roads, dress, and all things of this kind, all the prizes, and the luxuries of life, one and all, songs and pictures, and the polishing of quaintly-wrought statues, practice and therewith the experience of the eager mind taught them little by little, as they went forward step by step. So, little by little, time brings out each several thing into view, and reason raises it up into the coasts of light. For they saw one thing after another grow clear in their mind, until by their arts they reached the topmost pinnacle.[55]

But for Lucretius, as for every other classical philosopher, the topmost pinnacle is also the beginning of decline, of decay, of eventual disintegration. For as things come into being, so must they go out of being. Progress and degeneration are the two sides of the same cycle of genesis and decay.

Two

THE CHRISTIANS

In the beginning God created the heaven
and the earth.

Genesis

And therefore God created only one single
man, not, certainly, that he might be a solitary
bereft of all society, but that by this means the
unity of society and the bond of concord might
be more effectually commended to him, men
being bound together not only by similarity of
nature, but by family affection.

St. Augustine

The education of the human race, represented
by the people of God, has advanced, like that
of an individual, through certain epochs, or, as
it were, ages, so that it might gradually rise
from earthly to heavenly things, and from the
visible to the invisible.

St. Augustine

For once Christ died for our sins; and, rising
from the dead, he dieth no more

St. Augustine

As the world is the whole frame of the world,
God hath put into it a reproofe, a rebuke, lest
it should seem eternall, which is, a sensible
decay and age in the whole frame of the world,
and every piece thereof.

John Donne

1. THE AUGUSTINIAN METAPHOR

The Greek metaphor of genesis and decay is an integral part of the Christian philosophy of mankind. It exists, however, within the rigorous limits set by the Hebrew record of man's relation to God.

No more powerful and lasting fusion of idea-systems is to be found in all history than that between the Hebrew sacred writ and Greek metaphysics. From the fusion came the perspective of sacred developmentalism that was to govern Western thought on mankind until the late Renaissance, when it became secularized.

In this fusion of idea-systems St. Augustine played the principal role. Born pagan, converted in mid-life to worship of Christ, Augustine made full use of all derivations of *physis:* immanence, genetic continuity, telic growth, purpose, cumulative development, fixed stages or epochs, progress and degeneration, and even the all-important concept of what Aristotle had called the "motor cause." And he placed these concepts within the context of the developmental cycle. What Augustine did *not* borrow from pagan classical thought was the idea of recurrence of cycles; such recurrence was repugnant to his sense of the uniqueness and sacredness of the drama of Christ. But apart only from the notion of recurrence, the major legacy of Greek thought on change in time is to be found in Augustine's great *The City of God*.

The book was written during the years immediately following Alaric's sack of Rome in A.D. 410; it was written in large part to sustain the faith of Christians and to answer attacks on Christianity by its enemies. In it—forming it, really—is a philosophy of history, a theory of development, drawn from fusion of Hebrew and Greek traditions, that would remain the essential European envisagement of cosmos and society for more than a thousand years; until the seventeenth century when, in a modification of the metaphor of genesis and decay even more striking than Augustine's, the idea of indefinite progress was formulated. It is a philosophy of history *and* development, with mankind, the whole of mankind, as its subject: in it mankind is conceived as having been developing from the beginning through the will of omnipotent God.

Later philosophers of history would modify the Augustinian vision and, especially after the seventeenth century, secularize it; placing in "nature," "spirit," "civilization," or "dialectic" what they took from the God whom Augustine had made responsible for the First Principle. The unity of mankind that for Augustine came, and could only come, from the premise of the fatherhood of God would for later philosophers be sufficient unto itself, an inescapable attribute of what they would call civilization or society. As a first cause, God would in time disappear, his place taken by one or other of the secular determinisms of the eighteenth and nineteenth centuries.

But what would not be altered—at least not until the twentieth century with its revivals of Greek cyclical multiplicity—was the underlying Augustinian framework formed by contemplation of a single entity—mankind, civilization, society, call it what we will—undergoing over long periods of time a necessary sequence of unfolding, self-realizing stages of development. With St. Augustine began the practice—as regnant today as in his work—of using the histories of specific nations as stages or epochs in the life of the single, indivisible entity, mankind. As I say, for Augustine this device—and device it must be called—was made possible only on the premise of God's contemplation, through all time, of the human race made one and indivisible through God's creation of Adam, parent of all mankind, seed of its life and growth. But, as is often the case in the history of thought, what began in theistic terms became transmuted into secular terms.

The immediate point of departure of *The City of God* was Augustine's desire to rescue Christianity from charges that the troubles of Rome, which had reached awful culmination in Alaric's invasion of the city itself, were the fateful consequence of Constantine's act a century earlier making Christianity the official religion of Rome. *Post hoc propter hoc* was as familiar a human response then as today, and given the magnitude of Constantine's decree and the magnitude of the time of troubles in the century that followed, it is easy to be sympathetic to conservative pagans.

But of course they were wrong: wrong substantively, wrong even in the terms of classical-pagan philosophy, and wrong overwhelmingly in light of Christian doctrine. It is in terms of all three of these perspectives—substantive fact, classical philosophy, and Christian exegesis—that Augustine constructed his monumental refutation of anti-Christian polemics. He did this in a variety of ways: empirical, metaphysical, ontological, epistemological. His account of Rome's actual history, from the third century on, with its incessant military, political, and economic crises, is set in contexts of philosophy that Augustine had been immersed in prior to his momentous conversion. Augustine knew classical history, and he was steeped in classical philosophy.

But underlying all of his arguments is a philosophy of human history and development: one that sprang from a Christian premise that is a blend of Greek and Hebrew intellectual elements. On the basis of this premise the troubles of Rome are to be seen not as the offshoot of adoption of Christianity, nor as anything temporary or adventitious, but as the iron consequence of processes of decay and degeneration that had been set in motion long before Christianity had become Rome's religion. Exactly as Marx, fifteen hundred years later, would seek to prove to capitalists that their troubles came, not from temporary or alterable circumstances, but from endemic, ineradicable processes that, in one form or other, had always been part of the history of human society, so, in the fifth century, did Augustine seek to prove that Rome's difficulties sprang, not from official acceptance of the Good News, but from an inexorable cycle of genesis and decay that had begun with Adam—in whom, Augustine repeatedly tells us, the seeds of all subsequent human grandeur and defeat had been planted, so to speak, by God—and that would terminate in the not very distant future in the final destruction of the visible world and its works. It is in the course of his astonishingly learned and philosophically labyrinthine proof of this proposition that Augustine gives us the basic structure of what would be the West's unique succession of philosophies of history—through Orosius, Otto of Freising, Bossuet, and, after the secularization of the essential format, Condorcet, Comte, Marx, and countless others down to the present.

The epitome of the Augustinian vision of the history and development of mankind is to be found in the following brief passage: "The education of the human race," he begins in a phrasing that would continue virtually unchanged to the twentieth century, "represented by the people of God, has advanced, like that of an individual, through certain epochs, or, as it were, ages, so that it might gradually rise from earthly to heavenly things, and from the visible to the invisible." [1]

The analogy and its implied metaphor of growth are, of course, classical. Even the specific form in which Augustine uses the analogy—that is, the human individual, rather than plant or organic life in general—was a familiar one to Romans. As we noted above, the Stoics, particularly Seneca, had likened the genesis and decay of the world to a single human being's life. But an even more exact comparison with Augustine's figure is to be found in Florus, who lived in the reign of Trajan. The comparison in Florus is the means of a representation of Roman history from the beginning to the present.

"If anyone contemplates the Roman people as he would contemplate a man, and considers its whole age, how it had its origin, how it grew up, how it arrived at a certain vigor of manhood, and how it has since, as it were, grown old, he will observe four stages and degrees of its existence." [2] What follows in Florus' account is a detailed categorization of the major events and changes in Roman history, from the founding of Rome down to the reign of Trajan, into the specific ages of "infancy," "youth," "manhood," and, in his own time, "the old age of the empire." True, Florus saw in Trajan's reign a sudden restoration of energy to the empire, "as if youth were restored to it." How far this appended observation sprang from conviction and how far from respect for Trajan's personal vigor is hard to say. It does not matter. It may be taken for granted that, however long the interruption of decline into old age might prove for Rome, it did not enter Florus' head to suppose that such decline could be permanently averted. The decline of Rome was, for any Roman, as certain in the distant future as was the decline of any living entity.

If the metaphor of decline was used in so relatively prosperous an age as that marked by Trajan's reign, it may well be assumed that its uses multiplied a century later. The third century was, by any standard, a wretched one for the most part. The effects of military reverses, of economic depression, and of appalling political mismanagement were marked by a sense of impotence in high places of government and by a general malaise in the population at large, if contemporary records, such as they are, can be trusted. "Such miserable records as survive," writes Cochrane, "point to an intensification of anxiety as the empire plunged into more and more hopeless confusion; and men began to anticipate the actual end of the world." [3]

How better to explain it all than in the familiar, classical terms of the exhaustion and waning strength of old age? This, as is clear from much Christian writing in the period, was an explanation much favored by Church fathers, as well as by pagan thinkers.

There is no inherent, doctrinal reason why Christianity should have adopted a developmental view of mankind, one based upon the familiar cycle of genesis and decay. True, the ideas of the nativity, crucifixion, and resurrection may be seen as refractions of the ancient theme of the dying god, itself based on the analogy of the death and renewal of the plant. But this, plainly, is a very different thing from the philosophy of sacred, God-engendered developmentalism that began to form in the third century and that was to be given its masterful statement by St. Augustine in the early fifth century. And there is no other good explanation for this philosophy than the fact that the Christians were, after all, for the most part Roman: Roman in birth, Roman in loyalty, and Roman in cultural essence. And this meant, as for all Romans, a powerful substratum of Greek consciousness. Christianity is an amalgam of Hebrew writ and classical philosophy, and nowhere is this more evident than in its epic view of mankind, especially, now in the third century, of mankind's waning strength, its exhaustion of energies. Here is the great St. Cyprian on the matter.

> This truth, even if we remain silent and do not adduce the prophecies of the Holy Writ, the world itself attests, proclaiming by the evidence of universal decay her imminent collapse. No longer is there sufficient rain to nourish the crops, or heat in summer to bring them to maturity. Spring no longer makes provision for the sowing, nor autumn for her fruits. Less and less are blocks of marble wrested from the exhausted hills; less and less the worn-out mines yield their stores of gold and silver; daily the impoverished veins become shorter until they fail. The field lacks labourers, the sea mariners, the camp soldiers. Innocence departs from the forum, justice from the court, concord from friendship, skill from art, discipline from conduct.[4]

What cannot but arrest attention here is that St. Cyprian, Christian to the core in faith and morals, should have couched his lament, not in the rhetoric of apostolic righteousness, of good and evil, but instead in the rhetoric—familiar from Hesiod to Seneca— of organic decay. *Ad senescentem mundum*: this was his answer to the question of cause. St. Cyprian could well have had before him the text of Lucretius—which, to be sure, prophesied rather than described all of this—with its own reminder that "even the walls of the wide world all around will be stormed and fall into decay and crumbling ruin." And very possibly he did, for there must have been very few of the greater Christian theologians lacking in very considerable knowledge of the pagan philosophers. Certainly St. Augustine was not lacking in this respect. Much of the greatness of *The City of God* comes indeed from its imaginative rephrasings, its profound adaptations, of pagan philosophy to Christian uses.

Among these is the metaphor of genesis and decay. It is as fundamental in Augustine as it had been in Aristotle, Lucretius, or Seneca. On the metaphor is built the Augustinian edifice that we know as the Christian epic of mankind. We are given a view of Creation very different from that of the Jewish writ: made different by Augustine's insistence that in the Creation lay a plan or design; that God never deviated from this plan; that through the next several thousand years (Augustine followed scrupulously the chronology of Eusebius, which allowed limited duration to the world and man) this plan gradually fulfilled itself by the actualization of what was potential in the Creation; that throughout mankind's existence on earth there has been a slow, gradual, and continuous progress of knowledge, of material culture, and of the arts of civilization; that the development of mankind has taken place through fixed stages or epochs, each of them standing for a step in mankind's realization of its inherent essence; that, throughout, the human race has been torn in its history by endemic conflict, struggle, and war: conflict, above all, between the two Cities, the one ruled by egoism and self-love, the other by love of God and man. Divine, epical, cosmic in its dimension, this conflict is in a very real sense for Augustine the motive power, the "efficient cause," of all that has happened in the history of mankind and of all that will yet happen.

Now, however, the world and man are in their fixed and preordained period of decline. Such decline is the inevitable prelude to imminent destruction of the world, the ending of the cycle of genesis and growth, of decay and disintegration, that had begun when God created the world in accordance with, "not a new and sudden resolution, but by His unchangeable and eternal design." [5]

"Wonderest thou that the world is failing? Wonder that the world is grown old? It is as a man who is born, and grows up, and waxes old. There are many complaints in old age; the cough, the rheum, the weakness of the eyes, fretfulness, and weariness. So then as when a man is old; he is full of complaints; so is the world old; and full of troubles." [6]

In all of this, Augustine is, of course, classical to the core. The passage just quoted could have been written by any one of dozens of Greek and Roman philosophers, all of whom took it for granted that a time of severe troubles was the inevitable harbinger of the termination of a cycle of development.

Seneca, well known to all of the Christian theologians, had written that there will "one day come an end to all human life and interests. The elements of the earth must all be dissolved or utterly destroyed *in order that they all may be created anew in innocence, and that no remnant may be left to tutor men in vice.* . . . A single day will see the burial of all mankind." [7] (Italics added.)

With this Augustine was in full agreement. Where agreement with Seneca and with all the pagan philosophers had to end, however, was in respect to what follows this mundane cycle. For Seneca, as for his numberless philosophical predecessors in classical thought, an infinity of such cycles existed. But this belief, given the sovereign role of Christ, given the Hebrew-drawn conception of the sacredness and uniqueness of mankind and mankind's relation to God, was utterly foreign, unacceptable, to Christian consciousness.

2. THE REPUDIATION OF CYCLES

There is one monumental, transcending difference between the classical and the Christian view of the cycle of genesis and decay. In the former, it is set in the context of infinite multiplicity, plurality, and recurrence. In the Christian view, however, the cycle of genesis and decay is single, unique, never to be repeated. There is the one cycle of human existence that began in Adam, that will terminate sometime in the not distant future, and that is all.

There will be renewal of life, yes. What Seneca referred to in the passage above as creation "anew in innocence" is assuredly a part of the Augustinian view of things. But not creation anew on this earth. "Is it a little thing that God hath done for thee," asks Augustine, "in that in the world's old age, he has sent Christ unto thee, that He may renew thee then, when all else is failing?" [8] Cyclical renewal, if we like, but in the Christian scheme of things, renewal, once effected at the conclusion of this single unique cycle, will be eternal and unchanging; that is, for the elect. The purity and felicity that man has not known since the primal Fall in the Garden will be restored to the virtuous, in whatever age they may have lived, but it will not be in the form of the beginning of yet another cycle of earthly genesis and decay. It will be in the form of restoration eternal, in the City of God. The wicked of all ages will, of course, also know eternity, but theirs will be an eternity of torment and pain, the consequence of having known the right but chosen its opposite.

That the idea of recurrent cycles must have been a strong idea in Augustine's day is attested by the skill and care with which he seeks to refute it. And refute it he had to. For how convincing could the news be of Christ, his suffering for and redemption of mankind, if there continued to lurk in the minds of converts any approximation of a view in which there would be, over infinity, an infinite succession of Falls, Nativities, and Redemptions? True, this would be to distort the cyclical doctrine as the Greeks and Romans had set it forth—a doctrine of development of things rather than of infinitesimal repetition of persons and events—but Augustine could take no chances here. The mere thought of the cycle of Christian genesis and decay repeating itself was an abhorrent one.

There was, moreover, the nature of the record that Augustine and all Christians drew from the Hebrews. This record was a sacred one in the sense that it sprang from God's direct dealings with the Jews, with Adam, Abraham, Noah, and others. "It is what the Lord said and the Lord did that Scripture history chiefly aims to exhibit—it is His guidance of a particular nation in an essentially special way that is its subject. . . ." [9] There is divine guidance in the Hebrew record and, with this, divine necessity. I shall come back to this point shortly, for the idea of historical necessity, or of historical inevitability, as we have had it in the West down to the present moment, is a compound of the idea of divine necessity, as found in the Old Testament, and of the kind of internal, self-perfecting necessity that is to be found in the Greeks, especially Aristotle.

What must be stressed at this point, however, is the irreconcilability of a sacred, God-given history—the kind to be found in the Old Testament, the kind that Christianity took over from the Jews —and a view of sacred events and sacred persons endlessly repeating themselves in cycles of time.

At the heart of Augustine's explicit repudiation of the classical idea of recurrent cycles of development is a shrewd and altogether sound realization that anything infinitely repeated loses not only its uniqueness but also its majesty—and thereby its appeal. How evocative could the "good news" be in the minds of those who worshipped Christ, who felt purified and renewed in Christ, if one were committed by other belief to the vision of an infinite succession of Christs appearing and reappearing to save man? As I have said, such a representation of the classical doctrine of cycles is not strictly accurate, for there is no evidence that in that doctrine any repetition of *specific events and persons* was involved. But the distinction between history and development is a subtle one at best, and even assuming that Augustine was himself aware of precisely what the cyclical theory actually implied, he did not err in meeting its argument in the powerful terms of *the* event of all history: the appearance of Christ.

But it was not enough for Augustine, philosopher and rhetorician extraordinary, to rest the argument against cyclical recurrence on the ground alone of its repugnance to believers in Christ. The actual context for the refutation of recurrence in *The City of God* has to do, not with Christ as such, but with that momentous cosmological question—of such obsessing concern to all classical philosophers—how did it all begin? How, as John Donne many centuries later was to re-phrase the matter, a Creation of All out of Nothing? [10]

For Augustine this question could only be answered by reference to God, the absolute being to whom all things are possible, even, and especially, things that defy all principles of observation and logic. Moreover, Augustine declares, what has happened has happened within a finite period of time, specifically within a period of slightly less than six thousand years. Those documents which assign greater antiquity to the world are "highly mendacious" and can be proved so, Augustine argues, by enumeration of their own inconsistencies, quite apart from reference to "the sacred writings." What follows reveals Augustine as a shrewd debater.

How, Augustine asks, if an infinite time has held the history of mankind, do pagan philosophers vindicate "the truth of their history, which narrates who were the inventors, and what they invented, and who first instituted the liberal studies and the other arts, and who first inhabited this or that region, and this or that island?" They reply to this question by referring to other human existences, separated in time by an infinite recurrence of disasters and devastations, with each new existence arising out of human seeds left over from the previous existence. So they say. "But," writes Augustine, "they say what they think, not what they know." [11]

For can one really suppose that, given the disasters and destructions which according to the pagan cyclical theory periodically devastate civilization and depopulate the world, "some men would be left alive in the world" whose posterity would renew the population and who would then commence once again a cycle of development identical with that preceding? Here it is not Augustine the Christian but Augustine the skeptic amusing himself with what seems to him the self-evident absurdity of the doctrine of recurrence.

Then there is the answer that must be given those who ask why it was that God created mankind when He did, rather than some earlier time, as he could have, assuming the omnipotence and omnipresence Christians attribute to Him. But, replies Augustine, if there had elapsed, not the actual six thousand years, but

even sixty or six hundred thousand years, or sixty times as many, or six hundred or six hundred thousand times as many, or this sum multiplied until it could no longer be expressed in numbers, the same question could still be put, Why was he not made before? For the past and boundless eternity during which God abstained from creating man is so great, that, compare it with what vast and untold numbers of ages you please, so long as there is a definite conclusion of this term of time, it is not even as if you compared the minutest drop of water with the ocean that everywhere flows around the globe.[12]

Nor is it possible—save by adducement of the Divine—to deal with the problem of beginnings of time. If we take away from a time which has no beginning "terms of years so vast that they cannot be named by the most skilful arithmetician . . . and take them away not once and again repeatedly, but always, and what do you effect, what do you make by your deduction, since you never reach the beginning which has no existence?" [13] What is now demanded by these philosophers after scarce six thousand years might with equal weight be demanded "after six hundred thousand years, supposing these dying generations of men continue so long to decay and be renewed. . . ." Indeed precisely the same question might have been asked by those who have lived before us. "The first man himself, in short, might have, the day after, or the very day of, his creation asked why was he created no sooner. And no matter at what earlier or later period he had been created, this controversy about the commencement of the world's history would have had precisely the same difficulties as it has now." [14]

This controversy has been resolved by some philosophers, Augustine notes, by "introducing cycles of time, in which there should be constant renewal and repetition of the order of nature." There is no agreement among philosophers as to whether one permanent world passes through all these cycles or "whether the world shall at fixed intervals die out, and be renewed," but irrespective of this, the cycle, Augustine tells us, is the approved method of dealing with the problem of development and time.[15]

"And from this fantastic vicissitude they exempt not even the immortal soul that has attained wisdom, consigning it to a ceaseless migration between delusive blessedness and real misery." How, he asks, can anything be called blessed when it has no assurance of being so eternally? Further, such a soul must either be in ignorance of its incessant cyclical excursions, and therefore blind to approaching misery at the end of a cycle or, knowing, spend an eternity in fear of approaching misery. On the other hand, if we assume that the soul, being blessed, is spared these cyclical mutations and exists in eternal bliss, then, on the same logic, why can man himself not know a single existence, thus escaping the "circuitous paths" held forth by deceiving and deceived sages?

There are those who, in defense of their cyclical ideas cite what

Solomon says in the book of Ecclesiastes. But the words of that book—"there is nothing new under the sun . . . It hath been already of old time, which was just before us"—do not have reference, Augustine argues, to cycles of time and being. They may refer to the orbit of the sun, to the recurrence of human generations, even to nature's production of "monstrous and irregular" types which can, like normal things, resemble each other. Solomon's words refer to many things, for there is indeed nothing new under the sun. But not to cycles.

> At all events, far be it from any true believer to suppose that by these words of Solomon these cycles are meant, in which, according to those philosophers, the same periods and events of time are repeated; as if, for example, the philosopher Plato, having taught in the school at Athens which is called the Academy, so, numberless ages before, at long but certain intervals, this same Plato, and the same school, and the same disciples existed, and so also are to be repeated during the countless cycles that are yet to be—far be it, I say, from us to believe this. *For once Christ died for our sins; and, rising from the dead, He dieth no more.* (Italics added.)

As death has no dominion over Christ, neither has it over us, once we depart this world and attain to our eternal resting place. And this will be as true of those consigned to eternal hell as to those in heaven. "The wicked walk *in a circle.*" But this saying does not mean, Augustine assures us, that the life of the wicked, anymore than of the blessed, is to recur. What it means is that the path in which the philosophers' false doctrine of cycles runs is circuitous.

Thus the Augustinian criticism of the classical doctrine of recurrent cycles. His treatment of the doctrine is neither accurate nor fair, generally speaking. For, let us again emphasize, the idea of recurrent cycles among Greeks and Romans did *not* rest upon the claimed recurrence of Plato, the Academy, or of any other specific person or event—though there may well have been doctrines, even as there are today, suggesting this form of transmigration of souls —but, rather, upon the claimed recurrence of cycles of development: of institutions, cultures, nations, worlds; development, in short, of entities for which cyclical genesis and decay could be asserted, over long periods and in ways that referred to general patterns, not to specific individuals and events.

Did Augustine know this? Very probably. He was a learned scholar—in matters of Greek and Roman philosophy as well as of Christian doctrine. But he was, first and last, the Christian polemicist concerned with advancing Christianity, with defending it from its attackers, and with clearing from the scene all the thickets of pagan belief that might hinder the progress of conversion. It is within this context of purpose that we have to look for the elements of what was to become the Christian view of mankind, its rise and fall, its struggle of the two cities, and its cyclical movement from birth to death; above all its *necessity*.

3. HISTORICAL NECESSITY

One of the profoundest ideas ever to come to man's mind is the idea of historical necessity; the idea that what has happened in the past has been not merely actual but necessary: necessary in the sense that each change, each event, has followed with inexorable logic and purpose from the preceding change or event, and that the entire process from start to finish may be seen as the actualizing of some latent design, divine or secular. Historical necessity is a profound idea; it is also a dangerous idea. Once a pattern of history is asserted to be real and inevitable, what shrift can be given ideas and acts that stray, in caprice, ignorance, or heresy, from the appointed course of history? Very little, as the history of doctrines of historical necessity from Augustine to Marx makes clear in the European record.

There is, of course, fascination in contemplating the historically inevitable, in drawing from the data of history clearly evolving patterns. As Sir Isaiah Berlin has written:

> To understand is to perceive patterns. To offer historical explanations is not merely to describe a succession of events, but to make it intelligible. To make intelligible is to reveal the basic pattern; not one of several possible patterns, but the one unique pattern

which, by being as it is, fulfills only one particular purpose, and consequently is revealed as fitting into a specifiable fashion within the single, "cosmic," over-all schema which is the goal of the universe, the goal in virtue of which alone it is a universe at all, and not a chaos of unrelated bits and pieces. The more thoroughly the nature of this purpose is understood, and with it the patterns it entails in the various forms of human activity, the more explanatory or illuminating—the "deeper"—the activity of the historian will be. Unless an event, or the character of an individual, or the activity of this or that institution or group or historical personage, is explained as a necessary consequence of its place in the pattern (and the larger, that is, the more comprehensive the schema, the more likely it is to be the true one), no explanation—and therefore no historical account—is being provided.[16]

Needless to say, this is not a way of looking at history that Sir Isaiah is proposing, not a way of regarding the totality of events that he recommends. He is simply describing, and with utter fidelity, it seems to me, the doctrine of historical necessity. It is a doctrine—whether in the form of "Providence," "Spirit," "Dialectic," or "Manifest Destiny"—that has had numerous and often decisive consequences in Western thought. Although adumbrations of the idea of historical necessity are clearly evident in many areas of ancient thought, it is certain, I believe, that it was St. Augustine's *The City of God* that began a succession of works which is one of the most distinctive intellectual continuities in the West, a succession in which the names of Orosius, Otto of Freising, Bossuet, Condorcet, Comte, Hegel, Marx figure, and in which the names of such contemporaries as Berdyaev, Niebuhr, Sorokin, Toynbee, and others belong, in one degree or other.

Fundamental to this tradition of thought is, first, the envisagement of mankind as a whole, a super-entity composed of the individual life-histories of specific peoples—Egyptians, Jews, Greeks, Romans, *et al.*—and endowed, as it were, with existential reality. Second, within the life of this super-entity, mankind, there is to be discerned a single, unilinear pattern of development, with the individual life-histories of historic peoples forming its successive stages or epochs. And third, most important for our purposes here, is the conviction that the discerned pattern is a *necessary* one: made necessary ultimately by God, if we like, but made necessary too by the existence of forces contained in the process from the beginning. It is the union of all of these aspects in one single, great design that lights up *The City of God* and gives this book historical priority in the tradition I am referring to. The gulf between the God-intoxicated Augustine and the materialism-driven Karl Marx is a broad one, to be sure, but not so broad that it cannot be bridged by the single doctrine of history conceived as working itself out through what Marx was to call iron necessity. For Augustine the existence of an omnipotent God was fundamental, and this surely sets him far from a Comte or Marx. But this much granted, the theoretical distance is surely narrowed when we omit God for the moment and turn to the design or mechanism within which, according to Augustine, God's will expressed itself.

For although the Hebrew idea of a sovereign deity is Augustine's basic premise, what follows conceptually from this is not without strong elements of the Greek. We go back once again to the Greek idea of *physis*. Any being, physical or cultural, that is said to fulfill its *physis*, its "natural pattern of growth," grows, obviously, in a "necessary" way. It is *necessary*—accidents barred—that any living thing will grow in the way prescribed by its own nature. It is "necessary" that infancy precede puberty, that puberty precede adulthood, and so on. And, moving from our organismic model to classical developmentalism, it is "necessary," as Aristotle said, that monarchy precede oligarchy, that oligarchy precede a republican form of government, that democracy produce, in time, dictatorship in the name of the people. Similarly, in nineteenth century doctrines of social developmentalism it was held "necessary" by a Lewis Morgan that matriarchal forms of kinship precede patriarchal; or by a Tylor that animism precede totemism, and totemism, polytheism; or by Marx that feudalism precede capitalism, and capitalism, socialism.

But the kind of necessity that I am here speaking of is different; related, if we like, but different. For in confronting doctrines of historical necessity or inevitability we have something more than the developmentalist's insistence that there is a natural (and hence necessary) order of change in an entity. We have an insistence that *all that has actually happened*, in the sense of *all events and persons in time, has necessarily happened*; that, not merely the development of forms and types, but the history of events, acts, and motives, has been necessary.

Nothing of this sort existed in Greek and Roman historiography. Consider the words with which Herodotus prefaces his great *Histories*: "These are the researches of Herodotus of Halicarnassus which he publishes in the hope of thereby preserving from decay the remembrance of what men have done, and of preventing the great and wonderful actions of the Greeks and the Barbarians from losing their due meed of glory; and withal to put on record what were their grounds of feud." [17] Or consider the words of Thucydides on the Peloponnesian War: "Thucydides, an Athenian, wrote the history of the war between the Peloponnesians and the Athenians, how they warred against each other; having begun from its very outset, with the expectation that it would prove a great one, and more worthy of relation than all that had been before it; inferring so much as well from the fact that both sides were at the height of all kinds of preparation for it, as also because he saw the rest of Greece joining with the one side or the other, some immediately, and some intending so to do." [18]

Historiography for the Greeks (and this remained true of the historiography of the Romans, including the writings of Livy, Tacitus, and Suetonius, among others) served, in short, the same function that it generally does for us today: to set down, for secular reasons, exactly what happened and why. It was not an effort to record the divine or to descry some indwelling pattern of purpose and drama. The Greeks left the latter to tragedy.

But when we turn to the Hebrew tradition of historiography we have something very different. As Robert Flint writes, "It is what the Lord said and the Lord did that Scripture history chiefly aims to exhibit—it is His guidance of a particular nation in an essentially special way that is its subject—whereas the historians of Greece set before themselves for end simply the satisfaction of man's curiosity about the actions of his fellow-men." [19] Probably no people, Flint says of the ancient Jews, has ever been so conscious of itself as a product of time, "more thoroughly conscious of being rooted in, and growing out of, a marvellous past." And from first to last, from Adam through each person who followed, this consciousness of being special, of being worthy of note, was set in the context of the Hebrews' relation to a divine being who was the cause of each and every thing that had happened. What happened could not have happened differently because it was all the result of God's will and direction. We are thus in the presence of *sacred* history, unlike even the kind of "history" that Hesiod had set forth in his *Theogony*. The idea of historical necessity appears when the Hebrew writ is fused, as it is fused by Augustine, with the Greek idea of becoming, of realization of design. For while in Hebrew historiography we have the clear notion of divine governance, we do not have, it seems to me, the idea of indwelling *necessity*. There is plainly an active and pervasive Deity making decisions, setting forth opportunities and traps alike for individuals, from Adam onward, giving unremitting direction, making covenants, rewarding and punishing, in short, guiding and governing. But we do not have any sense of immanent plan unfolding, present from the start in the materials God created in the beginning, the end foredestined. Such a plan or design is not to be found for the good and sufficient reason that, in a quite different context, Leo Strauss has recently stressed: *the concept of nature does not exist*. Professor Strauss is, of course, using the word "nature" in its pristine Greek sense.[20]

In St. Augustine we do find the idea of an indwelling design. From the Greek, as we have seen, he acquired the idea of *physis*, or a pattern of growth resident from the start. From the Hebrew he acquired the idea of a sacred history, sacred and unique. In the union of these two momentous ideas we have the beginning of Western doctrines of historical necessity.

Given this union, it became possible for Augustine to arrange even historical events, specific acts, concrete personages, along with changes of the human condition, into fixed stages or epochs, all of them aspects of reality unfolding slowly through time in accord with prior plan that God never changed.

Repeatedly Augustine makes us understand not merely that everything has been ordained by God but that it was ordained before man ever made his appearance. That the whole plenitude of the human race was embraced in the first man, Adam, and that God foresaw, predetermined indeed, the two parts of Adam's nature that were to manifest themselves in time in the form of the Two Cities: the City of Man and the City of God. In the beginning, writes Augustine, "there was laid the foundation, *not indeed evidently*, but in God's foreknowledge, of these two cities or societies, so far as regards the human race." [21]

Over and over in *The City of God* does Augustine stress the following thesis: "He made in time, not from a new and sudden resolution, but by His unchangeable and eternal design." Or, as Augustine writes: "He willed to make in time, and this without changing His design and will." [22] Necessity comes, in short, not from the simplistic notion of God's sovereignty, but from the more complicated and subtle notion of God's sovereignty expressing itself in a predetermined plan, a divine *physis*, from which not even God ever strays.

The plan, to be sure, is God's. On this Augustine is ever insistent and emphatic. But the point is, he does distinguish between God's will and God's design for the human race. Necessity, in the Augustinian sense of historical necessity, flows from the idea of design, immanent design, a notion that is, of course, classical to the core. For a long time there remained a close union between the two ideas—God's will and God's "unchangeable and eternal design"—but the history of European philosophy of history can be written precisely in terms of the ever greater division between these two ideas. By the sixteenth century "God's will" has retreated somewhat from the scene of "God's design," and this is a retreat that becomes more and more evident until by the eighteenth century God's will has disappeared in the mists of deism and, by the nineteenth century, it is lost altogether. Then the idea of unchangeable design acquired secular footings, and God was a premise that could be dispensed with. Of such is the history of ideas.

Augustine is not a historian—though he knew a vast amount of history—but a philosopher of history. Mankind as a whole, not any particular people, is his essential subject—mankind which, he never doubts, is as substantively real and as unified in character as anything else of God's creation. It is the whole of mankind that he is constantly concerned with, and the concrete histories of the several peoples who, for Augustine, form mankind in its history from Adam onward, are important chiefly insofar as they exemplify stages in the development of mankind.

Augustine is the first to seek to divide the whole of human history into stages or epochs.[23] There is nothing very systematic about these epochs or stages into which Augustine divides the pageant of historical necessity. Depending upon which section of the book we are reading, the number of epochs is given variously as two, as three, and as six. To be fair to Augustine, these are not contradictory: merely greater or less extended ways of covering the same thing.

The twofold division of history is simply that of before Christ and after Christ, the preparation and the fulfillment, a very common division indeed among Christians, then and now. Augustine's threefold division of mankind's historical development is into "youth," "manhood," and "old age," one that he derived, as we know, from the pagan philosophers but one into which Augustine seeks to make events and acts fall that could never have been of interest to any Greek or Roman philosopher—events and acts drawn largely from Jewish writ. What is Greek or Roman about this threefold division, however, is Augustine's further characterization of the epochs as representing respectively the conditions of nature, law, and grace.

It is the sixfold division that puts Augustine more directly in the line of European philosophers of history, for in this he seeks to encapsulate both linkages of events and patterns of social change in each of the six epochs which form this sixfold division. I will not try to describe each of the epochs in any detail. The first epoch extends from Adam to Noah and is characterized by Augustine as the period when mankind's existence is taken up chiefly in satisfaction of material wants. The second runs, in terms of time and events, from Noah to Abraham; in this epoch the most signal cultural development is the division and proliferation of languages. Also, Augustine tells us, in this epoch concern with preservation of the past through written memory first became important to man. These two epochs form, in Augustine's words, the youth of mankind. The next three epochs form mankind's maturity; they begin with Abraham and conclude with the appearance of Christ, at once the purpose, the fulfillment, the triumph of the whole process of historical development. In each of these three epochs some distinctive addition is made to mankind's store of knowledge, to what Augustine calls the "education of the human race." The sixth and last of the epochs is the one reaching from Christ to Augustine's own time—reaching, actually, to the end of the world, an end that might require several more centuries of continued degeneration of the world but that was as inevitable for Augustine as any other episode in the epic of mankind. This last epoch is the old age of mankind, accompanied by the familiar stigmata of debility and waning of energy yet also by the wisdom (wisdom in knowledge of Christ and the Good News) that commonly accompanies old age.

Such is the panorama of stages or epochs. In his delineation of the genesis and decay of mankind Augustine gives us reference to such peoples as the Jews, Babylonians, Egyptians, Assyrians, Greeks, Romans, and a few others, their totality representing for him the principal manifestations of the history of "mankind." Considered as an effort to encompass even what was known of human history and geography in Augustine's day, the substance as well as the outlines of the epochs are primitive and even rather absurd. For, remember, it is not the histories of Jews, Assyrians, Romans, and other discrete peoples that Augustine is writing, but *the history of mankind,* and there are countless peoples omitted altogether from Augustine's account, peoples known well to the Romans—the Chinese, for instance, with whom Rome had been trading for centuries, and scores and scores of others.

Again, however, it is necessary, in Augustine's defense, to remember that no philosopher of history, from Augustine to Marx, or even to the present moment, has ever pretended that in dealing with "mankind" or "the human race" or "civilization" he was encompassing within his narrative each and every people that has ever existed, or whose existence is known from the records. Smile though we may at some of Augustine's inclusions and omissions, the selective mechanism is ever at work, and has to be, whenever anyone, however vast the sum of knowledge he may have at his disposal, seeks to discern in mankind—considered as an existential being—or in civilization or in culture a unified pattern of development.

There are two other aspects of Augustine's doctrine of historical necessity that we should look at briefly before leaving this momentous subject, aspects that go well beyond philosophy of history to the whole of the contextual and sociological study of events, ideas, and acts that is a part of the very warp of modern scholarship. Here I follow gratefully some insights on Augustine I have drawn from the late Charles Norris Cochrane.[24]

Given his overarching doctrine of the *necessity* of human history, of the history that began with Adam and would end with the destruction of the world, it was inevitable that Augustine would regard each specific episode, act, and idea as also necessary; *necessary to time and to place*. Augustine was thus able, in the first place, to dismiss all ideas of mere "fortune," or of the purely casual, the fortuitous, and the accidental when he came to deal with his genealogies of event and personage. Each was necessary to time and circumstance when it occurred and could not for Augustine be imagined to have occurred at any other time or in any other place; not without violating the laws of linear time. Second, and following from this, is Augustine's insistence upon the contextual relevance of all that has happened.

With respect to the first point, we find Augustine declaring:

"What we call the fortuitous (*casum*) is nothing but that, the reason and cause of which is concealed from our view." In short, that our common inability to perceive the correct, often concealed, relationships of things and events is elevated into a pernicious doctrine of fortune or else cast into the bin of the accidental and contingent. History, far from being an account of unique and separate events is, for Augustine, "a tissue of births and deaths" in which generations succeed one another in fixed and regular order.

This leads to the second, the contextual, point. In the regular, measured sequence of generations and ages, each man, each act, has significance that can only be inferred in terms of the age in which the man or act appears. The notion of a man "out of his age" is a vicious and irrelevant abstraction for Augustine, as Cochrane has emphasized. No man, whether Abraham or Noah or any other, could act save in terms of the point in history, the age, in which he lived. To have expected from human beings before Christ the same awareness that can, through the Church, be expected of them since Christ is absurd on the face of it and a violation of time and space as expressed in the Christian *logos*. Those destined to fill the ranks of the damned in eternity are not the pre- or non-Christians as such; far from it. Heaven will be inhabited by many who lived before Christ; hell will be populated by many who lived after Christ, who knew his doctrine and professed to follow it. The criteria of division between the saved and damned are never wholly clear in Augustine, but this much we know: what was good or evil in a human being must be judged in terms of the conditions "necessary" to that human being's time and place in history.

4. THE TWO CITIES: CONFLICT AND RESOLUTION

We come now to another vital element of the Augustinian epic of genesis and decay: the motor-force or, as Aristotle would have phrased it, the efficient cause of the whole epic. This we find in *conflict*. Actuating, giving movement to the drama of historical necessity that is the history of mankind is the relentless, convulsive struggle that has taken place from the very beginning between the two natures of man, base and noble, expressed most memorably in Augustine's City of Man and City of God. Augustinian conflict between these spheres is the archetype of all the motivating conflicts—those between Good and Evil, Egoism and Altruism, Oppressor and Oppressed—that Western philosophies of history have been built around for the past fifteen hundred years.

For how can immanent development take place—irrespective of the fact that it represents an indwelling plan—apart from forces which are persisting, dynamic, and directive, and which are integral elements of the entity undergoing development? How can movement in time, the march of history, be declared necessary and inevitable unless it be generated out of forces which lie within the nature of man, or within his relationships to other men? There is no major philosophy of history in the Western tradition from Augustine on that is without this all-important mechanism of endemic conflict of elements. And always resolution of the conflict is seen—whether in earthly or heavenly terms—as bound up with the nature of the conflict itself.

Conflict, as I mentioned in the preceding chapter, was a prime interest of Greek philosophers in their explanations of flux, growth, and change. This was true of the pre-Socratic philosophers, so many of whom, as we noted, took from their observations of the political scene in which they had had careers visible processes like conflict and compromise and, as it were, endowed them in the physical scene, where they were held to participate in the *physis* of things. From politics to physics is a not unfamiliar route in the history of mankind's explanations of the physical world.

And of all experiences in social and political life, conflict is surely one of the deepest seated and most universal. It is hardly a matter for wonder, then, that throughout Greek and Roman thought elemental forces of conflict were arrayed alongside those of flux, motion, attraction, as endemic in physical behavior.

Paralleling the vital role of conflict as a physical process in ancient thought was its role in many of the religions that reached the

Greeks and Romans from the East, from Persia particularly. Not, of course, that conflict among the gods and goddesses was foreign to the Greek and Roman worshipper, but in the religions I am thinking of we have conflict elevated—as it is *par excellence* in Zoroastrianism, with its eternal struggle between Spenta Mainyu and Angra Mainyu—to a theological principle in which the essence of good is in incessant war with the essence of evil.

In Augustine conflict is, at one and the same time, cosmic, theological, and historical. If he rejected those religious views, found in paganism and Christian heresy alike, in which the powers of evil and good are made equal and eternal, he did not reject the notion of conflict between these powers or forces within a finite period of time, namely that period that has elapsed since Adam.

As Thomas Merton has written: "God [in Augustine's view] created Adam as a pure contemplative . . . In Adam all men were to be, as it were, 'one contemplative' perfectly united to one another in their one vision and love of the One Truth." But, as we know, Adam sinned. "Adam's fall was a collapse into division and disharmony. All mankind fell from God in Adam. And just as Adam's soul was divided against itself by sin, so all men were divided against one another by selfishness. The envy of Cain, which would have been impossible in Eden, bred murder in a world where each self-centered individual had become his own little god, his own judge and standard of good and evil, falsity and truth." [25]

There are really, it would appear, two distinguishable conflicts to be found in Augustine's rendering of the Christian epic. There is the endemic conflict *within* the City of Man—the selfish struggle, the covetousness, the hate, and strife of man against man. Towering above this setting of conflict, however, is the vast and eternal conflict between the City of Man and the City of God. This conflict, one judges, preceded Adam's fall—at least in God's contemplation—and presumably it will continue to exist in the same purview after the destruction of this world, into eternity indeed. I say "one judges" and "presumably," for it is by no means clear from reading Augustine's references to the conflict in *The City of God* to what extent he had conquered in his own mind those impulses toward Manicheanism, that commitment, indeed, that had preceded his conversion to Christianity. Did Adam's sin really begin the conflict within the City of Man and between this City and the City of God, with the final conflagration of the world to end conflict forever; or is there in Augustine a sense, Manichean in origin if not substance, of conflict eternal? I confess I am no more able to deal with this matter than I am able to deal with the question of what happens to the eternal dialectic, in the Marxist's vision, once communism is reached, with its resolution of the conflicting forces that, in universe and society alike, are posited as constitutive and timeless.

We are, in any event, interested solely in Augustine's philosophy of history, his history of the world since Adam, and if I have implied more than I know about the problem of conflict in Augustinian theology it is only because, as I have said, Augustine's theology is a rich source of the persisting and eventually secularized interest in conflict as the actuating force of history that we find in the centuries following Augustine.

The human race, Augustine writes,

> we have distributed into two parts, the one consisting of those who live according to man, the other of those who live according to God. And these we also mystically call the two cities, or the two communities of men, of which the one is predestined to reign eternally with God, and the other to suffer eternal punishment with the devil. . . .
> When these two cities began to run their course by a series of deaths and births, the citizen of this world was the first-born, and after him the stranger in this world, the citizen of the city of God, predestinated by grace, elected by grace, by grace a stranger below, and by grace a citizen above.[26]

Thus the two great Cities. The conflict between them is, as I have said, the essential framework of St. Augustine's masterpiece. If there is, within the absolute sovereignty that Augustine ascribes to God, the absolute omniscience and omnipotence that the Augustinian God enjoys through all eternity—room for the idea of *eternal* conflict between good and evil—it lies in the conflict between these two communities.

But there is, as we have noted, another arena of conflict: this one is *within* the City of Man. What Augustine writes here is premonitory of what an entire school of natural law philosophers in the seventeenth century would lay down in their texts as the natural condition of man, requiring the same restraints from the civil state that Augustine and his successors for a thousand years held to be the obligation of the Church. Here is what Augustine writes of the conflict *within* the City of Man:

> But the earthly city, which shall not be everlasting (for it will no longer be a city when it has been committed to the extreme penalty), has its good in this world, and rejoices in it with such joy as such things can afford. But as this is not a good which can discharge its devotees of all distresses, this city is often divided against itself by litigations, wars, quarrels, and such victories as are either life-destroying or short-lived. For each part of it that arms against another part of it seeks to triumph over the nations though itself in bondage to vice.[27]

Let us make no mistake on one point. Augustine is not castigating mankind in wholesale fashion for its war-making, its internal struggles, its litigation, and its grasping for gain and glory. He distinguishes between those things that men "justly" aspire to on earth. He differentiates between wars fought in the hope of establishing peace and those fought for no end beyond war itself, its rewards and booty. When victory goes to the party with the juster cause, "who hesitates to congratulate the victor, and style it a desirable peace. These things, then, are good things, and without doubt the gifts of God." But such "goods" and "evils" are, in the long run, transitory, a part of the human condition that must in time become obliterated.[28]

Conflict is endemic in the earthly community because

> the founder of the earthly city was a fratricide. Overcome with envy, he [Cain] slew his own brother, a citizen of the eternal city, and a sojourner on earth. So that we cannot be surprised that this first specimen, or, as the Greeks say, archetype of crime, should, long afterwards, find a corresponding crime at the foundation of that city which was destined to reign over so many nations, and be

the head of this earthly city of which we speak. For of that city also, as one of their poets has mentioned "the first walls were stained with a brother's blood," or, as Roman history records, Remus was slain by his brother Romulus. And thus there is no difference between the foundation of this city and of the earthly city, unless it be that Romulus and Remus were both citizens of the earthly city.[29]

The difference between the two Cities, each of which has partial and fleeting manifestation on earth, is the difference, as Thomas Merton has told us, between two loves. "Those who are united in the City of God are united by the love of God and of one another in God. Those who belong to the other city are indeed not united in any real sense: but it can be said that they have one thing in common besides their opposition to God: each one of them is intent upon the love of himself above all else." [30]

Or, in Augustine's own classic expression: "These two cities were made by two loves: the earthly city by the love of self unto the contempt of God, and the heavenly city by the love of God unto the contempt of self." [31]

Augustine, who varies the symbolism of the two cities, refers to the incessant conflict between them on earth as being like two streams carried along in the same river. "But in this river, as I may call it, or torrent of the human race, both elements are carried along together—both the evil which is derived from him who begets, and the good which is bestowed by Him who creates us." And it is in this torrent, with its two composing streams of good and evil, that we may see the whole of the human race in time, from its beginning to its inevitable, foredestined ending. What is good and blessed in man has manifested itself ever since Adam. So has that with which good conflicts, evil.

5. PROGRESS AND DEGENERATION (2)

Few misconceptions are more tenaciously held in modern thought than that relating to the Christian idea of progress. It is widely believed, and has been since at least the seventeenth century, that the intellectual tradition which flowed from St. Augustine did not, and by its very nature could not, allow for the cultural progress of mankind on earth. For, it is argued, given the premises of Augustinian Christianity, only degeneration can have prevailed on earth from the time of the Fall. Everything has been involved in a long linear decline from the purity and bliss known, and then lost, in the Garden of Eden. Only the final ending of this world and the ascent to heaven of the elect will terminate the miseries which are an inalienable part of the human condition. So runs the common view of the matter, and although it would be too much to declare it totally false, it must be regarded nonetheless as seriously deficient. For the fact is, there is a very clear conception of progress—material, cultural, intellectual—in Augustine. Moreover, this view of progress is developmental, that is, based upon man himself, immanent, cumulative, and necessary.

God might have begun the human race by creation of several men, Augustine tells us, but He chose instead to produce it from the one individual, Adam, whom He created. It is different with other, lower animals. "He created some solitary, and naturally seeking lonely places—as the eagles, kites, lions, wolves, and such like; others gregarious, which herd together, and prefer to live in company—as pigeons, starlings, stags, and little fallow deer, and the like: but neither class did He cause to be propagated from individuals, but called several into being at once." [32]

When it came to man, however, God began the process of the propagation of his species with the creation of but a single representative, from whom in time all of his issue would become the human race.

> And therefore God created only one single man, not, certainly, that he might be a solitary bereft of all society, but that by this means *the unity of society and the bond of concord* might be more effectually commended to him, men being bound together not only by the similarity of nature, *but by family affection*. And indeed He did not even create the woman that was to be given to him as his wife, as he created the man, but created her out of the man, that the whole human race might derive from one man. [33] (Italics added.)

It is again the Greek in Augustine when he tells us, drawing from the classical doctrine of plenitude, that the entire diversity and fullness of the subsequent human race was embraced in the nature of the first man. This is as true of the goodness of mankind as it is of the evil. There is nothing, Augustine tells us, "so social by nature, so unsocial by its corruption" as mankind, and it is the conflict indeed between these two spheres of sociality and unsociality—what Kant was to call man's "unsocial sociability"—that has supplied the motive force of mankind's actual development.

"And human nature has nothing more appropriate, either for the prevention of discord, or for the healing of it, where it exists, than the remembrance of that first parent of us all, whom God was pleased to create alone, that all men might be derived from one, and that they might thus be admonished to preserve unity among their whole multitude." [34]

Thus the beginning of that most Western of ideas: the unity of the human race, of mankind, of civilization. Thus the beginning too of the conflict between good and evil, concord and discord, justice and injustice that would, for long after Augustine, seem the inherent, inalienable conflict in the human condition.

The human race, from its simple and unitary beginning, has developed in the same way that the individual develops: through "certain epochs, or, as it were, ages, so that it might gradually rise from earthly to heavenly things, and from the visible to the invisible." This, as I suggested earlier, is the essential Augustinian metaphor of change in time. We can now turn to Augustine's explicit rendering of mankind's cultural and intellectual advancement. This is, as it was for the Greeks, not the less real an advancement for its having occurred after the Fall, after man's expulsion from the garden of felicity and blissful ignorance. Augustine puts mankind's advancement in the characteristic terms of the blessings it has received from God's hands.

The first of the blessings and the very condition of all other advance in time is man's capacity to propagate his kind at will. God "did not inhibit after man had sinned, but the fecundity originally bestowed remained in the condemned stock; and the vice of sin, which has involved us in the necessity of dying, has yet not deprived us of that wonderful power of seed, or rather of that still more marvellous power by which seed is produced, and which seems to be as it were inwrought and inwoven in the human body." [35]

The second of the blessings is man's mind and, with it, the capacity—his own alone—to create all the wonders that are to be seen in the history of civilization. "For over and above those arts which are called virtues, and which teach us how we may spend our life well, and attain to endless happiness—arts which are given to the children of the promise and the kingdom by the sole grace of God which is in Christ—has not the genius of man invented and applied countless astonishing arts, partly the result of necessity, partly the result of exuberant invention, so that this vigour of mind which is so active in the discovery of not merely superfluous but even of dangerous and destructive things, betokens an inexhaustible wealth in the nature which can invent, learn, or employ such arts?" [36]

And here, almost in the fashion of a Sophocles or a Lucretius, Augustine sets forth in ode-like form the marvellous increases that have taken place over time through man's employment of his own inventiveness.

What wonderful—one might say stupefying—advances has human industry made in the arts of weaving and building, of agriculture and navigation! With what endless variety are designs in pottery, painting, and sculpture produced, and with what skill executed! What wonderful spectacles are exhibited in the theatres, which those who have not seen them cannot credit! How skilful the contrivances for catching, killing, or taming wild beasts! And for the injury of men, also, how many kinds of poisons, weapons, engines of destruction, have been invented, while for the preservation or restoration of health the applications and remedies are infinite! To provoke appetite and please the palate, what a variety of seasonings have been concocted! To express and gain entrance for thoughts, what a multitude and variety of signs there are, among which speaking and writing hold first place! What ornaments has eloquence at command to delight the mind! What wealth of song is there to captivate the ear! How many musical

instruments and strains of harmony have been devised! What skill
has been attained in measures and numbers! With what sagacity
have the movements and connections of the stars been discovered!
Who could tell the thought that has been spent upon nature,
even though, despairing of recounting it in detail, he endeavoured
only to give a general view of it? In fine, even the defence of
errors and misapprehensions, which has illustrated the genius of
heretics and philosophers, cannot be sufficiently declared.[37]

Now, the important point in the above passage is that these
wonders that Augustine is extolling are, precisely as they were for
Sophocles and Euripides nearly a thousand years earlier, and precisely as they would be in the modern literature of progress a thousand years later, *wonders that man himself had accomplished.*
Granted that everything for Augustine is ultimately directed by,
having been caused by, God; it is yet testimony to the strength of
the idea of cultural progress in the ancient world, and to the metaphoric rendering of "the education of the human race," that Augustine should take time out, as it were, from celebration of God's
omnipotence to tell us of what "the genius of man invented and
applied" in the course of his history on earth.

And note too the fateful combination of cultural advancement
and moral obliquity—the same combination that we found,
though not universally, in Greek and Roman thought. For he is
careful to emphasize, at the very end of the passage in which he
extols the creations of mankind, that only through their association with some aboriginal but continuing flaw in mankind could
these marvellous achievements in time commence to wither, to
decay, and to face extinction in final dissolution. This aboriginal
and continuing flaw is, of course, the sin which led to expulsion of
Adam and Eve from the Garden. For Hesiod—and for countless
others down through the Stoics in the Roman world—the commencement of moral decay, of spiritual decline, may have been
less dramatic than it was in the Judaic-Christian account of the
Fall (though, for all that, the myth of Pandora in Hesiod gives
good competition), but the important point is this: Whether for
Greek or for Christian, *the conception of moral and spiritual*

decline is inextricably tied up with man's possession of faculties which are crucial to his material and cultural progress on earth. On all of this Augustine is very explicit indeed. The flaw of pride, covetousness of gain, lust for knowledge, call it what we will, that is, for Augustine, a basic part of Adam's being and which transmits itself to all his issue in mankind as a whole, has been instrumental in the accumulation of secular wonders which Augustine has extolled in the passage quoted above. So would it be in the long tradition that followed Augustine, sacred and secular alike, down to the present day in the West.

There is still another aspect of Augustinian respect for the wonders of this mundane cycle of existence. This is to be seen in his glorification of the human body and of the physical setting of human life. Both must come as a shock to readers brought up on the conviction that in Augustinian Christianity there lay, could have lain, only contempt for both as against the sole reality and value of transcendental existence. But it is Augustine, not some *philosophe* of the eighteenth century, who has written the following passage; it appears just after his celebration of man's mental faculties and of his cultural achievements; he is writing now of the strength and symmetry of the human body:

> Man has not been created stooping towards the earth, like the irrational animals; but his bodily form, erect and looking heavenwards, admonishes him to mind the things that are above. Then the marvellous nimbleness which has been given to the tongue and the hands, fitting them to speak, and write, and execute so many duties, and practise so many arts, does it not prove the excellence of the soul for which such an assistant was provided? And even apart from its adaptation to the work required of it, there is such a symmetry in its various parts, and so beautiful a proportion maintained, that one is at loss to decide whether, in creating the body, greater regard was paid to utility or to beauty. Assuredly no part of the body has been created for the sake of utility which does not also contribute something to its beauty.[38]

To the above Augustine adds that were it possible to accomplish what anatomists and dissectors of bodies have not yet been able to accomplish, that is, to go beneath the surface and to expose to medical view "the intricate web of veins and nerves, the vital parts of all that lies under the skin," the wonderful combination of utility and beauty in the human body would be even more striking.

And the physical world! One would have to go to Lucretius for anything in the ancient world to compare with the following apostrophe to the wonder and beauty of nature:

> Shall I speak of the manifold and various loveliness of sky, and earth, and sea; of the plentiful supply and wonderful qualities of the light; of sun, moon, and stars; of the shade of trees; of the colours and perfume of flowers; of the multitude of birds, all differing in plumage and song; of the variety of animals, of which the smallest in size are often the most wonderful—the works of ants and bees astonishing us more than the huge bodies of whales? Shall I speak of the sea, which itself is so grand a spectacle, when it arrays itself as it were in vestitures of various colours, now running through every shade of green, and again becoming purple or blue? Is it not delightful to look at it in storm, and experience the soothing complacency which it inspires by suggesting that we ourselves are not tossed and shipwrecked? [39]

Reference to Lucretius in my remarks above was not by chance. The last sentence in Augustine's ode to nature is almost word for word the sentence with which Lucretius begins the second book of his *On the Nature of Things*.

Granted that Augustine, in his celebrations of nature, of the human body, of the human faculties, and of the progress of culture, is in the larger view extolling the wonders of God. There is no question of the fact that for Augustine everything proceeds from God and that the principal purpose of *The City of God* is that of reminding his readers of God's omnipotence. But from the point of view of the historian of ideas what is of equal importance is the whole set of propositions by which Augustine advances his argument of God's majesty. For these are the propositions which, when they have become detached from Augustine's premise of the indispensability of God, as they were indeed to become detached in the seventeenth and eighteenth centuries, would be decisive in so much of the modern conception of harmony and progress.

Let us be clear on one point before concluding treatment of Augustine's conception of progress. This conception is set, like the classical conception, in a context that requires decay and disintegration for its full presentation. We end where we began with St. Augustine: with the metaphor of genesis *and* decay. For what has developed over nearly six thousand years is now necessarily in its process of decline: prelude to ending of the whole cycle.

The world, he tells us, is "broken down by such destruction that it has lost even the semblance of attraction." Each state, like each thing in nature, has the life allotted to it by God. So "what wonder then if some time or other there should be an end of a single city? And yet peradventure the city's end is not come now; yet some time or other come it will." [40] Augustine is much too shrewd to predict the date of the world's ending, or the destruction of Rome herself. He is even willing to grant that Rome may have some good years yet ahead. What has so recently happened, in Alaric's invasion of the city, is but portent, not the final event. But that all signs point clearly to this final event is not in doubt.

"As the end of the world approaches, errors increase, terrors multiply, iniquity increases, infidelity increases; the light, in short . . . is very often extinguished; this darkness of enmity between brethren increases, daily increases, and Jesus is not yet come." [41]

All that is now being awaited is for all accounts on this earth to be settled, for those to be judged and condemned to eternal hell who "are not written in the book of life." When these accounts are settled and judgments rendered, when the deterioration of the world's frame and the decay of its substance have reached their final point, "then shall the figure of this world pass away in a conflagration of universal fire, as once before the world was flooded with a deluge of universal water." [42]

• • •

For approximately twelve hundred years the essential elements of the Augustinian cycle of genesis and decay remained the guideposts of the European mind. That men during the so-called Dark Ages, the period from the late seventh century to the eleventh, should have continued to be obsessed by the Christian prediction of the world's ending, following the Augustinian metaphor, is hardly a matter for surprise. Much that went on in those centuries must have seemed very confirming evidence indeed.

Continued belief in the Augustinian metaphor becomes more surprising, however, as the decades and centuries accumulate without the prophesied destruction of the world occurring. Even more important in the surprise occasioned is the fact of the pronounced change in men's attitudes toward secular pursuits that we see taking place from about the twelfth century through the Renaissance: towns built, universities founded, trade routes opened, guilds proliferating, trade and industry beginning to flourish, technological inventions, explorations in many parts of the non-European world, interest in the fine arts spreading, and, above all, the accumulating passion for knowledge—not just sacred knowledge but knowledge of world and man. We used to date most of this from the Renaissance, but we know today that its clear beginnings are to be seen in the high Middle Ages. It is difficult for the modern mind to reconcile the sheer exuberance, the buoyant vitality behind the technology, art, learning, and literature of the period with continued belief in the slow and relentless degeneration of the world. But the belief seems to have been universal.

Inevitably there were individuals such as the remarkable Roger Bacon in the thirteenth century who seemingly did not give much thought to the ultimate extinction of this world or to processes of decay around them. Roger Bacon, like his namesake Francis Bacon three centuries later, was fascinated by knowledge: mathematics, chemistry, astronomy, and physics. He was eager to reform the program of the universities, to found schools which would not be limited to the professions alone. In addition to his efforts to demonstrate the unity of the fields of knowledge, he proposed the establishment of actual experiments in the physical sciences, the better to advance the pace of men's learning. And yet, all this notwithstanding, there is no lessening of Augustinian conviction in

Roger Bacon that processes of degeneration continue, that the end of the world lies ahead, and that whatever advances occur in men's knowledge of the world in the remaining centuries, these will not be, cannot be, other than incidental so far as the direction of things is concerned.

That minds such as Roger Bacon's and, later, Erasmus's, Machiavelli's, Rabelais's, Montaigne's, and Bodin's should have been devoted to learning, should have been impressed by the advancement of learning and the arts, is not, as we reflect on it, really extraordinary, even in terms of the dogma of decay and degeneration. After all, Augustine himself, as we have seen, did not doubt the marvels of mankind's secular advancement, and did not doubt that the advancement sprang from man's own mind and spirit. Nor did Augustine think that such advancement of learning, such cultivation of arts, had ceased even in his own day. The Augustinian metaphor of genesis and decay carried with it implications of advancement of knowledge *paralleling* decay of spirit and soul. So had the metaphor in the writings of the pagans. There is therefore nothing really astonishing about the coexistence in savants of the late Middle Ages and early Renaissance of ideas of both advancement and degeneration.

Admittedly, the coexistence of the ideas in the English Elizabethan period comes as somewhat more of a shock. For there have been few ages in all human history as fertile in ideas, literary achievements, philosophical contributions, and, for present purposes even more tellingly, in the genteel arts of living. No one can look at Elizabethan architecture, handicraft, jewelry, clothing, fairs, and the like without concluding that here was a people in whom joy of living, optimism, and dedication to the pursuits of this world were paramount. We do not, in short, think of this period, with its Spenser, Marlowe, Francis Bacon, and Shakespeare, as a period in which preoccupation with decay should have remained regnant. But that it did admits of no doubt. Elizabethans, as Rowse has emphasized, were fascinated, in scores of ways, with the stigmata of decay and degeneration. The idea of death and destruction of the body haunted them.[43]

The idea of the decay and death of the world similarly haunted many of the theologians and philosophers of the age. In 1580 appeared a treatise entitled *A Blazing Starre*, by an obscure divine named Francis Shakelton. One gathers from it that he, like so many of the Christian philosophers who preceded him from Cyprian on, thought that the ancient pagans, Aristotle and Galen among them, had had no idea whatsoever of the necessity of the decay of all things in time. He seems to regard the idea as a purely Christian one. No matter. It is what he says that is important here. Shakelton holds, with Augustinian confidence, the view "that this world shall perish and pass away." We need but consider the parts of which the earth is composed, the elements in their own incessant decomposition and destruction, to realize that this must be the case.[44]

This was a point that interested still another Elizabethan, Godfrey Goodman, who wrote in 1616 in his *The Fall of Man*: "Whereunto I will adde the weaknesse of the elements, decay of the heavens and a generall imperfection in al things now, in this last old and cold age of the world." [45]

Even the remarkable Purchas, whose account of the explorations of the world and whose pride in the expansion of men's knowledge of the earth's surface is rightly taken as one of the hallmarks of the Elizabethan quest for knowledge, wrote: "It cannot be without some great worke of God, thus in the old and decrepit Age of the World, to let it have more perfect knowledge of it selfe." [46]

Less surprising perhaps is the appeal of the idea of decay to John Donne. There was no doubt in his mind that heaven as well as earth must decay, even that men today are shorter in stature, weaker in muscle, than were men at an earlier time in history, and that man's weakened mind (weakened, that is, in comparison with the greater minds of the ancients) is an infallible sign of the senescence of the species. Donne wrote:

> As the world is the whole frame of the world, God hath put into it a reproofe, a rebuke, lest it seem eternall, which is, a sensible decay and age in the whole frame of the world, and every piece thereof. The seasons of the year irregular and distempered;

the Sun fainter, and languishing; men lesse in stature and shorter-lived. No addition, but only every yeare, new sorts, new species of wormes, and flies, and sicknesses, which argue more and more putrefaction of which they are engendered. . . .[47]

Donne goes back to the very observation that we have already noted from St. Cyprian: *Ad Senescentem mundum,* "to the age and impotence of the world," must be attributed all the calamities, exhaustions, and enfeeblements that surround us. Cyprian's words were uttered, we will remember, in the dread third century, when everything seemed to suggest the downfall of Rome and all mankind. Donne's approving quotation of Cyprian's words is, however, during one of the greatest, most prosperous, and most intellectually creative ages in the history of Western civilization. Such, we can only conclude, was the immense power of the metaphor of growth and decay.

Godfrey Goodman, whom I have already cited, who was by his own account "a poor country parson" yet served as chaplain to the Queen, took the view—partly Augustinian—that the decay of nature had commenced with Adam's fall. From man decay entered into all nature. The course of man and nature has been one of continuous decline from the perfect state of youth it knew at the beginning to the degeneration of old age. Goodman argued that the farther anything proceeds from its source, the more corrupt it must become, as water becomes more impure the farther it runs from the fountain. "And as we see decline and decay in individual parts of nature, as for instance in man, so the universe itself must partake of the nature of its parts and pass through the cycle of youth, old age, and death." [48]

In all these observations we are dealing, obviously, with those for whom the Christian interpretation of history remained governing. But what, it will be asked, about those in whose works we are able to see the Elizabethan mind slipping away from Christian orthodoxy: Francis Bacon, for example?

That Bacon was a "modern" in most respects admits of no doubt. His *The Advancement of Learning* is in many ways a paean, profound, learned, future oriented, to the wonders of man's knowledge. Just so is his *Novum Organum*, properly read, an effort to show what men must do by way of perfecting a *method* of inquiry in order that the advancement of learning may continue untrammeled by the various idols of the cave, the tribe, the theater, and the marketplace. No one, before or since, has exceeded Bacon in his dedication to the idea that men may learn, may advance through knowledge, may attain power over nature through her mastery by intellect.

But for all that, Bacon, like any other Elizabethan, had a due sense of the mutability of things, of their corruption as well as genesis. He is among those who argue a different, a chronologically contemporary, referent of the word "ancient" in his discourses. Among all the fetters on proper intellectual inquiry, he writes, is "reverence for antiquity." But we are the true "ancients," ours is the "actual antiquity," Bacon declared.

As for antiquity, the opinion touching it which men entertain is quite a negligent one, and scarcely consonant with the word itself. For the old age of the world is to be accounted the true antiquity; *and this is the attribute of our own times, not of that earlier age of the world in which the ancients lived;* and which, though in respect of us it was the elder, yet in respect of the world it was the younger. And truly as we look for greater knowledge of human things and a riper judgment in the old man than in the young, because of his experience and the number and variety of things which he has seen and heard and thought of; so in like manner from our age, if it but knew its own strength and chose to essay and exert it, much more might fairly be expected than from the ancient times, inasmuch as it is a more advanced age of the world, and stored and stocked with infinite experiments and observations.[49] (Italics added.)

And in his *Essays* Bacon gave the figure different emphasis and a darker hue. It is in his "Nemesis: Of Vicissitude of Things" that the following words appear: "In the youth of a state, arms do flourish; in the middle age of a state, learning; and then both of them together for a time; in the declining age of a state, mechanical arts and merchandise. Learning hath its infancy, when it is but beginning and almost childish: then his youth, when it is luxuriant and juvenile: then his strength of years, when it is solid and reduced: and lastly, his old age, when it waxeth dry and exhaust." [50]

So thought Bacon, and there were none of his age, not even Montaigne nor the mighty Shakespeare to give him dispute—to give the Christian epic dispute. That mankind, knowledge, government and all the arts must decay even as these had undergone development and progress was a proposition compelling in its logic and, looking out over the world, amply confirmed by experience.

THREE

THE MODERNS

The comparison we have just drawn between
the men of all ages and a single man is
applicable to our whole problem of the ancients
and the moderns. A good cultivated mind
contains, so to speak, all minds of preceding
centuries; it is but a single identical mind which
has been developing and improving itself all the
time . . . ; but I am obliged to confess that
the man in question will have no old age; he
will always be equally capable of those things
for which his youth is suited, and he will be
ever more and more capable of those things
which are suited to his prime; that is to say, to
abandon the allegory, men will never degenerate,
and there will be no end to the growth and
development of human wisdom.

Fontenelle

1. THE METAPHOR AS PROGRESS

The epigraph to this chapter is by common assent the first expression of the modern idea of progress; the idea that civilization has
progressed in the past, is now progressing, and will continue to
progress into the illimitable future. It occurs in an essay written in
1688 by the French intellectual, Bernard Le Bovier de Fontenelle,
as a contribution to the controversy that has become known as the
Quarrel of the Ancients and the Moderns, an elegant donnybrook
of the seventeenth century that we shall return to in a moment,
for it is vital to any understanding of the initial premises of the
modern philosophy of progress.

But first let us savour briefly the familiar analogy and metaphor.
The idea of progress is generally regarded as the very cornerstone
of intellectual modernism. Is it not therefore irony of the first

water that its first formulation should occur in the context of a metaphor that was the very heart of the Augustinian view of mankind's development that goes back indeed to the classical age? I say irony simply because if there is one over-all characteristic of seventeenth and eighteenth century thought it is the conviction that at long last human thought has escaped the trammels of classical and medieval dogma alike. The mind boggles at the thought of trying to enumerate all the political and social differences between Fontenelle's age in Europe and the age in which St. Augustine wrote his *The City of God*. But these differences notwithstanding, the essential metaphor is the same.

I am not suggesting that the modern idea of progress is the same as either the Christian epic or the classical cycle. Assuredly, a conviction that mankind will go on developing and improving forever into the illimitable future is a substantially different idea from those ideas that rest upon not only the premise of advancement but the premise also of decay and eventual death. Of this there is no question.

But it is surely of more than merely antiquarian interest that this modern idea of progress, with all its differences relating to the envisagement of the future, rests nonetheless, in its main outline and content, upon the identical analogy and metaphor that we have seen to underlie Western conceptions of change in time ever since the classical philosophers. That, by a kind of rhetorical trick, the attribute of decay is plucked by Fontenelle from the metaphor, that he assumes, in his own words, that he is abandoning the metaphor merely because he ascribes to mankind an endless future of developing knowledge, hardly affects the main point: which is that the statement he gives us of human progress rests almost wholly upon the historic metaphor.

Granted all the intellectual contexts in which Fontenelle's statement occurred in 1688, contexts of expanding commerce, deepening humanism, spreading control of nature, and the like, the key fact, the overriding observation, would seem to me to be Fontenelle's reliance upon, not new masses of historical data, not novel scientific insights drawn from the great age of science in which he lived, but the self-same image, the identical figure, that had been used, with different effect, to be sure, by St. Augustine and by those both prior and subsequent to him. This fact, despite all that Bury and a long line of historians of the idea of progress have said about the idea's being a novel emergent in the Western mind, a repudiation of and antithesis to both classical cycle and Christian epic, is, from any realistic point of view in the history of ideas, the most important aspect of the idea of progress.

If designation of the future were the *sole aspect* of importance in the metaphor of growth, the matter would be different. But, as is clear enough by this time in my argument in these pages, this aspect is in most respects the least important aspect: least important in the idea of cycles, in the Christian epic, and in the idea of progress. It is least important in that larger view of the metaphor and its derivative ideas which encompasses, as we have seen, the vital concepts of growth and development, continuity, necessity, unfolding purpose, telic end, and so on.

And all of these concepts are as deeply embedded in the idea of progress as they were in either of the two great world-views that preceded them. For, like the two great earlier perspectives, the idea of progress is, in its most vital implication, a framework for the assessment of the relation of past, present, and future. J. B. Bury has properly called the idea of progress a synthesis of the past and a prophecy of the future. So were the perspectives of the cycle and the Christian epic. Bury, however, like most historians of the idea of progress, chose to see it as something which lay more or less germinally in the thought of the ancient and medieval worlds, always ready to burst forth save for the gigantic *interferences* of, first, the classical idea of cycles and, second, the Christian transhistorical view of human destiny.

But a far more realistic view of the matter would seem to me to lie in conceiving the idea of progress, as we find it in the seventeenth and eighteenth centuries, as but a modification—momentous to be sure—of the same largely metaphoric view of growth and development contained in classical and Christian ideas. I repeat: no one can take away from the significance of a view of progress extending indefinitely into the future. But, from the strict point of view of the history of ideas, neither can anyone detract from the significance of the common metaphoric premises of all three statements. In the long run, and with reference to areas of thought that we shall explore in the second part of this book, these premises regarding history and change are of greater importance than the single element of contemplation of the future.

Let us go back now to the circumstances of the appearance of the idea of progress in the seventeenth century. These were, as I noted, the rather heated arguments that formed the so-called Quarrel of the Ancients and Moderns.[1] I stress these circumstances, for they gave the essential character to the seventeenth-century statement of the idea, which was intellectual alone, not social or political or moral. The latter derivations were to be added in the next two centuries.

On one side in this controversy were such minds as the great Boileau in France and Jonathan Swift in England. When the question was raised, who are superior in profundity, insight, and literary excellence, the great minds of the ancient world—Homer, Aeschylus, Socrates, Aristotle, Vergil—or the reigning minds of the seventeenth century? these two men, among others, argued forcefully in terms of the ancients. Swift, whose *The Battle of the Books* is probably the one authentic classic of the whole controversy, made it very clear where he stood. No lover of modernism in any of its forms, political, economic, or intellectual, Swift could only react with irony to the idea that the literary works of his contemporaries, who were, of course, the "moderns," could possibly match the best of what had been written in the ancient world. But however sympathetic we might be to Swift on the basis of the evidence, it has to be admitted that in the terms of strict debate— and also of subsequent history—his irony and learning were insufficient. The field was won by the moderns; won in the phrasing of the metaphor but with an alteration of it hardly less momentous than that Augustine had given it.

Behind the seventeenth-century modification of the metaphor, giving context and significance to it, are two major currents of thought. First, there is Cartesianism, with its celebrated proof of the uniformity of the laws of nature, a uniformity that, Descartes and his followers emphasized to all believers in an intervening Providence, has been constant since the beginning of time and would so remain forever. Second, less explicit perhaps, but not less influential in the thought of that century and the two centuries following, was a dedication to pure knowledge—to philosophy and science—that has not since been excelled if even equalled. It was as characteristic of the seventeenth century to put all matters in the light of the primacy of intellect and knowledge as it had been of earlier centuries to put them under religion or as it would be in a later century to subordinate them to purely economic forces. It is wholly indicative of the century that Descartes should have made his "I think; therefore I am" the cornerstone of his epistemology and metaphysics alike. (It is also, however, indicative of the point I am making in this section that his famous statement comes almost verbatim from St. Augustine.)

Belief in, dedication to, and a sense of the all-sufficingness of scientific and philosophical knowledge is a powerful force in the century. There is another aspect of this. Plainly, knowledge builds on itself, for if knowledge persists at all, it must—so the argument went—be additive, or cumulative. This was not a novel idea. From the Middle Ages one of the favorite figures of European rhetoric had portrayed each generation standing, like a dwarf, on the shoulders of the giant represented by the learning of all preceding generations.[2] If knowledge is indeed cumulative, then must it not follow, given the constancy of the laws of nature, that what is to be found in the seventeenth century has to be superior to the knowledge of all preceding centuries since it has the benefit of theirs and also of ours? More important, and closely related, is a further proposition: if through the uniformity of nature's laws and the cumulative character of knowledge, there has been improvement continuously over the past down to the present, does it not follow with inexorable logic that the progress of knowledge must continue into the indefinite future?

This, of course, is where the significance of the Quarrel of the

Ancients and Moderns enters history, and it is in these terms that we turn briefly to the manner in which the metaphor of genesis and decay was stripped, as it were, of its centuries-old property of decay, leaving only genesis and growth. It was probably Pascal whose influence proved decisive in this modification of the metaphor, even though he did not carry the implications of the modification quite as far as did Fontenelle and Perrault two decades later.

In his *Fragment of a Treatise on Vacuum*, published in 1647, Pascal continued Francis Bacon's musings on what both felt to be the illogic of calling the Greeks and Romans the "ancients" when in clear fact *we*, their posterity, are actually older in terms of time and accumulated knowledge. It is, Pascal tells us, just as had Bacon, an illogic that engenders false respect for the opinions of those who preceded us. By so respecting these opinions we are indeed holding false to what it was in the Platos and Aristotles of antiquity that made *them* the superior of those who had preceded them. "For what is more unjust than to treat our ancestors with greater deference than they showed to those who preceded them, and to entertain for them that inviolable respect which they have merited from us only because they entertained no such respect for those who possessed the same advantage over them?" [3]

Given the unblinkable fact of the persistence of human knowledge from age to age, does it not follow, asked Pascal, that whereas the Greeks and Romans knew only what they and *their* predecessors had learned, we, with the advantage of two thousand years, know what they knew and, in addition, all that has since been added to their knowledge? And it is here that Pascal reintroduces the familiar analogy of mankind to the education of the individual, the familiar metaphor of genesis and growth:

> Whence it follows that, by a special prerogative, not only does each individual man progress from day to day in the sciences, but mankind as a whole constantly progresses in them in proportion as the universe grows older, because the same thing happens in the succession of men in general as in the different ages of a single individual man. So that the whole succession of men, throughout

the course of so many centuries, should be envisaged as the life of a single man who persists forever and learns continually: whence we see how unjustly we respect antiquity in our philosophers; for, seeing that old age is the age which is farthest from childhood, who does not see that the old age of this unversal man should be looked for, not in the times nearest his birth, but in those most remote therefrom? [4]

Clearly, then, the metaphor as we find it in the passage from Fontenelle with which this chapter began, was far from unique in his phrasing in the seventeenth century. What better image could possibly have been found by the moderns in their quarrel with the traditionalists, with those who said in effect: continuity, time, advancement notwithstanding, we still believe that no one in our age, and no one in the twenty centuries intervening, has been able to equal the genius of Aeschylus, Sophocles, Plato, Aristotle, and the others of the ancient world whose works we continue to read. For, to this the moderns—the Pascals, the Fontenelles, the Perraults—could say: granted their greatness, still, do we not come after them; do we not know them, and is it not probable that, knowing them, we are able to build on them, see farther than they?

There was another aspect of the matter that in a sense clinched the argument for the moderns. This was the Cartesian assumption of the uniformity of nature, to which I have already referred. If the ancients did indeed have intellects superior to ours, declared Fontenelle, "then their brains must have been better ordered, fashioned of firmer or more delicate fibres, filled with a higher percentage of animal spirits." [5] But on what evidence can such a surmise possibly stand? For has it not been shown unchallengeably by Descartes and others, asks Fontenelle, that nature is uniform in her workings; that she does not vary her prescription from generation to generation?

Here, however, a problem presented itself: the Dark Ages, the period of European history that stretched—in the proud rationalist consciousness of the age in which Fontenelle lived, at least—from the fall of Rome down until about the sixteenth century.

(Not until the "rediscovery" of the Middle Ages in the nineteenth century would this period come in for anything but the disdain and hatred that we find in seventeenth and eighteenth characterizations of it.) How, given the all-too-manifest existence of the superstitions, ignorance, and cultural desolation of the Dark Ages, asked the rationalist Fontenelle, could the theory of nature's uniformity and the dependent theory of the continuous progress of knowledge be sustained? If the progress of knowledge is to be foreseen as certain in the future, it must be seen as having been certain and continuous in the past. The seeming exception or interruption constituted by the Dark Ages was therefore crucial, as Fontenelle shrewdly realized. But he has a ready answer. The Dark Ages, he tells us, prove nothing; nothing, that is, decisive to the principle of continuous progress of mankind. "Would a man with good beginnings of science and belles-lettres even were he to forget them as the result of some illness, would that mean that he had become incapable of them?" [6] Certainly not. The knowledge would remain, even though temporarily rendered mute or distorted, and growth in this man's mental constitution would go on.

In the same year in which Fontenelle wrote his essay, another of like subject and argument was written by Perrault in which he addressed himself to the same point: the problem of the apparent discontinuity represented by the Middle Ages; and Perrault used a different analogy to get around the difficulty. Despite the appearance of superstition unrelieved that medieval Europe presents to us, despite the surface of ignorance, tyranny, and churchly oppression, true knowledge actually continued in its development, but this development went underground, as it were, "like those rivers which are suddenly swallowed up, but which, after having flowed underground for a space, come finally upon an outlet in some neighboring province, when they are seen to reissue with the same abundance with which they vanished from sight. The outlets through which the sciences and arts are restored to the earth are the happy reigns of great monarchs, who, by reestablishing peace and tranquillity in their states, cause to reflourish there all the graces of learning." [7]

The importance of this metaphoric substantiation of the "real" continuity of knowledge, despite the "appearance" formed by history is, of course, immense so far as the theory of progress is concerned. For, insofar as progress is a principle or theory instead of a mere hope for the future, it must be shown, as the French rationalists clearly understood, to be a part of the natural scheme of things, one of the provisions of nature for mankind and the development of mankind's learning and knowledge. History, in the sense of everything that has visibly happened, did not, as the example of the Dark Ages made clear, support the principle of certain, continuous progress. And, as both Fontenelle and Perrault realized (and, after them, all other theorists of progress, including Condorcet, Comte, Hegel, and Spencer) the Dark Ages formed by no means the only example of its kind. There were many others in the long history of mankind.

So a distinction had to be made; a very fundamental distinction: the distinction between what happens *naturally* and *normally* in the development of knowledge and, by contrast, what happens all too often in the concrete histories of peoples and areas. It is the nature of human knowledge, so the rationalist argument ran, to progress constantly—cumulatively and surely. But, as with all forms of growth, interferences can obtrude themselves—interferences in the forms of war, despotism, ecclesiastical dominance, dogmatic rigidities, and the like. And when these interferences obtrude themselves, as they so plainly had during the Dark Ages from the seventeenth-century rationalist point of view, the progress of knowledge must come to a halt—temporary so far as the long run is concerned, but a halt nonetheless, at least on the surface.

Now, the important point in this rationalist argument is, of course, the assumption that what is natural and normal is the *progressive development* of knowledge. Conceivably, looking at the rather grim panorama of history, with all the despotism, war, and superstition that the rationalists saw only too clearly, a different proposition might have emerged: a reverse proposition, one which declared in effect that the progress of knowledge is *not* a normal or natural process in time but rather something so infrequent and sporadic that it might be preferable to assume the contrary of the idea of progress: to assume that what is "normal" or "natural" is inertia or stagnation, leaving the infrequent bursts of progress as the matter to be explained.

But from at least the time of publication of Bacon's *Advancement of Learning*, and gathering momentum in the seventeenth century, the theory prevailed that it is progress that is normal and natural, even certain in the long run, and that the task of statecraft is simply therefore that of removing obstructions to this natural progress of knowledge. And it was this aspect, of course, that in the eighteenth century was to make the theory of progress such a marvellous ally for those concerned with revolutionary overthrow of existing institutions.

The distinction I have just referred to is, in essence, the one we observed earlier: the distinction made by the Greeks between "growth" and "history." The Greeks made growth, as we saw, a normal attribute of all things, social and cultural included. And the task of reason, or science, was that of discerning the patterns of growth peculiar to all living things, including polities and economies and cultures in general. History, however, in the sense of the concrete data dealt with by a Thucydides or Xenophon, might or might not reveal such patterns of growth. Aristotle had made the powerful distinction between the "necessary" and the "accidental," meaning by the latter the fortuitous, yes, but also on occasion the *actual:* that which actually happened (e.g. a hail storm in July, a desiccating drought in spring) in contrast to what was normal or natural.

So also with respect to mankind and knowledge. Augustine, working from the premise of an omnipotent God, had tried to fuse the actual events and actions of history with the concept of *physis* he drew from the Greeks and from which, as we saw, his own theory of development was drawn, one presented not merely in terms of things and conditions—man's material and non-material culture—but also in terms of epochs of the events and personages which had characterized the history of man from Adam onward.

But the rationalists of the seventeenth and eighteenth centuries, like the rationalists of the fifth century B.C., were not disposed to deal with past, present, and future in the terms of an ever-guiding Providence. Their objective was a theory of the development of mankind's knowledge that would be based upon what is constitutive to mankind itself, not to an external deity. If the progress of mankind was to be made certain in theoretical terms it must be premised on man, his passions, interests, and reason. No more than their Greek forerunners did the seventeenth-century philosophers doubt that in knowledge, in human wisdom through the ages, there was a self-engendering drive to cumulative improvement. True, the record does not often show this cumulative, continuous improvement. But this is because of the incessant obstructions that human beings in their cupidity or ignorance or superstition have placed in the way of this improvement, which is always waiting to be released from its obstructions. For mankind as a whole, as for the single hypothetical human being living through all ages that forms the analogy, there are intermittent fevers, sicknesses, debilities. These must be eradicated, cured.

A final word here on the analogy itself. St. Augustine could only have shaken his head in wonder at the illogicality of using it to support a theory of the constant and cumulative development of knowledge in the past, but of then departing from its logic by declaring that "the man in question will have no old age," that mankind will forever remain in its prime, "and there will be no end to the growth and development of human wisdom."

But, then, a Plato or Seneca could only have shaken his head at the illogicality of Augustine's using the analogy from birth to death, but then refusing to allow the existence of succeeding cycles of existence.

2. THE EXPANSION OF METAPHOR

After the age of Fontenelle the idea of progress becomes widened in scope, moving from the accumulation of human knowledge to which it had been confined universally in the seventeenth century to an ever-wider purview, one that before the eighteenth century was ended came to include governments, economies, social institutions of all types, even morality and human happiness. More important, the concept of *civilization* became a vital one in the eighteenth century, a concept which was made to include manners as well as ideas, institutions as well as knowledge. The philosophers of the eighteenth century set the idea of progress ever more widely in the context of civilization rather than knowledge alone, just as in the nineteenth century the idea was cast in terms of society or culture.

It was the great Leibniz, as early as 1697, who gave metaphysical sanction, as it were, to what had been, or what might have seemed, but the artifice of intellectuals. Arguing from the principle of plenitude as well as of natural growth, Leibniz declared that to comprehend the true fullness of perfection of nature we must see it in terms of its potentiality as well as its actuality. "Although many substances have already attained a great perfection, yet on account of the infinite divisibility of the continuous, there always remain in the abyss of things slumbering parts which have yet to be awakened, to grow in size and worth, and in a word, to advance to a more perfect state. And hence no end of progress is ever to be reached." [8]

In the next century there would be those to sneer at and to caricature Leibniz's words. Yet it is clear that he was only arguing from precisely the same premises of immanence, of continuity, and of latent, emergent being that have been, historically, indistinguishable from the metaphor of growth. He is saying exactly what Herbert Spencer would say in the nineteenth century and what in different wording Marx, Comte, and many others would say: that, given the principle of development, of potentiality in unceasing drive toward actuality, progress was—and I use here Spencer's words because they are precisely applicable to Leibniz—"not an accident but a beneficent necessity."

Leibniz said something else that would prove indispensable to the major developmentalists of the eighteenth and nineteenth centuries, including Darwin. "Nature," he wrote in matchless

apothegm, "never makes leaps." Banish the thought of discontinuities and fortuitous jumps which might make a true science impossible. Nature never makes leaps. Always she proceeds in continuous, gradual, and cumulative fashion. "Everything goes by
degrees in nature, and nothing leaps, and this rule as regards
changes is part of my law of continuity." [9] Of course, as we have
seen, it was exactly in terms of the premise of continuity that
Fontenelle and Perrault were able to declare human progress certain and necessary, and it was to justify the principle of continuity
that they, in effect, declared the whole Middle Ages a kind of
nightmare or fiction, not a part of nature's true provision. Nevertheless, it was Leibniz, with his immense philosophical prestige
and his impeccable metaphysical style, who, above any other single
figure, gave sanction to that most important attribute of growth
applied to civilization: continuity.

It was in terms of this same proposition of continuity of growth
in time that Leibniz also provided Western thought with the
formula for prediction of the future that it has followed right
down to our present moment. In 1714 he wrote, in his *Principles
of Nature and Grace*, "The present is big with the future, the
future might be read in the past, the distant is expressed in the
near." [10] Nothing about the proposition is really novel, of course;
it was in these terms that Aristotle, and before him, the Pre-
Socratics, fused past, present, and future. If civilization—or anything, for that matter—is indeed subject to the principles of
growth, then it follows inexorably that the present is big with the
future, just as the past was once pregnant with what is now actual
in the present. And if all this is true, then does it not follow that
in addition to discerning the curve of development from past to
present, it is possible by the same logic to extrapolate this curve of
development into the future? Leibniz thought so. And so, in the
generations to follow, did Turgot, Condorcet, Comte, Marx,
Tocqueville, and Spencer, all of whom, in their predictions of
equality, Positivism, socialism, the mass state, individual freedom
—as the case might be—were but finding, with Leibniz's apothegm in mind, the future in the present.

The idea that beneath the crimes and follies of history, actual history, there is a deep current of natural progress, needing only to be aided in its flow, only to be freed of the earthworks of superstition and tyranny, could not help but prove an attractive and valuable one to the French *philosophes* at the end of the eighteenth century. To their hatred of church, aristocracy, guild, and feudal tradition on political grounds, on grounds of utopian dream, there could be added a vision of human development in which all these institutions were to be deemed not simply moral evils but obstacles to the natural course of progress of civilization that would prevail if only these groups and institutions could be extirpated.

Hence the vision that sits like a beacon light over so much of the eighteenth century, especially in France but to be seen also in Germany and England, in which Progress is held to be the natural and normal trend of mankind but which, for its free and uninterrupted flow, requires from time to time the obliteration of obstructing institutions and beliefs. The conviction of progress as the normal tendency of man was united with the belief in the existence of a natural order and also in the existence of a "natural history" that all things follow until they are arrested or diverted by artificial circumstances. I shall come back to eighteenth-century "natural history" shortly, for it is the indispensable background for our understanding of the form that was to be taken by the nineteenth-century idea of social development or social evolution. For the present, however, it is important to continue with the concept of progress and its ineffaceable metaphoric premises.

Kant gave the idea of progress a mighty boost when, in reply to some exceedingly shrewd doubts on the matter expressed by Moses Mendelssohn (who had written that human beings seem never to take steps forward without soon sliding back with double rapidity to their former state), he wrote: "I will therefore venture to assume that as the human race is continually advancing in civilization and culture as its natural purpose, so it is continually making progress for the better in relation to the moral end of its existence, and that this progress, although it may be sometimes interrupted, will never be entirely broken off or stopped." [11]

No other single statement better illustrates the degree to which, within the bare space of a century, the idea of progress passed from a descriptive generalization embracing knowledge alone to one comprehending the whole of civilization and human culture, including even morality. Moreover, this progress is absolutely certain in the long ages ahead. In his *Idea for a Universal History* Kant declared that despite the appearance of the merely contingent and sporadic in human history, we may see the movement of mankind as a whole "to be steady and progressive though slow evolution of its original endowment."

> The history of mankind can be seen in the large as the realization of Nature's secret plan to bring forth a perfectly constituted state as the only condition in which the capacities of mankind can be fully developed, and also bring forth that external relation among states which is perfectly adequate to this end.[12]

What Kant is seeking in his study of universal history is a secure underpinning for the whole principle of progress. This is an effort that bore much result in his work and that of others. He compares his enterprise with that of Kepler and Newton who had reduced the seemingly contingent and erratic motions of the planets to definite laws and then explained these laws by a "universal natural cause." We will note in passing, however, that whereas Kepler and Newton had managed to arrive at principles unknown to classical and Christian philosophers alike, Kant reaches his "universal natural cause" strictly within the framework of a kind of secularized Augustinianism. Uniting all of Kant's asserted principles of the evolution and progress of mankind is the same metaphoric conception of growth that underlay the works of Augustine and his followers.

"All natural capacities of a creature are destined to evolve completely to their natural end." Here is the essence of the analogy that we have been concerned with. There follows his application of it to mankind: "In man (as the only rational creature on earth) those natural capacities which are directed to the use of his reason are to be fully developed only in the race, not in the individual." And then, in a final burst of Augustinianism, this time with respect to means, he writes: "The means employed by Nature to bring about the development of all the capacities of men is their antagonism in society, so far as this is, in the end, the cause of a lawful order among men." [13]

Kant wrote also a little work which he titled "Conjectural Beginning of Human History." It is an essay in that form of investigation so dear to the hearts of eighteenth-century philosophers, the "conjectural" or "natural" or "hypothetical" history, which the philosophers rigorously contrasted with the ordinary kind of history-writing. I shall have much more to say of this mode of investigation in the next chapter, for it is the immediate forerunner of the nineteenth-century theory of social evolution. For the moment, however, I wish only to stress the fact that "conjectural" history, whether in Kant or any other writer of his day, was a means of demonstrating the reality of progress as a fixed principle. By fixing attention upon what was thought to be the *natural* provision for progress in mankind and distinguishing this from the plethora of accidents, mishaps, and follies that formed the *appearance* of human history, it was possible to give evolutionary justification for the principle of social and moral perfection in time. Thus Kant can write, in words which are to be echoed throughout the next century and more, that "whether man has won or lost in this change [that is, from the primitive to civilized state] is no longer an open question, if one considers the destiny of his species. This consists in nothing less than progress toward perfection, be the first attempts toward that aim, or even the first long series of attempts, ever so faulty." [14]

Kant's words appeared in 1786, and they may be taken as sufficient evidence that the search for a "law" of progress, far from being, as it is sometimes thought to be, a preoccupation of the nineteenth century, was part and parcel of the Enlightenment's desire to found its proposals for reform upon what was understood to be a law of motion of human society. Men's conscious attempts to reform government were important; no one of the great rationalists ever denied this; but of overriding importance was the conviction —to be found in minds as dissimilar as Kant, Adam Smith, and

Rousseau—that such reforms were to be conceived as the making actual in society what was latent, what was inherent in nature's provision for progress.

Eleven years later, in France, appeared Condorcet's remarkable *Progress of the Human Mind*, written while he was in hiding for his life from the secret police of the Jacobins whom he had offended. Here too we learn that

> nature has set no term to the perfection of human faculties, that the perfectibility of man is truly indefinite; and that the progress of this perfectibility, from now onwards independent of any power that might wish to halt it, has no other limit than the duration of the globe upon which nature has cast us. This progress will doubtless vary in speed, but it will never be reversed as long as the earth occupies its present place in the system of the universe, and as long as the general laws of this system produce neither a general cataclysm nor such changes as will deprive the human race of its present faculties and its present resources.[15]

But Condorcet does not limit himself to general propositions. The greatness and also miraculousness (considering the book-bare attic in which he was forced to write) of his volume lie in the union of what might be called psychological principles and anthropological overview. For, like Kant, Condorcet seeks to ground the necessity of the progress of civilization in the unalterable characteristics of the human mind, in its restlessness, its curiosity, and its faculties generally. But he goes beyond this, and we are treated also to an outline of the cultural stages through which mankind has passed in its progress to the present. Space does not permit a detailed description of these, and it must suffice to say that within them we find, in careful and sequential development, the beginnings of human society in clans and tribes, a theory of the probable origins of language, writing, and the arts which first formed civilization; the transition from the pastoral to the agricultural stage; the founding of governments and, with them, modes of despotism under which man has so long suffered and which have slowed down his rate of progress; the beginnings of rational philosophy and of science in the ancient world; the growth and spread of commerce, cities, and ever-widening enlightenment of men, all the way down to Condorcet's own period of history, which he places in the ninth stage of humanity's progress, and from which the tenth and last, and greatest, stage was even then, he was convinced, Jacobins or no, being formed in embryo, to be given birth by the mighty French Revolution. It is in his final chapter, on the tenth stage, that we are offered Condorcet's vision of what the imminent future would be like: its equality of opportunity, its liberty, its rationality, its democracy, and its universal education.

It is a mark of not simply prophetic passion but of scientific conviction that Condorcet was able to forecast this benign future while hiding from the Jacobin police, and if I stress this it is only to emphasize again the point so often overlooked in histories of social thought, that the effort to ground the progress of civilization in psychological and sociological law—that is, to rescue it from mere utopian caprice and give it scientific sanction—commences in the eighteenth, not the nineteenth century. This is true even though philosophers like Comte and Marx in the latter century were fond of supposing that *they* were the scientists of progressive development, and that all that had preceded them was altruistic sentiment, utopian speculation.

Throughout his delineation of the nine stages of progressive development in the past and present, Condorcet constantly emphasizes the barriers, the hurdles, the interferences, that progress has had to cope with. Always in the past, he writes, there have been the power-driven ways of despots, wars, calamities of one kind or other induced by human ignorance, inequality, economic exploitation, and, perhaps above all, the superstitions of religion, the machinations of priests. In the present age, Condorcet writes, mankind shows, with the events of the Revolution in France leading the way, the first real evidence of finally liberating itself from all of these toils and traps. And once liberated from them, there cannot help but be progress at a pace never before known.

For those who may still think that the eighteenth century merely hoped for, or dreamed of, progress, the following passage from Condorcet is instructive:

The history of man from the time when alphabetical writing
was known in Greece to the condition of the human race today in
the most enlightened countries of Europe is linked by an uninterrupted chain of facts and observations. . . . Philosophy has
nothing more to guess, no more hypothetical surmises to make; it
is enough to assemble and order the facts and to show the useful
truths that can be derived from their connections and from their
totality.[16]

How often those very words would be written, with the air of fresh
announcement, in the following century!

It is occasionally implied that Condorcet sang alone the
eighteenth-century chorale of universal progress. Such is far from
the case, however. I have mentioned the mighty Kant: there was
also Herder, one of the most undervalued philosophers of civilization, it seems to me, in modern Western thought. There is almost
nothing that would be contained a century later in the so-called
"historical" schools of the social sciences that cannot be found systematically stated by Herder. Uniting all of his observations on the
development of civilization, its ideas, traits, and institutions, is the
certainty of a unilinear trend of progressive development for mankind at large. Like most of the other philosophers of progress he
avails himself, of course, of the familiar analogy of infancy, youth,
maturity, and old age, using it, as he tells us, "to point out a high-
way on which the history of cultivation . . . could be traced with
certainty." Storms, setbacks, revolutions of violence there will be
indeed. These, Herder tells us, are "necessary to our species, as the
waves to the stream, that it become not a stagnant pool. The genius of humanity blooms in continually renovated youth, and is
regenerated as it proceeds, in nations, generations, and fami-
lies." [17]

Hegel, a scant generation later, repeated this thought. The
"childhood," "youth," "manhood," and "old age" into which
Hegel divided the historical development of civilization—more
accurately, the spirit of freedom through the ages—betokened the
advancement of mankind as a whole; an advancement made inexorable by the very constitution of humanity. But such progress

could only have been achieved through conflict and through inter-mediate deaths of specific civilizations. We may compare the total-ity of the process, Hegel writes, to the plant, from seed to fruition, but "commencement and result are disjoined from each other." What is begun by a single people is passed on to still another people, with the first succumbing to the "poison-draught" of the very elixir it created; for the single people "the taste of the draught is its annihilation, though at the same time the rise of a new prin-ciple." [18]

And this essentially is the view of the progress of mankind that lasts throughout the nineteenth century—and even today. When Comte declared progress an iron law of civilization, he was careful to specify civilization as a whole. "To me," wrote Comte, "it ap-pears that the amelioration is as unquestionable as the develop-ment from which it proceeds." But this, he continues, is "taking the human race as a whole, and not any one people. . . ." [19]

Darwin was writing precisely in this vein when, in *The Origin of the Species*, he spoke of "an innate tendency toward progressive development" in the species. Not, obviously, for each and every species that has ever come into being, but only for the totality of species conceived as a long chain of being from the beginning of things. Similarly, when Darwin wrote that "in all cases the new and improved forms of life tend to supplant the old and unim-proved forms" [20] he was referring, just as Hegel and Herder did in regard to peoples and civilizations, to a mode of conflict built into the nature of progressive development.

And, finally, there is Herbert Spencer's celebrated declaration: ". . . progress is not an accident, not a thing within human con-trol, but a beneficent necessity." So many times has this passage been laughed at, treated with contempt, marked as the utterance of someone wholly blind to the miseries and mishaps around him. But Spencer was as well aware as most scholars—almost as aware as Marx and Engels—of the economic and social distresses of his age. He did not declare that these distresses, or the system that en-compassed them, were good, or signs of progress. What Spencer said in his famous essay *Progress: Its Law and Cause* was merely that, taking the human race as a whole, from beginning to present, from present to anticipated future, a line of progress could be clearly discerned, and that while individual species, peoples, and civilizations have fallen, and will continue to fall, progress for humankind as a whole is "not an accident but a necessity." Brash though the words may appear out of context, I can think offhand of no philosopher of progress and development in the nineteenth century who would have disagreed with them in context.

Spencer serves as well as anyone to emphasize again the essentially metaphoric and analogical footings of the theory of progress as we find it in modern writing. The investigations of such biologists as Wolff, Goethe, and von Baer have established the truth, Spencer writes, "that the series of changes gone through during the development of a seed into a tree, or an ovum into an animal, constitute an advance from homogeneity of structure to heterogeneity of structure." [21] And here we come to perhaps the most famous paragraph in the nineteenth century on the subject of progress, a paragraph moreover that serves as a bridge to our concern in the next section of this book, the theory of development.

> Now, we propose in the first place to show that this law of organic progress is the law of all progress. Whether it be in the development of the earth, in the development of life upon its surface, in the development of society, of government, of manufactures, of commerce, of language, literature, science, art, this same evolution of the simple into the complex, through successive differentiations, holds throughout. From the earliest traceable cosmical changes down to the latest results of civilization, we shall find that the transformation of the homogeneous into the heterogeneous, is that in which progress essentially consists.[22]

There were many in the nineteenth century who believed that Spencer—Mr. Spencer as he was admiringly known even to those closest to him—was the first human being in history to have rendered progress from an ideal to a scientific law. We can only respect the honor in which Herbert Spencer was held by so many of his contemporaries. But to believe that Spencer was the first to put progressive development in the form of law is signal injustice to the many who preceded him: Comte, Hegel, Kant, Condorcet, Leibniz, and others all the way back to the Greeks who were the first to liken the growth of human culture to the unfolding of the seed. True, it would never have occurred to a Greek or Roman philosopher to extend the principles of progressive development beyond the cyclical recurrence of genesis and decay. But the idea that growth was progressive in the upswing of the cycle, in the trajectory from seed to maturity, was as unquestioned by Greek as by Victorian philosopher. And for both, the principal aim of the science of man was that of describing and explaining this process of development.

3. PROGRESS AND DEGENERATION (3)

But the idea of progressive development is far from being the whole story in the eighteenth and nineteenth centuries. So accustomed are we to thinking of these centuries in the undiversified terms of the progressive view of historical change—of optimism, hope, confidence in future, etc.—that it comes as a surprise when we are reminded that side by side with the prophets of progress stood those who saw anything but amelioration in the human condition and its future. The historian F. S. Marvin has somewhere referred to the nineteenth century as the Century of Great Hope. So it was. But it was, almost equally among educated minds, the Century of Foreboding: foreboding of the results of the very values and processes which to utilitarians, democrats, socialists, and humanitarians promised certain progress.

In preceding chapters we have noted the degree to which intimations of progress and degeneration coalesced in earlier ages. Greek and Roman conviction of cyclical genesis and decay carried with it conceptions of progress from the past as well as premonitions of degeneration in the future. And Augustine, as certain as anyone could be of anything that the end of the mortal world lay ahead, could yet write an inspired paean to mankind's cultural and intellectual progress from the past.

It is now necessary to call attention to the fact that though we may ordinarily think the eighteenth and nineteenth centuries were progress-intoxicated, there were nonetheless prophets of different inspiration in these centuries. Among them were some of the profoundest minds of their time, minds that have done a great deal to shape twentieth-century thought. The reaction to the pieties of progress that we generally think of as arising in the twentieth century—and as the reaction to such recent events as economic depression, political totalitarianism, and two massive world wars— is hardly more than a widening acceptance of ideas of decay, moribundity, and endemic defeat that we have no difficulty in extracting from the works of such men as Bonald, Tocqueville, Donoso Cortès, Burckhardt, Max Weber, and others in the nineteenth and very early twentieth centuries.

Even, however, in the eighteenth century we find some very emphatic doubts of progressive development in the human condition, some skepticism that an idea drawn in the first instance from the generalized accumulation of knowledge in the past could realistically be made the basis of either syntheses or prophecies when it came to the wider matters of morality, governments, and human happiness.

Nowhere in the eighteenth century were doubts of progress more widespread, more profound, than in that remarkable group of Scottish moral philosophers that numbered among its members such minds as David Hume, Adam Ferguson, Adam Smith, Lord Kames, Lord Monboddo, and others. Despite the infinitely greater attention that the French Enlightenment has received from historians, one would be hard put to defend the proposition that it carried with it greater brilliance, much less greater profundity, than the Scottish Enlightenment of the same period.

In his *An Essay on the History of Civil Society*, published in 1767, Adam Ferguson, then professor of moral philosophy at the University of Edinburgh, made it very plain that he could discern no consistent line of progress whatsoever in the history of nations. One full section of his book is devoted indeed to what he calls "the decline of nations." Another deals with the effects of corruption, of social decay. Moreover, he is far from convinced that time brings with it improvement in the affairs of men.

We are generally at a loss to conceive how mankind can subsist under manners and customs extremely different from our own; and we are apt to exaggerate the misery of barbarous times, by an imagination of what we ourselves should suffer in a situation to which we are not accustomed. But every age hath its consolations, as well as its sufferings. In the interval of occasional outrages, the friendly intercourses of men, even in their rudest condition, is affectionate and happy.[23]

The progress of societies to greatness, Ferguson writes, "is not more natural than their return to weakness and obscurity is necessary and unavoidable." Ferguson notes how frequently mankind, or a single civilization or nation, is made analogous to the life-cycle of the individual; now progress is drawn from it, now the very opposite. "But it must be obvious that the case of nations and that of individuals is very different." [24] There is no more reason inherently to expect progress with the passage of centuries than to expect its opposite.

Ferguson's contemporary, David Hume, was equally skeptical. So rare, Hume thought, are the actual evidences of intellectual advancement in human history that we might with better cause regard fixity and inertia rather than progress as the normal condition. There is little reason to conclude either from reason or observation that the world is eternal or uniform. Many things "prove strongly the mortality of this fabric of the world, and its passage by corruption or dissolution from one state or order to another." [25] If the world is indeed like an organism in its growth then it follows that old age and decrepitude are inexorable.

But acceptance of the metaphor of growth and decay does not mean for Hume that human reason and observation can conclude anything definite with respect to progress or decline within the relatively short period of time that has been taken up by human history. Any effort to discern either linear progress or linear

degeneration within the period of man's known history is doomed
to failure. There is no evidence that men today are physically
different from men many thousands of years ago. In this Hume is,
of course, one with Fontenelle and the defenders of the moderns.
But Hume breaks with them on concluding from this sameness of
physical type a constantly increasing knowledge and civilization in
history. All that we can safely conclude, he thinks, is that there has
been a constant pattern of rise and fall, of genesis and decay, of
efflorescence and desuetude of human cultures. Taking the universe at large, and even allowing that it must have its cycle of
growth and decay, "it must still be uncertain whether, at present,
it be advancing to its point of perfection or declining from
it. . . ." [26]

Hume was by no means alone in his century. For every Abbé
de Saint-Pierre, every Kant, every Condorcet fascinated by the
marks of progress alone, there was a Voltaire to point to the melancholy fact "that in the course of many revolutions, both in
Europe and Asia, peoples which once were well organized have
fallen into a state of near savagery." [27] Nor would this undulating
character diminish, Voltaire thought, in the future; civilization is
forever imperiled by the possibility of degeneration. And whatever
the larger view of the fate of mankind that we may find in a
Gibbon or a Montesquieu or Volney, there was assuredly ample
reflection within this larger view on the decline and decay that
seize specific civilizations.

One of the best-read volumes of the late eighteenth century in
France was the Count de Volney's *Ruins*, a charming little work
that opens with the author's sad contemplation of the ruins of
Palmyra. "Thus," writes Volney, "perish the works of men, and
thus do nations and empires vanish away. . . . Who can assure us
that desolation like this will not one day be the lot of our country?" [28]

Still, for all the air of melancholy with which Volney's book
begins, there is—and this indeed is the very theme of the book—
hope eternal for man if he will but only learn the lessons of history. For, as Volney gazes at the ruins of Palmyra, an apparition

appears, who uncovers for the author the principal causes of the breakdown of civilizations in the past, which, unless averted, will lead to Europe's decline in the future. These causes are the familiar ones of ignorance, superstition, ecclesiastical fetters, and political despotism. If man will but eradicate these and allow liberty, human rights, and the natural order of goodness to prevail, the whole to be set in a context of rationalist education, then nothing will prevent progress continuing forever.

What is true of Volney's depiction seems to me almost universally true of the French Enlightenment: genuine consciousness of corruption, decay, and decline in history, including the present that surrounded the *philosophes,* but along with this consciousness a profound faith that if only, for the first time in history, the *interferences* to progress could be removed by wise legislation or enlightened despotism, the natural order of progressive development would take over. I think this is true even of Voltaire. He could be savage in his denunciation of the crimes and follies of past and present, in his occasional categorical repudiation of all that surrounded him (though much of this served purely specific and tactical purpose), but there is little doubt that for Voltaire human progress would be assured if there were to be inaugurated a regime of individual freedom, rationalism, and total liberation from the traditional authorities and dogmas inherited from the past.

The same is true of Rousseau. If we follow the progression of argument from his first *Discourse,* on the arts and sciences and the corrupting influence they have had on man's character in history, through the second *Discourse,* on inequality, where he accounts for cultural corruption in terms of the rise of private property and artificial social inequality, through the third *Discourse,* on political economy, to the great *Social Contract,* we discover that like most of the other philosophers of his time Rousseau had a perfectly clear notion of the natural tendency of man toward goodness and toward political progress. What else indeed are the prescriptions contained in the third *Discourse* and the *Social Contract* but very detailed predictions, in effect, of the progress that will ensue once the scene has been cleared of the social rubbish deposited by history through the ages and ages of superstition and despotism mankind has had to endure? It is sometimes said that Rousseau proposed the abnegation of all human polity and culture and man's return to the state of nature. Rousseau made no such proposal. What he proposed was the restoration of the kind of freedom that man had once enjoyed in his earliest stages of cultural development *through the building of the political community founded on the General Will.* Given this type of community and the type of economy, religion, system of education, and family life he tirelessly advocated, Rousseau's belief in progress was as vital as that of any other philosopher of this day.

There was, to be sure, a cult of "exoticism" in the eighteenth century, chiefly in France; one that looked to the lives of the South Sea Islanders, for example, as these were vastly idealized in a very popular literature of the day, and contrasted these lives in an imagined state of nature with the culture of Europe.[29] And, as in Hesiod's *Works and Days* or in Ovid's *Metamorphoses,* or even in Augustine's rendering of the Garden, there is the powerful suggestion of an ineradicable conflict between moral goodness and culture. The cult of Nature was a reality in the eighteenth century. But then, as we have already noted, it is a reality pretty much throughout history. It cannot be said, however, that any of the major philosophers of the century took this theme very seriously. Even Rousseau, who found the history of the arts and sciences to have been throughout allied with the baser instincts of man, and who referred to the "natural decorum" of the uneducated and the lowly in his time, believed that once the good state was formed, the arts and sciences could then, for the first time in history, serve mankind well and be united with morality.

It is a different matter, however, when we come to the nineteenth century. What we find, commencing in the aftermath of the French Revolution, is a conviction that impending tragedy lies in the very conditions that for utilitarians and rationalists, for liberals generally, and for radicals universally spelled mankind's progressive emancipation from the past. Thus in the writings of the post-Revolutionary Conservatives we find ourselves confronted by a more or less tragic view of life set in time perspective.[30] It is a view that draws its melancholy forecast of future, not from extraneous or fortuitous factors, but from the very substance of history, from the very forces that the rationalists had hailed as promising liberation and the new empire of reason. In this view history is conceived as being periodically seized by deep moral crises which do not—as the thinkers of inexorable progress argued—automatically resolve themselves but remain instead to haunt and mock man's hopes of secular salvation.

What we see in this view of history is the specter of cultural disintegration and moral disenchantment. Major values seem to be in process of corruption, a process caused by conditions that no mere social reconstruction, even revolution, is likely to offset. There is a preoccupation with social dislocation—of community, class, authority, and sacred values—that arises out of centuries-old tendencies—of centralization, leveling, secularization. Where the progressive rationalist had tended to deprecate the crises and disorders in history, to see them, even as Marx and Spencer did, as necessary, if ugly, steps toward the new and good, the alienated philosophers saw these rather as "wounds" in the social organism which would not necessarily heal themselves.

We may take Bonald as the exemplar of the conservative distrust of modern European development. Curiously, Bonald is, despite his hatred of modern forces, more optimistic than Tocqueville and Weber were to be. For, he argues, the Revolution can be seen as a gigantic and awful lesson. More, it can be seen as a form of illness in which the accumulated poisons have been allowed to run out of the social body. We are approaching a major crisis in the development of society, writes Bonald. The French Revolution was, like all revolutions, both religious and political (Bonald's characterization of the French Revolution in these terms is the probable source of Tocqueville's later and classic treatment), and it was the result of powerful laws "governing the preservation of societies, to be compared to a terrible and salutary crisis by means of which nature roots out from the social body those vicious principles which the weakness of authority had allowed to creep in. . . ."[31]

Will this crisis turn Europe providentially from the course it has held since the sixteenth century, a course compounded of individualism, rationalism, the sovereignty of the people, secularism, industrialism, and the like, or will these by now deeply implanted elements of modernism stay fixed? There is no certainty. "Anarchy has been dethroned and the armies of atheism are defeated; but the precedent lives on after these successes and the principles survive the precedent." [32] Generations have been reared, Bonald reflects, on the errors and poisons of the spirit of dissent and rationalism that began in the wake of the feudal period, the period that Bonald, like most of the conservatives, revered.

What conservatism introduced into European thought after the two great revolutions, democratic and industrial, had begun to transform the European landscape, was a profound doubt that human betterment did indeed consist of the qualities we referred to earlier as modernism, qualities which the philosophers of progress like Comte, Marx, Spencer, and the utilitarians generally saw as the beneficent heritage of social development out of the past. Now, increasingly, there appears a vein of thought in Western Europe that saw, not progressive amelioration in the tides of individualism, secularism, democracy, and industrialism, but slowly accumulating disaster for the West, possibly for mankind everywhere.

We see this vein of thought in the great Tocqueville. Liberal to the core in his sensibilities and political values, a participant in the Revolution of 1848, no lover of the reactionaries of his day, Tocqueville, as we know, saw a double-edged fate in the development of social equality which, for him, was the single great tidal current of European history from the early Middle Ages on. There were, he conceded, many noble results to be seen in the leveling of classes and the spread of individualism, mass culture, and equalitarianism. And he did not for a moment suppose that the heritage of the Age of Reason and of the two revolutions, democratic and industrial, could be thrown away; nor did Tocqueville even desire it. But no one can miss the fact that what sets off *Democracy in America* (a work as much, if not more, about France and Europe as about the United States, a point Tocqueville himself emphasized) from most other books on democracy in the nineteenth century is the *tragic* element that Tocqueville finds in democracy. All that is potentially good is also potentially bad. Equality liberates but also enchains—in a new type of despotism that democracies alone have to face. Individualism emancipates but it also alienates—in new forms of selfishness, spiritual isolation, and insatiable restlessness. Secularism opens the mind to new worlds of conquest but steadily weakens the desire to prosecute them. Public opinion triumphs over the tyranny of princes but becomes itself a greater repression of individual thought than anything to be found in the Spanish Inquisition. And power becomes ever greater in the political form of democracy than ever it was in the hands of divine right monarchs.

So it goes. "Shall we ever," Tocqueville asked in 1848, at the time of his very success in the Revolution of that year,

> as we are assured by other prophets, perhaps as delusive as their predecessors, shall we ever attain a more complete and far-reaching social transformation than our fathers foresaw and desired, and that we ourselves are able to foresee; or are we not destined simply to end in a condition of intermittent anarchy, the well-known and chronic and incurable complaint of old peoples? As for me, I am unable to say: I do not know when this long voyage will be ended; I am weary of seeing the shore in each successive mirage, and I often ask myself whether the *terra firma* we are seeking does really exist, and whether we are not doomed to rove upon the seas forever! [33]

To a Marx or Spencer such words could have seemed but the outcroppings of pernicious traditionalism, of fear of change, of distrust of the iron laws of development. But to more than a few other powerful minds of the nineteenth century, Tocqueville's words bespoke their own conviction that in the alleged manifestations of progress there lay the canker of impending doom, self-engendered doom, for the West, possibly for all mankind.

Space does not permit any detailed summarization of the view of degeneration that lay side by side with the view of progress in the nineteenth century. Let it suffice here only to refer to Burckhardt, who saw the future in the hands of the *simplificateurs terri-bles*, those men of power fashioned by democracy's twin forces of bureaucracy and militarism; to Frederick Le Play, for whom the triumph of democracy, liberalism, and laissez-faire industrialism was the very negation of morality and human happiness; to Nietz-sche, in whose eyes Europe was becoming ravaged by the new barbarians, nurtured by the decadence, philistinism, and idle romanticism of the democratic and industrial order; to Georges Sorel, author of *The Illusions of Progress*, enemy of the whole strain of progressive rationalism in European philosophy and let-ters, and caricaturist of those who professed to find linear meaning in history[34]; to Max Weber, who had dark premonitions of European freedom and humane culture being suffocated by spread-ing rationalization of society, thought, and mind; and to Émile Durkheim, who made it a very principle that the advancement of the arts and crafts of civilization is linked with the increase of unhappiness and the loss of the secure contexts of belief and membership in which alone man finds refuge from *anomie*.

Even in the United States, so often thought of as being, in the nineteenth and early twentieth centuries, almost single-mindedly buoyed up by belief in progress and in all the intellectual traits associated with it, there are profound skeptics of progress: John Quincy Adams, who liked little of the modern temper and was anything but optimistic of the future; Nathaniel Hawthorne, with his contempt for the whole progressive-utopian spirit; Fenimore Cooper and his hatred of the industrial and democratic forces that were destroying aristocratic traditionalism; and, of course, Herman Melville whose *Moby Dick* is one of the most powerful testaments ever written to the omnipresence and timelessness of evil.

And at the end of the nineteenth century in America there were the two Adams brothers, Henry and Brooks, both of whom reacted strongly against faith in the progressive development of human society. Henry Adams, reflecting much of his illustrious forebear's distrust of modernism, came increasingly to the view that what history actually reveals is not progress but regress; not inevitable fullment over time of potentiality, not enhancement of energy, but a running down of vitality comparable to that proclaimed in the second law of thermodynamics. Entropy, not progressive expansion and differentiation, is at the heart of the historical process, as it is of the physical.

The law of development is as central in Henry Adams' thought (and in Brooks Adams') as we have found it to be in Comte, Buckle, and Spencer, whom both the Adams had read with admiration. So is the metaphor of growth and the analogy of society to an organism. If Henry Adams, under the mechanical impulsions of the age of science in which he lived the final years of his life, saw fit to deal with growth and decay in terms of physics rather than the terms of biology, the over-all objective was the same. What is important is that he rejected utterly the implications of progress, for present and future, that others were drawing from the metaphor of growth. Like the progressive developmentalists, he could divide the past into rigorous stages of development. He saw, first, the age of instinct; next the age of religion; then the age of science; and, finally the age of the supersensual, just beginning. Each ensuing age was shorter than its predecessor, and the final age threatened to be the shortest of all; then chaos. Throughout the evolutionary process there was a gradual depletion of human energy. The next hundred years, he thought, would see an "ultimate colossal, cosmic collapse." For him the supreme irony of it all was that civilization, the very assemblage of institutions, values, and beliefs that so many others regarded as the very definition of progress, was in fact a manifestation of decay—decay of the raw, primal energy that alone betokened man's true individuality and creativeness. Modern man, far from being at the apex of human development was actually "the most advanced type of physical decadence."

Somewhat different was Brooks Adams' presentation of the principle of decay. Whereas Henry had put the whole of history in a single, unitary framework of decline, Brooks tended rather to see history in the classical terms of recurring cycles of growth and decline. What he called "the law of civilization and decay" is a framework for the assessment of any one of a multiplicity of national or cultural histories. As a recent study suggests concerning Brooks Adams' theory of history: "Limited to human history, the law of civilization and decay was cyclical in nature, with each separate civilization or society running the gamut from concentration to decay. When one society became extinct, another rose to take its place until such time that it too had failed to acquire, by trade or war, new sources of energy." [35]

Even so, for all Brooks Adams' envisagement of history as characterized by recurrent cycles, he seemed to regard his own age, much as Henry did, as probably the final one in human history. Writing to his brother Henry, Brooks Adams put his despair for modern civilization in unambiguous terms:

> Out of it all observe that for the first time in human history there is not one ennobling instinct. There is not a barbarian anywhere sighing a chant of war and faith, there is not a soldier to sacrifice himself for an ideal. How can we hope to see a new world, a new civilization, or new life? To my mind we are at the end; and the one thing I thank God for is that we have no children.[36]

Nor, obviously, have accents of lament and melancholy disappeared from our own day. Side by side with the progress-minded intellectual for whom modernism connotes, even as it did for a Condorcet, Marx, or Spencer, liberation from the less mature, less progressive past and is a harbinger of even greater benefits in the future, with the inevitable spread of Western technology, democracy, and secularism over the world—side by side with this intellectual sits the intellectual who renounces these things, who sees not progress operating, but Brooks Adams' principle of decay, of entropy, and a future formed by decline and disintegration.

So, *mutatis mutandis*, was it in Aristotle's day; so was it in Augustine's.

PART II

THE THEORY OF SOCIAL DEVELOPMENT

Four

THE THEORY OF NATURAL HISTORY

Let us begin then by laying facts aside, as they
do not affect the question. The investigations we
may enter into in treating this subject, must not be
considered as historical truths, but only as mere
conditional or hypothetical reasonings, rather
calculated to explain the nature of things, than
to ascertain their actual origin; just like the
hypotheses which our physicists daily form
respecting the formation of the world.

> *Rousseau*

In most cases it is of more importance to
ascertain the progress that is most simple, than
the progress that is most agreeable to fact; for,
paradoxical as the proposition may appear, it is
certainly true that the real progress is not always
the most natural. It may have been determined by
particular accidents which are not likely to occur
again, and which cannot be considered as forming
any part of that general provision which nature
has made for the improvement of the human race.

> *Dugald Stewart*

1. NATURE VERSUS CONVENTION

Out of the eighteenth century's general interest in intellectual and
cultural progress came a more specialized concern with the *process*
of human development: that is, the successive steps or stages
through which mankind had passed to reach its present eminence. All of a sudden the atmosphere was filled with the words
"origins," "stages," "advancement," and "development." Such
terms were by no means limited to those who found the present
morally and politically satisfying. Far from it. Whether one chose
to regard the surrounding culture as good for the most part or un-

relievedly bad, the task confronting any moral philosopher who sought to explain this culture was the same. This task was quite literally to show how the present had come to be as it was, to demonstrate the provisions in nature—the nature of man and the nature of society—by which civilization had developed from primitive origins to its existing stage, and what might be done to aid this process of development in the interest of a more perfect society.

The framework of this interest in development was called variously "natural history," "conjectural history," "hypothetical history," and "deductive history." [1] Whatever the phrase used, the method was the same: to cut through the morass of customs, superstitions, traditions, and prescriptive laws, which to most of the rationalists of the age seemed to be the very stuff of the historic social order, to the underlying forces of the natural order. What was wanted was a conception of man's advancement through the ages in the terms of what was fundamental and natural to man, rather than in the terms of ordinary or conventional history.

The first point to make about the eighteenth century's cherished natural history is that it is part and parcel of that century's general adoration of the idea of nature. There are many meanings of the word "nature" with reference to man and society. But by all odds the most encompassing, the most widely used, is clearly that of the *pristine condition* of a thing, be it an organism, man himself, or an institution. "Pristine" is used here not in any chronological sense, although that is often involved, but rather in the sense of a thing's condition before it has in any way been corrupted by adventitious circumstances. To get to the nature of anything is to get to its shape and substance before these have been altered by exposure to elements and forces not bound up in its own being.

The reason why philosophers of the classical age and the eighteenth century alike so often looked imaginatively back to the origin of things was that it was thought that these in their supposed primal state might reveal the true essence, the *nature*, of things. But no classical philosopher or eighteenth-century rationalist ever supposed that "the natural" existed solely in primal times. *Nature*, whether with respect to man's own character, his religion, law, property, or the state, could be understood through the resources of reason, supplemented by comparative observation. That there was to be had, if reason and power could but accomplish it, a "natural" economy or polity permitted no doubt at all to any *philosophe*. And this did not at all mean "returning" to the state of nature. Nature was ever present, and could be made visible if only enlightened political action would remove the underbrush of convention and historical tradition that hid nature and her laws.

The Greeks, as we noted, made a fundamental distinction between *physis* and *nomos*. This distinction took on special significance in Attica after the Cleisthenean reforms at the end of the sixth century B.C. when, given the powerful currents of social and moral change induced by these reforms and also by the spectacle of the radically different ways of foreigners now able to visit Athens, philosophers, among them the Sophists, endeavored to distinguish the "natural" from the merely "conventional"; that is, the way of nature from the way of mere use and wont. And in this endeavor the affinity between the "natural" and the "rational" became very close indeed, for how else could the natural be discovered, lying buried and concealed by convention, save through the resources of reason? [2]

Equally powerful was this affinity in the seventeenth and eighteenth centuries in Western Europe. To cut through mere *appearance* (which could be identified with the plethora of conventions and habits by which man lived willy-nilly, through historical use and wont) to *reality* (which for social and moral philosophers could be identified with underlying nature) was, as the great Descartes had shown, possible through reason alone. For an institution to be "against nature and contrary to reason" meant, especially in the eighteenth century, that it was marked for extinction once the forces of enlightened power ever gained control.

Nature, then, in eighteenth-century as in ancient Greek thought carries with it the clear idea of an ideal-type, a character of an entity, physical or social, that is its true essence and that *will mani-*

fest itself provided only that corrupting, deflecting, or interfering circumstances of one kind or other do not obtrude. Whether for purposes of analysis or action, what is necessary is to cut away all that now hides nature in order to know it and then to achieve it. This is the central theme of the philosophy of nature in the eighteenth century, as seen in writings as distinct from one another as those of the physiocrats, Rousseau, Adam Smith, Diderot, Adam Ferguson, and others.

It is possible, I would suggest, to separate liberals from radicals in the French eighteenth century in terms of the amount of action that was held to be necessary to achieve the natural order. On the one hand were those such as the physiocrats in France and Adam Smith in England who assuredly were not lacking in a sense of contrast between traditional order and that order appointed by nature which lay beneath the former, but who thought that it would be sufficient to work toward the educating of monarchs and legislatures. Among the physiocrats, Quesnay was responsible for a small treatise on what the natural order actually consisted of—he even supplied a sketch of it in the form of a *tableau*—and he, along with other physiocrats, thought that this simple, logical order of commerce, industry, and agriculture, and order appointed by nature, could be legislated into existence if only there were a political ruler sufficiently enlightened and powerful to undertake the work of discarding the traditional order. In England, Adam Smith, whose *The Wealth of Nations* was to prove vastly more influential than any of the works of the physiocrats, also limned the natural order and its contrasts with the traditional. One of the most humane and compassionate minds of the eighteenth century (anything but the lackey or devotee of capitalists that he has sometimes been caricatured as being), Smith thought it to everyone's advantage—the advantage of rural laborer, artisan, as well as merchant—to be freed from the labyrinth of customs, statuses, and regulations that now covered over the natural rights and freedoms which were waiting, so to speak, for their release—release by wise parliamentary action.

But the idea of nature could support proposals of a far more radical type. If one saw the natural order so heavily overladen by convention and tradition, so reinforced by the power of government, clergy, and aristocracy, that working through any existing institution appeared futile, there was left the way of revolution, of total destruction of the existing social order. And this way recommended itself to more than a few in the eighteenth century—to those who might have taken seriously Rousseau's advice, in his *Discourses* and his *Social Contract*, to cease trying to patch up the scene and to clear it utterly as Lycurgus had in ancient Sparta. It was this utilization of the concept of nature that was to prove so powerful in the laws and decrees of the Revolution after the Jacobins came into full ascendancy.

2. NATURAL VERSUS CONVENTIONAL HISTORY

The idea of a natural history flowed directly from eighteenth-century usage of *nature*, and much of the full flavor of the Greek *physis* was thereby restored. For *physis* meant, it will be recalled, not merely pristine condition to the Greek but a "way of growing." More important and crucial to present discussion, it meant a way of growing that was inseparable from, natural to, the thing in question; that proceeded from the very character and structure of the entity rather than from external forces. To uncover the *physis*, the normal course of development, of the state was, as we noted, Aristotle's objective in his *Politics*.

To uncover the "natural history" of things—the physical world, organic life, ideas, and institutions—was the objective of a great many philosophers in Western Europe in the latter part of the eighteenth century. Sometimes this mode of inquiry was called "hypothetical," sometimes "conjectural," and sometimes "reasoned" (as in the French *raisonnée*), but one and all these terms referred to a mode of investigation that was regarded as scientific in the highest degree, that was distinguished rigorously from conventional history, that is, the mere history of concrete places, times, and personages, and that could seem to an Adam Smith or a Rousseau absolutely necessary to reach the kind of understanding required by intelligent social action.

Let us turn now to a few examples of this "natural history." High among them is Rousseau's remarkable second *Discourse on the Origin of Inequality*, and within it we can start with his notorious and much misunderstood statement: "Let us begin then by laying the facts aside, as they do not affect the question." [3] Few statements in all the literature of politics have been as often caricatured as this one. Is it not, his enemies have so often asked, vivid testimony to his anti-rationalism, his clear renunciation of reasoned discourse, and his retreat to intuitive unreason? The answer is, it is not! What it is at bottom is a characteristically Rousseauian way of expressing a methodological point perfectly familiar to Adam Smith, Adam Ferguson, and scores of others in that age who were engaged in like enterprises. And this point is: if we are concerned with uncovering the moral, psychological, and spiritual *nature* of man, in contrast to the conventionalized appearances man makes in history as peasant, nobleman, priest, etc., we have no alternative but to lay aside the kinds of data that deal only with man in these appearances.

Consider the passage that follows the sentence quoted above. The investigations we are making, writes Rousseau, must not be considered as "historical truths" but rather as "hypothetical and conditional" reasonings "calculated to explain the nature of things . . . just like the hypotheses which our physicists daily form respecting the formation of the world." [4] What we must do is put aside the kind of testimony we receive from sacred or lay history alike, since this concerns man only as he actually has been and is, and look instead to "what might have become of the human race if it had been left to itself." This, Rousseau emphasizes, is the question dealt with in the *Discourse on the Origin of Inequality*.

What follows is a treatise at once psychological, anthropological, and, in its way, sociological. Hypothetical, speculative, Rousseau may have called his investigation, but it should not be supposed that he proceeded solely from the resources of imagination.

Rousseau, if not by any means the most learned of *philosophes*, was nonetheless well read in the scientific literature of the day and as well acquainted as the next writer with the extensive body of material that had been growing since the sixteenth century on the cultures of exotic or preliterate peoples. The apparatus of scholarship rarely shows—a happy trait of eighteenth-century philosophic and scientific writing!—but there are scores of references in the *Discourse* that rest upon observations drawn from the comparative psychology and ethnology of that day.

How, Rousseau asks, can we distinguish, in the study of man, "what is fundamental in his nature from the changes and additions which his circumstances and the advances he has made have introduced to modify his primitive condition?" [5] This question is the real point of departure of the *Discourse*. He gives us, in its answer, no simple-minded, stark contrast between a happy state of nature and a corrupt civilization, as the misrepresentations of Rousseau so often have it, but instead a remarkable panorama of the evolution of mankind as this might be reconstructed from the data of comparative psychology and ethnography and, to a lesser extent, of the ancient classical historians. Granted that the underlying motive of the *Discourse* was polemical, even revolutionary, and based upon belief in the inequity and corruption of modern civilization, we still are forced to recognize the work for what it is: the natural history of human society.

Far from declaring earliest man happy and good, and the first condition of humankind the most natural to its psychology, Rousseau specifically declares that earliest man was *neither* virtuous nor wicked, that the moral categories had, and could have had, no relevance to his estate. And, as Professor Lovejoy years ago made emphatic in his own study of this discourse,[6] Rousseau does *not* declare the first condition of man, the so-called state of nature, the happiest one for man. Free though the first stage was from the kinds of ills that torment man today, Rousseau notes, it nevertheless had its own dangers and terrors, the result of man's lack of protection from climate, wild beasts, and catastrophes of one kind or other. It was not, however—this in answer to Hobbes—a time of man's war against man, for war, Rousseau declares, did not emerge until a later stage of civilization had been reached.

Gradually human culture begins, we are told, through man's inherent "faculty for self-improvement, which, by the help of circumstances, gradually develops all the rest of our faculties, and is as inherent in the species as in the individual." [7] Reason united with instincts, or passions, formed the lasting mechanism through which man developed stage by stage in civilization. In time the simplest elements of morality made their appearance through instinct, necessity, and reason. Even more gradually appeared language. The origin and development of language was a subject of great interest to philosophers of that day, one of the best of treatises on the subject being an essay by Adam Smith. Rousseau's own analysis is sophisticated; he recognizes the immense problem represented by the transition from mere representation of sensation to expression of ideas, abstractions, and concepts, and he tells us that such a transition could have occurred only over great periods of time. The sex instinct, allied with compassion, which for Rousseau was as intrinsic to man as the sex drive, led to the gradual rise of love between the sexes, though in the beginning there were no fixed and permanent liaisons.

In fact there were no fixed liaisons of any kind, and it was because of this that inequality was at a minimum in the beginning, for how, asks Rousseau, could there have been extreme inequalities of a social kind when there were no fixed interdependences of human beings to breed these inequalities? It was a cardinal part of Rousseau's philosophical individualism to regard all interdependences with suspicion, and in his later *Social Contract* he made freedom synonymous indeed with the state's capacity, through the absolute General Will, to isolate man from all interdependences not of the state's own making.

We come now to the real beginning of Rousseau's view of cultural development. "Having proved that the inequality of mankind is hardly felt, and that its influence is next to nothing in a state of nature, I must next show its origin and trace its progress in the successive developments of the human mind." [8] Here, then, with the earliest stage of man described, with contexts formed in terms of the moral sentiments, language, and habits of thought that had already evolved, we are at the true beginning of Rousseau's "hypothetical history"—we would say evolutionary development—of social inequality. "I have nothing," he writes, "to determine my choice but conjectures: but such conjectures become reasons when they are the most probable that can be drawn from the nature of things, and the only means of discovering the truth." [9] So might Lucretius have stated it two thousand years earlier; so, in almost these very words, would the evolutionists of the nineteenth century, Darwin included, state the matter in their own efforts to recover, through reason and comparative observation, the decisive processes of the past.

Rousseau makes it plain, even as his successors in the next century would, that immense periods of time had to pass for everything to transpire that he is describing. He refers to "the almost insensible progress of things in their beginnings" and warns us that he must pass over very quickly in the *Discourse* "a multitude of ages; for the slower the events were in their succession, the more rapidly may they be described."

What led to the first major change in the condition of man, the transition from the first stage, which was the "state of nature," was the appearance of private property. This has all the decisiveness in evolutionary terms that it was to have for Marx and Engels in their own portrayal of the development of human society. "The first man who, having enclosed a piece of ground, bethought himself of saying 'This is mine,' and found people simple enough to believe him, was the real founder of civil society." [10] From how many crimes, wars, murders, and other horrors, Rousseau reflects, might mankind have been saved if that first "property holder" had been scorned, his stakes pulled up, his fences torn down. Where private property first appeared, when, and exactly how, we cannot of course know; such details are lost forever. But begin it did, and when private property began, so did other elements of civil society gradually begin to come into being: metallurgical arts; agriculture; organized, stable kinship systems; religion; villages and towns; trade and commerce; in short, all the arts and patterns of what we call civil society or civilization. And, along with these very slow and gradual advances, came the beginnings of human inequality. This was very different from that natural and reasonable inequality that first existed, for now inequality became artificial, out of all proportion to the true talents of the individuals involved, and steadily harsher as it became embedded in the forms of society.

An important point must be emphasized here. I have said that for Rousseau the whole process of the development of human culture required immense periods of time; there was nothing sudden about the appearance of any part of it, including the appearance of social inequality. Nor was there, in his view, any traumatic passage from the state of nature to civilization properly so called. On the contrary! It must again be emphasized that the first state, the pre-institutional state, of man was not, in Rousseau's view, the happiest for man. The happiest stage came *after* the earliest beginnings of human intercourse had been succeeded by the gradual appearance of institutions and the arts but *before* these had proliferated and also hardened to the point where they became tyrannical to man. It is the stage of development that follows man's emergence from "the indolence of the primitive state" and that precedes the rash of "petulant activity of our egoism" that for Rousseau was the happiest condition of mankind. The following passage makes plain the kind of moralism with which Rousseau larded his developmentalism.

> The more we reflect on it, the more we shall find that this state was the least subject to revolutions, and altogether the very best man could experience; so that he can have departed from it only through some fatal accident, which, for the public good, should never have happened. The example of savages, most of whom have been found in this state, seems to prove that men were meant to remain in it, that it is the real youth of the world, and that all subsequent advances have been apparently so many steps towards the perfections of the individual but in reality towards the decrepitude of the species.[11]

For Rousseau, let us emphasize, there was nothing wrong with the arts of civilization, with ideas, beliefs, and cultural pursuits generally, so long as people "undertook only what a single person could accomplish, and confined themselves to such arts as did not require the joint labor of several hands." The tragedy of mankind's development occurred, he tells us, when man, not content with the kind of solidarity that arose from human beings pursuing like individual enterprises, began to enter into ever more elaborate and complex mutual interdependences.

> From the moment one man began to stand in need of the help of another; from the moment it appeared advantageous to any one man to have enough provisions for two, equality disappeared, property was introduced, work became indispensable, and vast forests became smiling fields, which man had to water with the sweat of his brow, and where slavery and misery were soon to germinate and grow up with the crops.[12]

We smile today at the moralistic fervor in Rousseau, at his characteristically eighteenth-century preoccupation with happiness, at the Hesiodic and Augustinian overtones (and also Freudian) of implacable conflict between man's happiness and spiritual adjustment on the one hand and, on the other, the pressure of social and cultural interdependences. It is easy to categorize the *Discourse* as but an elaborate polemic with which to indict a political and social order that Rousseau detested. Here and there are phrases which make only too easy our dismissal of the treatise on the grounds of its dedication to some imaginary, utopian state of nature.

The second *Discourse* is all of these. But along with them it is a remarkably shrewd and learned effort to recapitulate the social and cultural development of man. Strike out the moralism, remove the evidences of eighteenth-century fascination with primitive exoticism, fatten the successive stages of development Rousseau gives us with the gobs of ethnographic data favored in the next century, and what we have is different only in scale from what the nineteenth century is to offer through its Morgans, Tylors, Engels, and Lubbocks in the way of the evolution of mankind.

Nor, despite the disclaimers I have just made for Rousseau, should even his moralism be left in the category of some kind of naturalistic repudiation of human culture. Rousseau, for all his vitriolic jibes at the culture that lay around him, for all his belief in, as it were, history-gone-wrong, was far from fatalistic about it. He was a man of the eighteenth century in his stout belief that things could be set right. Whatever the dour pessimism of the first two *Discourses*, his third *Discourse, On Political Economy*, and his *Social Contract* are proof enough that mankind can again be put on the correct course that its nature calls for. All that is required is destruction of the institutional accretions that followed remorselessly from the introduction of private property and the rise of social inequality.

Now let us turn to another masterpiece of the eighteenth century, one less electric in its revolutionary message, but hardly less revolutionary in its long-run effects upon European economy and polity: Adam Smith's *The Wealth of Nations*. Adam Smith was, like Rousseau, a moral philosopher, and although we tend to think of him today as the first of Europe's systematic economists, he himself regarded his great study of wealth as but a single aspect of the larger study of mankind. In his day he was as well known for his study of the origin and development of man's moral sentiments and, to a lesser degree, for his study of development of language, as he was for the work by which he will always be best known to posterity.

"The annual labour of every nation is the fund which originally supplies it with all the necessaries and conveniences of life which it annually consumes, and which consist always either in the immediate produce of that labour, or in what is purchased with that produce from other nations." [13] This is the beginning, familiar even today, word for word, to all who have studied economics. It is one of the most famous opening sentences in the literature of the social sciences. It is also one of the most misunderstood— misunderstood, that is, with respect to what it really introduces in Adam Smith's great work. What it actually introduces can be inferred directly, it seems to me, from the full title of the book: *An Inquiry into the Nature and Causes of the Wealth of Nations*. And of the words forming the full title, the key word is that most favored of eighteenth-century words, "nature." It is the *nature* of wealth that interested Adam Smith precisely as it was the nature of morality, government, language, civil society, man, and the cosmos that interested the other moral philosophers of Adam Smith's day. Shortly before publication of Smith's book in 1776, Quesnay and his group in France had dealt essentially with the same subject—though without the grandeur and brilliance of Smith's treatment—and had also concerned themselves with the nature of wealth, its natural or normal processes of accumulation, and the kind of polity best suited to these processes. To what extent the physiocrats directly influenced Adam Smith is of no concern here. The overriding point is simply that, like them, Smith directed his intellectual energies to a study of the *nature* of the economy; that is, to wealth and economy as these were, or would be, if all the distractions and interferences were removed: removed conceptually for purposes of observation and, in terms of public policy, removed actually for the greater prosperity of the people at large. *The Wealth of Nations,* as I have already observed, is in no sense a plea for any single group, manufacturers (whom Adam Smith, like other philosophers then and now, tended to dislike and distrust) or other. It is not primarily a plea for anything. It is, in the best eighteenth-century sense of the word, scientific; which is to say that it concerns the nature of things, in this instance the nature of wealth and of wealth-getting activities.

More to my present point, it is science in the Greek sense of the word. For, as the long sequence of chapters makes clear even in the table of contents, it is *nature in the sense of growth* that Adam Smith is most interested in. Like any Greek philosopher, Smith directs himself to the causes—material, formal, efficient, and final —of wealth. And also like any Greek philosopher he concerns himself with the forces—those of interference and diversion— through which the *natural* growth of wealth, the type of growth that is naturally inherent in wealth, tends to be checked.

Hence the diversity of illustrative material in the book—psychological, ethnographic, historical, and sociological—quite as we found this diversity in Rousseau's *Discourse.* For only by dealing with the psychology of man, his natural drives and impulses, could the mainspring of the process be uncovered; in this instance, the impulse to "truck and barter," the instinct of exchange.[14] From this fundamental and universal element in man, to be found everywhere Smith concluded from his ethnographic and historical data, the book takes its real departure. From this instinct to exchange there arises, also universally, in whatever degree, *division of labor*, the means whereby individuals improve their wealth-getting position by specializing in that which best suits their talents. And it is as cardinal a part of Smith's general moral philosophy as it is Rousseau's that human talents are *naturally* close to equal. Adam Smith was as confident as Rousseau or any other liberal mind of the century that the actual, historically-formed divisions of society, its classes, bore little relation to the underlying distribution of abilities of people.

These two fundamental and natural mechanisms, then, the instinct to "truck and barter" and the inherent drive to specialization, everywhere in the world are the origins of the processes of labor which create the wealth of any society. But it requires only a moment's observation to be aware of the fact that, first, nations are extremely unequal in their wealth (as are periods in history) and, second, that in no country, even the wealthiest, do the natural processes of growth of wealth operate unhindered. Everywhere there are interferences to this growth in the form of institutions and customs and beliefs which militate against it.

The third Book of *The Wealth of Nations* is titled "Of the Different Progress of Opulence in Different Nations." The first chapter in this Book, "Of the Natural Progress of Opulence" is the essential and unifying theme of the entire work: that wealth tends naturally to increase at a certain rate, provided that barriers to it do not come into existence. Unfortunately, barriers to this natural growth of opulence are to be found everywhere—from the most primitive society where sheer backwardness and superstition operate, to countries even such as those of Western Europe where progress is most notable.

Note in passing that Adam Smith is dealing with wealth in

quite the same fashion that Fontenelle and his contemporaries a
century earlier were dealing with knowledge: in each instance a
natural or normal tendency to cumulative progress is discerned in
the scheme of things, but the tendency has been everywhere ob-
structed by wars, ignorance, despotism, religious superstition, and
so on. Above all, as we have noted repeatedly, *institutions*, those
which have come into being through caprice and chance—which
have come into being "accidentally" so far as what is "necessary" is
concerned—have been the major barriers.

Here is Adam Smith on this very matter: "That order of things
which necessity imposes *in general, though not in every particular
country*, is, in every particular country, promoted by the natural
inclinations of man. *If human institutions had never thwarted
those natural inclinations*, the towns could nowhere have increased
beyond what the improvement and cultivation of the territory in
which they were situated could support. . . ." (Italics added.) [15]
In short, had the natural propensities of mankind been allowed to
develop in normal fashion there would not be the disproportion
between agriculture and towns, with the shortage of the former
posing so grave a threat, Smith thought, to much of Europe and
the world generally.

As he writes a little later in his argument:

> Had human institutions, therefore, *never disturbed the natural
> course of things*, the progressive wealth and increase of the towns
> would, in every political society, be consequential, and in propor-
> tion to the improvement and cultivation of the territory or coun-
> try. . . . [Italics added]
> According to the natural course of things, the greater part of
> the capital of every growing society is, first, directed to agricul-
> ture, afterwards to manufactures, and last of all to foreign com-
> merce. This order of things is so very natural that in every society
> that had any territory, it has always, I believe, been in some de-
> gree observed.[16]

Now we come to perhaps the single most influential sentence in
the entire *Wealth of Nations*, the sentence that was literally to
alter the polity of England in the nineteenth century: "But

though this natural order of things must have taken place in some degree in every such society, it has, in all the modern states of Europe, been, in many respects, entirely inverted." [17] The manners and customs of governments (Smith is here referring primarily to the Mercantilist policy) have, through either misguided purpose or untoward consequence, "necessarily forced them into this unnatural and retrograde order."

In short, the method followed by Rousseau in his highly polemical discourse on human equality is at bottom the method followed by Adam Smith in his study of human wealth. What we have in each instance is a limning of the *natural* features of the subject, the *natural* tendencies of growth which might be seen were it not for historical accidents or malign interferences in the ways appointed by nature. Rousseau's and Smith's works were to have signal consequences in practical affairs: the first in some of the legislation of the French Revolution which, taking its departure from Rousseau's very words, sought specifically to remove the historically accumulated interferences with equality; the second in successive Acts of Parliamentary legislation in England through which the natural order of competition and wealth was, in one or other degree, sought.

There were literally scores of other natural histories written in the eighteenth and early nineteenth century. Studies of the planets, the earth, organic life, man's psychological being, his moral sentiments, along with his polity, economy, social classes, religion, and kinship were to be found everywhere, written in the growth-terms of the century's cherished method of natural history. This is exactly what we find in Malthus: a *natural* history of population (which tends, he tells us, to increase geometrically) coupled with an account of the "interferences" such as poverty and disease which restrain it. And always distinction is made between natural history, a strictly scientific enterprise by the standards of the eighteenth century, and ordinary, conventional history, the contents of which Rousseau had in mind when he suggested laying the facts aside because they do not affect the matter.

David Hume provided authorship of both types of history; the first in his *The Natural History of Religion*, the second in his equally remarkable but utterly different type of enterprise, *The History of England*. The latter has been placed properly among the great works of history from Thucydides down to Mommsen and Motley. It was, for many years, the standard history of England. It is based meticulously upon the facts and data as Hume was able to get these from archives and other documentary sources. That it could have been written by the author of *The Natural History of Religion* is testimony to Hume's versatility as well as his genius. For there is hardly the hint of record, fact, or datum in Hume's study of religion. His effort here is to unfold the "history" of religion from the nature of religion; to deduce its most manifold characteristics in institutional or revealed religion from the set of simple, molecular elements that Hume's reason told him were at the original core of religion. It is history only in the sense of sequence and flow—but *logical* sequence and flow.

Nor should we omit reference in this connection to the work by Adam Ferguson, *An Essay on the History of Civil Society*, of which mention was made briefly above in regard to its doubts of moral progress and linear development. The very table of contents indicates the character of the book and its general relevance to the works we have mentioned in this section. There is, first, treatment of the general characteristics of human nature, of the passions, instincts, and primal relationships that might easily be reconstructed from the existence of the general characteristics of man's nature. This section is followed by a set of chapters on what Ferguson calls the "rude nations," and these are almost pure historical ethnology. In them he draws from the data provided by remote history and also from the records of the barbaric peoples as these were to be found in European accounts of explorations. Working from both the psychological data of the first section and the ethno-historical materials of the second, Ferguson gives us a natural history of mankind's advance from "rudeness" to "refinement." He deals with the influences of climate, of population, and wealth. He gives us individual, internal natural histories of civil liberty, the arts, literature, the professions, in each of which illustrative data are furnished from all parts of the world and from all ages.

The two great stages of primitive society are, we learn, the "savage" and the "barbaric," terms which the father of modern anthropology, Edward Tylor, would use unaltered a century later. Unlike Adam Smith, Ferguson uses a political rather than an economic scale of differentiation of stages of the early development of mankind. For Smith the early stages had been hunting and fishing, pastoral, agricultural, and commercial. But Ferguson rejects these in favor of a sequence bounded by political attributes.

But of the existence of a natural progression of types of society in time Ferguson is in no more doubt than Smith or Rousseau or any of the other natural historians. And like all of the others he makes as extensive use as possible of the materials furnished by ethnography. No adulator of the exotic or primitive (he rejected utterly any notion that the peoples of, say, Oceania are any more "natural" than are those of Western Europe), he nevertheless drew extensively on accounts of primitive peoples. These are our necessary guide to understanding the beginnings of mankind. "If, in advanced years, we would form a just notion of our progress from the cradle, we must have recourse to the nursery, and from the example of those who are still in the period of life we mean to describe, take our representation of past manners, that cannot, in any other way, be recalled." [18]

We will conclude this section with reference to one more work of the period; this one not itself a work in natural history but instead a matchless account of what was involved in the construction of natural histories. It is Dugald Stewart's *The Life and Writings of Adam Smith*, and I shall confine myself to that single part of it in which Stewart is at one and the same time explaining and expressing his admiration for the kind of inquiry contained not only in Smith's *Wealth of Nations* but more particularly in Smith's *Dissertation on the Origin of Language*, a short piece in which the author did essentially for language what he had done with respect to economic systems—that is, he constructed a developmental account. The essential purpose of each work, Stewart tells us, is to discover "by what gradual steps the transition has been made from the first simple efforts of uncultivated nature to a state of things so wonderfully artificial and complicated." [19]

We can refer to this mode of inquiry, Stewart says, by "the title of Theoretical or Conjectural history; an expression which coincides pretty nearly in its meaning with that of Natural History as employed by Mr. Hume and with what some French writers have called *Histoire Raisonnée*." In this type of inquiry the student does not bewilder himself, Stewart informs us, by digging from the erudition of scholiasts and antiquaries—for what good would such specialized data serve in the larger task of discovering the nature of mankind as a whole—and we find him, moreover, "borrowing his lights from the most remote and unconnected quarters of the globe, and combining the casual observations of illiterate travellers and navigators into a philosophical commentary on the history of law and manners." [20]

What is intrinsic to the method is deriving from what one knows of the "principles of human nature, or from the circumstances of society, the origin of the opinions and the institutions" that are relevant to the inquiry at hand. And in all of this what is vital is construction of a narrative which makes clear what the *natural* course of human history is, the course that has prevailed, or that would prevail, when "accidents" or "interferences" have not caused it to swerve from its appointed path: the path appointed, that is, by nature.

> In most cases it is of more importance to ascertain the progress that is most simple, than the progress that is most agreeable to fact; for, paradoxical as the proposition may appear, it is certainly true that the real progress is not always the most natural. It may have been determined by particular accidents, which are not likely to occur again, and which cannot be considered as forming any part of that general provision which nature has made for the improvement of the human race.[21]

Aristotle would have understood this point perfectly. So would Heraclitus before him. And so would a very large number of scholars and scientists since the eighteenth century, in many fields. We may today think most often of the kind of thing that paleontological museums offer when the phrase "natural history" comes into our minds. But this is but a derivative and highly specialized meaning. Epidemiologists and physicians continue to speak of the natural history of an epidemic or sickness (forgetting oftentimes in the process the presence of sick *people*), just as economists deal with the natural history of the business firm, sociologists with the natural history of revolution, crowds, crime-cycles, and so on. The distinction between the actual, minutely recorded, history of a thing and the history that we conceive as flowing from its very nature, when not deflected or otherwise interfered with, remains a vital distinction for most of us even though we rarely today make it as explicit as did the philosophers of the eighteenth century.

FIVE

THE THEORY OF SOCIAL EVOLUTION

The principle of development involves also the
existence of a latent germ of being—a capacity
or potentiality striving to realize itself. This
formal conception finds actual existence in spirit;
which has the history of the world for its
theatre, its possession, and the sphere of its
realization. It is not of such a nature as to be
tossed to and fro amid the superficial play of
accidents, but is rather the absolute arbiter of
things; entirely unmoved by contingencies, which,
indeed, it applies and manages for its own
purposes.

Hegel

The true general spirit of social dynamics then
consists in conceiving of each of these social
states as the necessary result of the preceding,
and the indispensable mover of the following,
according to the axiom of Leibniz,—*the present
is big with the future.* In this view the object of
science is to discover the laws which govern
this continuity.

Comte

No social order ever disappears before all the
productive forces for which there is room in it
have been developed, and new, higher relations
of production never appear before the material
conditions of their existence have matured in
the womb of the old society.

Marx

As it is undeniable that portions of the human
family have existed in a state of savagery, other
portions in a state of barbarism, and still other
portions in a state of civilization, it seems equally

so that these three distinct conditions are
connected with each other in a natural as well
as necessary sequence of progress. Moreover,
that this sequence has been historically true of
the entire human family, up to the status attained
by each branch respectively, is rendered probable
by the conditions under which all progress occurs,
and by the known advancement of several
branches of the family through two or more of
these conditions.

Lewis Morgan

The thesis which I venture to sustain, within
limits, is simply this, that the savage state in
some measure represents an early condition of
mankind, out of which the higher culture has
gradually developed or evolved, by processes still
in regular operation as of old. . . . That the
tendency of culture has been similar throughout
the existence of human society, and that we may
fairly judge from its known historic course what
its prehistoric course may have been, is a theory
clearly entitled to precedence as a fundamental
principle of ethnographic research.

Edward Tylor

1. SOURCES AND CONTEXTS

It is a short step from the eighteenth-century idea of progress and
theory of natural history to nineteenth-century perspectives of
social evolution. In both centuries the words "progress," "development," "advancement," and "natural history" were very nearly
interchangeable. This was as true indeed in the writings of the biological evolutionists—notably in Darwin's *The Origin of the
Species*—as in those of the social evolutionists. Of much greater
importance, the assumptions concerning the nature of change in
time which underlay the theory of natural history passed directly
into the nineteenth-century theory of social evolution.

I stress this point, for it is one of the more curious misconceptions of much modern writing in the history of social thought that nineteenth-century social evolutionism was simply an adaptation of the ideas of biological evolutionism, chiefly those of Charles Darwin, to the study of social institutions. While one must admit immediately that the ideas of social evolution acquired a certain luster from about 1859 on as the consequence of the immediate popularity of Darwin's work, they did not depend on it. Despite common myth which has Darwin's *Origin* shattering a Biblical innocence in the Victorian age, the book's main ideas were well known even to the literate lay public when it appeared, and the book went through some eight editions within the remaining period of Darwin's life.

In the first place, all of the principal works in the formation of the theory of social evolution had made their appearance before publication of Darwin's book. This was true of Comte, Hegel, Marx, and Spencer.[1] And even those which appeared shortly after publication of *The Origin of the Species* clearly involved work that had begun much earlier. I refer to the works of such men as Sir Henry Maine, Edward Tylor, and Lewis Morgan. None of these classics in social evolution refer to, or show any objective evidence of relation to, the line of study in biological speciation that came out of the eighteenth century and culminated in Darwin's great book.

In the second place, the difference between the theory of biological evolution and the theory of social evolution is substantial; it was substantial in the nineteenth century, especially after Darwin's and Wallace's researches appeared, and the difference increased after the long-ignored results of Mendel's remarkable studies in genetics became synthesized with the Darwinian theory of natural selection. This, too, is a point well worth emphasis, for too often we in the social sciences leave the impression that our studies of social evolution or development, even of social change generally, proceed from a theory and method common to biological and social sciences. But they do not. Allowing only for a few similarities in phrasing now and then, the difference in the nineteenth century between the theory of biological evolution and the theory of social evolution was profound. And, in very considerable degree, this difference persists to the present moment.

The difference consists essentially in this: whereas the biological theory became (very considerably in its Darwinian statement, wholly after it was fused with Mendel's great researches) a *populational* and *statistical* theory, the theory of social evolution was, and remains to this day, a *typological* construction. On the biological theory of evolution I can do no better than quote here some splendidly clarifying words of the contemporary Harvard biologist, Ernst Mayr:

> All organisms and organic phenomena are composed of unique features and can be described collectively *only* in statistical terms. Individuals, or any kind of organic entities, form populations of which we can determine the arithmetic mean and the statistics of variation. Averages are merely statistical abstractions; only the individuals of which the populations are composed have reality. The ultimate conclusions of the population thinker and of the typologist are precisely the opposite. . . . Many of the basic concepts of synthetic theory, such as that of natural selection and that of the population, are meaningless for the typologist.[2]

In the theory of social evolution, however, typological thinking figures prominently. This was vividly true of the nineteenth-century theories of such men as Comte, Marx, Spencer, Tylor, and others, but it is scarcely less true today. The subject in any given theory of social evolution tends almost invariably to be social class, kinship, culture, law, society as a whole, or one of the dozens of other types and structures into which the normative and institutionalized behavior of human beings falls. No doubt a considerable measure of the typological is inseparable from the study of social behavior of human beings, for it would be very hard to pretend that such entities as church, family, and nation are not real in the allegiances they inspire, in the authorities they wield, and in the transforming effect they have so obviously on the behavior of human individuals and "populations." How, given the constitutive place of institutions and social norms, could human behavior *not* be studied in at least some manifestation of the typological?

My aim here is not, however, either criticism or defense of the typological cast of the theory of social evolution. It is simply to stress, irrespective of all else, the profound difference between the theory of social evolution and the theory of biological evolution— the latter from, at least, Darwin on.

Darwin, it is important to emphasize, has elements of both the typological and the populational in his *Origin of the Species*. It is probably correct to say that he had largely ceased to be a typologist without, however, wholly becoming a population thinker. His single most important contribution to evolutionary theory was, of course, the idea of natural selection, an idea inseparable, as Mayr has noted, from population thinking. What we find in the *Origin*, however, along with this is continuation of several eighteenth-century ideas—most notably ideas of progressive development, uniformitarianism, and of the kind of genetic continuity that Leibniz had set forth in his famous phrase, *Natura non Facit Saltum*, "Nature never makes leaps." These were all ideas, as I shall emphasize later in the chapter, which were derived from that conception of change, as old as the Greeks, which we have dealt with thus far in our consideration of the whole metaphor of growth. The internal difficulties, the contradictions, which are to be found in Darwin proceed essentially from his realization that in natural selection alone, as a process, could the differences be explained which were presented by the biological records—a realization, however, coupled with his unwillingness to abandon premises which were drawn from a much earlier, and largely metaphoric, conception of change in time. Post-Darwinian evolutionary theory in biology has been built upon the solid base of natural selection as a process, to which was added, as I have noted, the line of work that began with Mendel and which focused on the mechanisms of the variations that Darwin simply took for granted in this theory of natural selection.

When we turn to the theory of social evolution, however, we have something very different, allowing only for those occasional similarities of concept which I have mentioned. The theory of social evolution in the nineteenth century—and this is true from Comte early in the century to the works of such men as Tylor and Morgan later—is built upon nothing comparable to the phenomena of variation which Darwin described in his theory of natural selection. It is built upon precisely that conception of organismic growth with which we have been concerned throughout the book. Such growth is *not* the model of Darwinian natural selection or of post-Darwinian theory in biology. Such growth *is* the model of the theory of social evolution—and it remains so even today in the social sciences.

No one stated this fact more explicitly than Herbert Spencer when he declared, in his essay "Progress: Its Law and Cause" written in 1857, that "the series of changes gone through during the development of the seed into a tree, or an ovum into an animal, constitute an advance from homogeneity of structure to heterogeneity of structure" and that "this law or organic progress is the law of all progress." [3] Spencer sought to show that even in the biological realm, in the succession of species and genera, his law of growth held, and this perhaps is the greatest single difference between him and Darwin—though there were indeed likenesses, and the two men admired each other.

Before we turn to the specific conceptual elements of the theory of social evolution, there is one other possible misconception that should be specifically set aside. In the same way that much interpretative writing seeks to make the theory of social evolution a byproduct of biological evolutionism, so is there a good deal of writing that puts social evolutionary theories under the rubric of the nineteenth-century's great interest in historiography. It is often said that it was the explosion of historical scholarship in the century that suggested to social scientists the possibility of dealing with society and its institutions "historically."

But this view holds no more water than does the one we have just examined. For, as in the first, the record is very clear indeed that the theory of social evolution has nothing to do with the kind of historical scholarship associated with the names of such titans as von Ranke, Mommsen, Motley, and Prescott. True, most of the social evolutionists—Comte himself to begin with, but also Marx, Maine, Lubbock, Morgan, and Tylor—occasionally used the phrase "historical method" to describe their labors. But, as Comte carefully explained in his *The Positive Philosophy*, by history he meant "abstract history," history divorced from all particularity of the events, actions, personages, places, and periods that was the very substance of what the historians were concerned with. By "abstract history" Comte meant precisely a method for the study of human evolution, progress, or development.

There is, in short, exactly the same differentiation between the theory of social evolution and historiography in the nineteenth century that we observed in the first chapter between the theory of cycles and the historiography of a Thucydides.

More immediately and directly, exactly the same differentiation that we have just observed exists also between what the eighteenth century called "natural history" and "conventional history." And this is the most essential point in setting the context and sources of nineteenth-century social developmentalism. The theory of social evolution is no more than the eighteenth-century theory of natural history—broadened, extended, ramified, and filled with a volume of ethnographic data not known to such men as Ferguson, Smith, and Rousseau (and also largely, though not wholly freed of the tendentiousness of eighteenth-century natural history), but the same basic theory, nevertheless.

Auguste Comte, in most respects the subtlest and most theoretically sophisticated of all the social evolutionists in the nineteenth century—and also the most candid—was well aware of all this. In his *The Positive Philosophy* he makes very plain that his evolutionary portrayal of human knowledge and society rests upon, not biological evolution (of which he had very mixed and skeptical views), not historiography, but the "noble theories" of such men as Condorcet, Hume, and most particularly the whole school of Scottish moral philosophers whom he admired greatly. No one was better aware than Comte of the straight line that stretched from Aristotle's *Politics*, with its picture of the natural growth of the state, down to his own envisagement of social evolution.

2. THE ELEMENTS OF SOCIAL EVOLUTION

The theory of social evolution is more commonly dealt with in terms of the patterns of assertedly universal origins and stages which the evolutionists put forward than in the terms of the major premises regarding the nature of change which underlay these origins and stages. It is the premises that will form the subject of this section, for they, rather than the other, more obvious aspects, have proved to be the really durable and the most influential features of evolutionary theory.

What are these premises? They are drawn, all of them, from the metaphor of growth, from the analogy of change in society to change in the growth-processes of the individual organism. Six seem to me the most constitutive and far-reaching in their relation to the theories of the major social evolutionists in the century.

Change is natural. Natural, that is, to the entity chosen by the evolutionist for his study. None of the theorists of social evolution ever made the mistake of supposing that change is in fact constant in a given area or period of time. None was blind to the manifest facts of inertia and fixity in history. But, recognizing this, the social evolutionists nonetheless assumed that change in time is natural, is normal, and that when fixity is encountered it is either to be categorized as abnormal, as a kind of monstrosity, or else it is fixity of appearance only, with reality to be understood in terms of underlying forces of change which required only further time for their manifestation.

For all of the social evolutionists the overriding problem in the study of society was that of finding proper reconciliation between what Comte called *statics* and *dynamics*.[4] The great error of all preceding theories of society, Comte wrote—and his words were to be echoed by all of the others—is that they introduced a false dichotomy between order and change. Order, Comte declared, is order-in-change; and change is simply the incessant realization of a higher level of order. Comte made statics and dynamics the two broad areas of his new social science, sociology, but he never failed to insist, in his numerous elaborations of these two divisions, upon their inseparability when it came to actual observation of things.

What was true of Comte was equally true of the others in the century—Hegel, Marx, Tocqueville, Spencer, Morgan, Newman, and Tylor, to name the principal exponents of the theory of development—who similarly proceeded from the assumption that change is as natural to a social entity as any of its elements of structure. The entity for Comte was human knowledge fundamentally, although he widened this in later work to civilization in its entirety; for Hegel the entity was freedom; for Marx the means of economic production through the ages; for Tocqueville it was democracy in the West; for Spencer each of the whole range of society's principal institutions; for Newman (who resurrected Augustinian developmentalism, though in very sophisticated ways indeed, ways which had full currency in his century) it was Christianity; for Morgan the entity was the idea of kinship, of property, and of civil government; and for Tylor it was culture generally, religion specifically.

In each of these outstanding theories of development the naturalness of change in time to the entity under consideration was taken for granted. In each the basic objective was the same: to show the roots of ongoing change in the several key forces which constituted the entity in question. I repeat, it was the *entity*—be it civilization in the large or a given institution or cultural form—for which natural development in time was claimed. It was *not* the sum total of geographic areas on earth. In these, as the evolutionists were well aware, divergences, exceptions, and instances of stagnation or fixity could be seen in abundance. Just as Fontenelle and other philosophers of progress in the seventeenth century contemplated the continuous growth of knowledge through the ages, but in full recognition of frequent obstructions to such growth in any given area or period of time, so did the nineteenth-century social evolutionists recognize such abnormalities, but without relinquishing their conviction that change is normal to mankind's institutions and its provisions are firmly embedded in the structure of each.

Change is directional. This, of course, is a conclusion, not in itself an observable fact. Change we may define as *a succession of differences in time within a persisting identity.*[5] All three aspects of this definition are crucial; and crucial only in their relatedness. A mere array of differences is just that; not necessarily change. The passing of time is just that; not change. And, obviously, persisting identity apart from anything else is the opposite of change. Taken together, however, these elements form what we call change.

We *see* the succession of changes, and I stress the plural. It requires analysis and deduction, however, or metaphor, or analogy, to bind the plurality of observed changes into a single, ongoing process. And it requires still further analysis and deduction to reach the conclusion that this single, ongoing process has beginning, middle, and end—that is, direction in time.

For each of the social evolutionists it was essential that this direction be specified for whatever entity development was claimed. And it is in this specification that we are given the sequence of stages which for most of us today remains the single most distinctive aspect of the theory of social evolution.

Hence Comte's Law of Three Stages, under which human knowledge could be seen as having passed from the religious to the metaphysical to the positive (or scientific). Not only did knowledge in its fullness pass through these stages but so did each of the disciplines—astronomy, physics, chemistry, biology, and sociology (the latter a term that Comte used for the single science of society)—pass through the same three stages. Later Comte adapted the Law to cover not merely knowledge but the arts and institutions of civilization.

Hence, too, Hegel's panoramic view of the spirit of freedom moving from its beginnings, very limited beginnings, in the Orient with ever widening scope to what he believed to be its ultimate and widest manifestation in the Prussia of his day. Hence Marx's depiction of the direction of economic evolution from ancient slavery (with some form of primitive communism preceding this) through feudalism to capitalism and, in due time, to socialism and communism—mature communism. Past, present, and future could thus be given connection in a single, directional series.[6]

Tocqueville dealt with the direction of political change from the first beginnings of "the spirit of equality" in the Middle Ages through the constantly enlarging dimension of democracy, a dimension that he also projected into the future, where he saw the clear possibility of mass society surmounted by despotism, both characteristics having been present in at least embryonic degree from the start. Unlike the other developmentalists, Tocqueville wrote little about mankind generally, and it has to be said that he is the most nearly "historical" of them all—confining himself as he did to Europe alone from the Middle Ages on. But developmentalism in the sense in which I am describing it here is nevertheless a cardinal feature of Tocqueville's treatment of democracy.

I need not elaborate further in any detail. Sir Henry Maine, restricting himself to legal institutions, saw the direction of evolution as from status to contract. Spencer had an evolutionary direction for everything. The most general was his "homogeneity to heterogeneity," a process of directionality that covered political society as well as the fertilized germ cell. But, within this, there was to be discerned the more specific patterns of growth in each institution. Lewis Morgan put the direction of evolution in several ways: "savagery" to "barbarism," to "civilization" being the most encompassing. Government he saw passing from the "personal" to the "territorial," property from the communal to the chattel to the individual and contractual; kinship from the consanguineal through several intervening stages down to the modern, Western form. Durkheim, in his first major work, *The Division of Labor*, took the subject of social solidarity for evolutionary treatment, finding the normal direction to be from "mechanical solidarity" to "organic solidarity." [7] And so it went. No one can miss the fact that in every instance—there is no exception—the direction of change found by the evolutionist was toward the specific set of qualities possessed by Western Europe alone. I shall have much more to say about this in the next chapter, but we should not overlook the ethnocentric overtones of the allegedly universal patterns of development uncovered.

Change is immanent. It is immanent, that is, in the entity being considered. This is true, the social evolutionist argued, of society as a whole but also of each of the major constituent institutions of society. As I noted above, the prime objective of the theory of social evolution was to discover the provisions for change which lay in the nature or structure of whatever it was that was being observed. This made focus on immanence or internality inevitable.

Actually immanence is the core attribute of the whole theory of social evolution. All of the evolutionists were aware of forms of change which were not immanent to the subject at hand. All were aware of adventitious impacts, events, accidents, interferences— the entire record of history, in contrast to evolution. But, as I have stressed, social evolution as a theory was premised upon the study of *entities*, not the totality of the geographic and historical record of man. In the institutions of religion, of property, of kinship, of economy, lay forces, it was argued, which engendered growth.

How else could change be directional save in terms of inherent forces within culture, within each of the institutions, which in their interaction provided the necessary dynamism? [8] Admittedly, natural, immanent growth could be arrested or deflected—could be and frequently was. It was still important to discover that kind of change which, assuming no interferences or mutational accidents, could be seen as inherent, as a function of the system itself, even as is the growth of an organism.

Here, as in other connections, Leibniz's ideas are profoundly relevant, as most of the great nineteenth-century developmentalists—Comte and Darwin among them—were quick to perceive. "When I speak of the force and action of created beings," Leibniz had written in 1714, "I mean that each created being is pregnant with its future state, *and that it naturally follows a certain course if nothing hinders it.*" [9] (Italics added.) When Leibniz wrote these words, he was thinking of what he called "monads," the essential components of reality in Leibnizian terms, and which, he said, "cannot naturally be hindered in their inner determinations, since they include the representation of everything external to them."

Later writers, however, and this includes the nineteenth as well as the eighteenth century, were willing to let go of Leibniz's "monadological" assumptions and retain gratefully his proposition that in any structure or entity there is a pattern of growth in time that springs from its inner composition. The prime task of nineteenth-century development theory was, as I have noted, to ascertain the course or direction of change in whatever entity or system was under consideration, but more was required here than merely describing what appeared to be the curve of development in the past. For unless such development could be shown to arise from the very nature of the society or institution under consideration, how could such development be declared to be a fixed law—as Comte, Marx, and Spencer, among others, so declared it?

What had made indefinite human progress certain to philosophers of the eighteenth century was the fact that it came from forces internal to mankind, not from willful or adventitious elements external to mankind. The same assumption of immanence is present in the nineteenth-century theory of development.

Comte's so-called laws of social dynamics, Spencer's "development hypothesis," Marx's "economic law of motion of modern society" had in common a conviction on the part of their authors that the processes of cumulative, directional change with which they were concerned were immanent to the social systems that were being studied. "No social order ever disappears," wrote Marx, "before all the productive forces for which there is room in it have been developed, and new, higher relations of production never appear before the material conditions of their existence have matured in the womb of the old society." [10] Marx was, as is plain, as much concerned with the microcosmic as with the macrocosmic in his search for the "economic law of motion" of society. Under the microcosmic fall his investigations of the internal structure of capitalism, as he found it in its "most developed form" in England, and his imagined discovery of the elements, the internal structural elements, that formed the motive power of the law of motion that could be seen in macrocosmic terms through ages of the past as well as of the present. Precisely as eighteenth-century students of "natural history" assumed that in each social system there is a natural or normal pattern of change embedded within—one that will manifest itself in time provided nothing interferes with its course —so did Marx assume that in capitalism there is a natural course of development, one that can be decelerated temporarily by alien forces or accelerated by, for example, a revolutionary vanguard of the proletariat, but that cannot, in the long run, be abrogated by human decision.

For Comte the laws of social dynamics worked with relentless force simply because they were founded on "the chief properties of our species; properties which, latent at first, can come into play only in that advanced state of social life for which they are exclusively destined." [11] Prior to his own time, prior indeed to himself, Comte thought with serene self-conviction, the philosophy of progress and the philosophy of order had been separated from one another. It was, Comte thought, his supreme contribution to knowledge to show that "social dynamics" and "social statics" are but two different perspectives of observation of the same phenomenon, human society in progressive development that comes inexorably from qualities contained within.

So, however, thought each of the other titans of developmentalism in the nineteenth century. What would happen to democracy in the future, as in the past, thought Tocqueville, flowed directly from the internal nature of democracy: its fixed and ineradicable contradiction between the values of equality and freedom, its ineffaceable tension between individualism and majority rule. Given these structural elements, was it not possible to deal with democracy in much the same way that we have seen Marx deal with capitalism and Comte human knowledge and culture? Or, within the Augustinian tradition, Christianity?

When John Henry Newman wrote, just prior to his momentous conversion to Roman Catholicism in 1845, his *Development of Christian Doctrine,* he was using, consciously and self-admittedly, the concept of development to prove that irrespective of all that had happened *to* Christianity since the sixteenth century, there was an inner power and logic of Christianity that determined its over-all development and that made Christianity of the modern age, for all its manifest differences from the Christianity of the apostles, the clear, lineal, developmental product of the earlier form. But, Newman went on, much in the manner of the biologist, just as there is development that comes from within a system of ideas, so is there corruption. How, Newman asked, are we to distinguish between the two? "The most ready test is suggested by the analogy of physical growth, which is such that the parts and proportions of the developed form correspond to those which belong to its rudiments. . . . That development, then, is to be considered a corruption which *obscures or prejudices its essential idea,* or which *disturbs the laws of development* which constitute its organization, or which *reverses its course of development*; that is *not* a corruption which is *both a chronic and an active state,* or which is *capable of holding together* the component parts of a system." [12]

On the basis of these developmental premises Newman constructed what he called seven tests by which genuine development could be distinguished from corruption. His objective was Christianity, the determination of what was valid and genuine in contemporary Christianity, and, as we know, it was his conviction that in Roman Catholicism lay what was truly developmental, truly emergent from the original apostolic primitivism of Christianity, that formed the stated background of his abandonment of Anglicanism and his conversion to Roman Catholicism. There is an element of the delicious in reflecting on Newman's great *Essay.* Its purpose was as strategic, even tactical, as Augustine's had been fifteen hundred years before. And just as Augustine had used pagan-secular intellectual arguments to turn the tables on the enemies of Christianity, so did Newman. There is not one single crucial element of the nineteenth-century perspective of developmentalism missing from his argument in behalf of the present character of Christianity. Truly, the uses of the idea of evolution were manifold in the nineteenth century!

Change is continuous. I use this important term not in the common sense of the constant or omnipresent, but in the stricter and older sense of logical gradation of steps within a single series. The denotation may be purely mathematical or taxonomic, or it may be genetic and sequential as in growth. The idea of continuity is, as Arthur Lovejoy has made profoundly clear in his *The Great Chain of Being*, one of the fundamental ideas of Western thought, as richly evident in Greek, Roman, and medieval philosophy as in the thought of the modern world. Often the idea of continuity bespoke linear gradation only, as from the smallest conceivable being on earth to God himself, with no possible space in the series left unfilled. But, from the Greeks on, the idea of continuity also could bespeak gradations of growth, cumulative, genetic, and thus the very opposite of the broken or discontinuous.

Natura non Facit Saltum had been Leibniz's pithy way of expressing the law of continuity. And the proposition "Nature makes no leaps" made its way from Leibniz's monadology to areas as far flung and distinct as Marx's theory of revolution and Darwin's theory of natural selection. The importance of the concept of continuity in the theory of development is obvious. How else can change be declared directional, predictable, save on the grounds of its continuity. Either the present is, in Leibniz's words, big with the future (as past was big with present) or it is all kaleidoscopic and incapable of scientific ascription of causality. Such was the implicit argument.

Darwin made his entire system rest upon the concept. "As natural selection acts solely by accumulating slight, successive, favorable variations, it can produce no great or sudden modifications; it can act only by short and slow steps. Hence the canon of *Natura non Facit Saltum*, which every fresh addition to our knowledge tends to confirm, is on this theory intelligible." [13]

What this theory of infinitesimally small and continuous variations meant, as Darwin well realized, was that all living species have been connected with the parent-species of each genus, "by differences not greater than we see between the natural and domestic varieties of the same species at the present day; and these parent-species, now generally extinct, have in their turn been similarly connected with more ancient forms; and so on backwards, always converging to the common ancestor of each great class. So that the number of intermediate and transitional links, between all living and extinct species, must have been inconceivably great. But assuredly, if this theory be true, such have lived upon the earth." [14]

The trouble was, however, as Darwin was forced to realize, the geological record, even in those parts of the earth where strata of fossils were most numerous and apparently continuous, did not even begin to support the theory of innumerable, finely graded, transitional links and, with these, the theory of non-saltatory, continuous variations in time. There is thus an entire chapter in *The Origin of the Species* with the title "On the Imperfection of the Geological Record." There is some evidence that Darwin had originally expected to find, in some sections of the earth, a "perfect" geological record; that is, one supporting the theory of continuous variation. Failing to find such a record in geology, he found instead reasons why the geological record really shouldn't be expected to be perfect in this respect—a number of such reasons. "But," Darwin wrote, in charming ingenuousness, "I do not pretend that I should ever have suspected how poor was the record in the best preserved geological sections, had not the absence of innumerable transitional links between the species which lived at the commencement and close of each formation, *pressed so hardly on my theory.*" [15] (Italics added.) The absence of links pressed so hardly, that is, on the theory of developmental continuity.

Biologists had, of course, a virtually unlimited amount of time in the past with which to make gross differences the cumulative and continuous results of minute differences. If a given transition must have required a million or ten million years for achievement in terms of continuity, there was no signal problem in allowing for such time in the nearly infinite reaches of geological and biological time.

Social scientists did not have this endless past, and could not, as could biologists, abstract their theories of change altogether from the records of history. This fact notwithstanding, the theory of continuity held the field in nineteenth-century social evolution quite as stoutly as it had two centuries earlier when the defenders of the moderns used the same theory in their controversy with the advocates of the ancients during the "battle of the books."

A full quarter of a century before *The Origin of the Species* appeared, Comte also quoted Leibniz approvingly, endorsing without question or qualification the view that "the present is big with the future," and that "nature never makes leaps." We may take advantage, writes Comte, of Condorcet's device of "supposing a single nation to which we may refer all the consecutive social modifications we actually witness among distinct peoples." Observe here that the modifications Comte refers to are modifications of *classificatory* difference, a matter I shall emphasize later. They are not modifications in the sense of actual change. Nonetheless they provide the basis of Comte's theory of continuous change. It is, he asserts, "the slow, continuous accumulation of these successive changes (*sic*) which gradually constitutes the social movement, whose steps are ordinarily marked by generations, as the most appreciable elementary variations are wrought by the constant renewal of adults." [16]

How does Comte reconcile his assertion of the continuity of change with the facts of discontinuity, of interruption, which he realized full well were the stuff of history in specific areas and among identifiable peoples? By recourse to the same analogy that had formed the means by which the eighteenth-century philosophers distinguished between "natural history" and "conventional history": the analogy of natural growth and of the aberrations and pathologies to which natural growth is occasionally subject. "In our search for the laws of society, we shall find that exceptional events and minute details must be discarded as essentially insignificant, while science lays hold of the most general phenomena which everybody is familiar with, as constituting the basis of ordinary social life." [17] Such exceptional events are likened specifically to the monstrosities that biologists have to deal with. But just as biology does not seek to pattern its own laws of natural growth in the organism around the aberrant and monstrous, neither will the sociological study of cultural development. Whatever the sporadic testimony of fixity, of reversion, and divergence in the actual histories of peoples, the study of social dynamics will proceed on the assumption of continuity of change—that is, natural or normal change.

So was Marx an apostle of genetic continuity. This is incontestably true, despite a theory of revolution that many would regard as an assertion of the very opposite of continuity. Here is Marx's rendering of the Leibnizian law of continuity:

> And even when a society has got on the right track for the discovery of the natural laws of its movement—and it is the ultimate aim of this work to lay bare the economic law of motion of modern society—it can neither clear by bold leaps nor remove by legal enactments the obstacles offered by the successive phases of its normal development. But it can shorten and lessen the birth pangs.[18]

Marx, let it be emphasized, knew a great deal of history, actual history, the histories of specific nations and peoples, most especially of the English and of the English working classes. But as Marx himself makes meticulously clear, the essential subject matter of *Capital* is not the actual history of the English or any other people. It is what he calls "natural history," the natural history of the entity or system that is capitalism, the system which, as he also tells us candidly, he has constructed out of "personifications of economic categories, embodiments of particular class relations and class interests." [19]

But does not Marx's view of revolution, it may be asked, reflect a renunciation of the slow, gradual, and cumulative idea of evolution, and of the assumption of continuity on which it is based? The answer to this question is certainly in the negative. For, Marx and Engels—at least in their systematic theory—saw revolution as but a final, triumphant, and more or less dramatic stage of growth just as continuous in its sequence of stages as anything to be found in Comte, Darwin, or Spencer. Revolution, in the Marxian sense, is feasible and theoretically rational only when the shape of the new social order is already substantially formed within the womb of the preceding order. We may again quote Marx's words: "No social order ever disappears before all the productive forces for which there is room in it have been developed, and new, higher relations of production never appear before the material conditions of their existence have matured in the womb of the old society." [20] This, Marx—the systematic Marx—believed as firmly for the advent of socialism as he did, retrospectively, for the advent of capitalism. Acceleration of a process, even by armed uprising, does not bespeak discontinuity.

Change is necessary. Because social development was directional, immanent, and continuous, it had—logically had to have—still another attribute: necessity. Necessity is one of those golden words in the nineteenth century, nowhere more golden than in the theory of development. As I noted earlier, it is easy to caricature Herbert Spencer's resounding declaration of the "beneficent necessity" of progress, but the fact remains that he was saying, with perhaps unique flourish, only what each of the other titans of social evolutionism said in Spencer's age.

Here again it is necessary to remind ourselves that no one of the social evolutionists was speaking of history in the aggregate when he spoke of necessity; nor was any of them blind to the existence of the casual and fortuitous. Each of them—Marx with capitalism, Morgan with polity, property, and family, Comte with human knowledge, and so on—was but declaring that a given sequence of development was necessary *to the nature of the system or systems* he was studying. Free of the accidental and the merely casual, it was *necessary* that a given institution have developed through time as comparative researches showed that it had in fact developed. This was the argument of evolutionary necessity.

We can see it in Hegel's *Philosophy of History*, the title of which is a misnomer, since it is the underlying *development of the idea of freedom* that Hegel is concerned with in this book, just as Comte is interested in the idea of knowledge, Newman in the idea of Christianity, and Morgan in the idea of government, of property, and of the family.

Development, Hegel tells us, is "a property of organized natural objects." Their existence, Hegel continues, "presents itself not as an exclusively dependent one, subjected to external changes, but as one which expands itself in virtue of an internal, unchangeable principle; a simple essence—whose existence, i.e., as a germ, is, primarily simple—but which subsequently develops a variety of parts, that become involved with other objects, and consequently live through a continuous process of changes. . . ." [21]

For Comte the development of knowledge from the religious through the metaphysical to the positive was necessary in its pattern because of the very pattern of the human mind itself. It was *necessary*, Comte argued, that physics precede chemistry, that chemistry precede biology, that biology precede sociology in the filiation of the sciences: necessary because of the successive degrees of conceptual dependence. And it is *necessary*, he tells us repeatedly in *The Positive Philosophy*, that sociology now pass from its metaphysical stage to its positive or scientific stage—necessary because of the pattern of development.

Even Darwin saw necessity in progressive development—one more instance of the persistence in his mind of essentially eighteenth-century conceptions side by side with a theory of natural selection that could ill afford them. Although, Darwin writes, there is no very good evidence of any "innate tendency towards progressive development" in the species, still, Darwin concluded, such progressive development may be regarded as "*necessarily*" following from the action of natural selection, which always he assures us, works toward the good of each being. The result is that "each creature tends to become more and more improved in relation to its conditions. This improvement *inevitably* leads to the gradual advancement of the organization of the greater number of living beings throughout the world." [22] (Italics added.)

Necessity means, in short, logical necessity; logical in the sense of the relation of the development to the structure of the thing developing—be it capitalism or Christianity. When St. Augustine introduced this momentous idea into the realm of history, he had behind him, of course, not merely the idea of the all-powerful, all-seeing God of the Jews but also the idea of necessity he drew from Greek philosophy. Given both, it was possible, as we saw, for everything in human history to have been necessary; and Augustine ceaselessly reiterates this. But when we are dealing with necessity in the nineteenth-century social evolutionary sense, we are dealing—quite as we are with respect to *directionality, immanence*, and *continuity*—with an entity that has been abstracted, so to speak, from the totality of things.

Marx, as we know, flattered himself that he had liberated himself from Hegel's priority of the idea, that he had, as it were, turned the matter right side up, making material things prior and fundamental. Let us not question the "materialism" in the Marxist scheme of things. But no one examining Marx's and Engels' treatment of capitalism, and also of feudalism and of the classical system of slavery they had preceding the others in time, can doubt that in each instance it is the *idea* of capitalism, etc., that Marx is dealing with.[23] Capitalism for Marx has the same kind of abstract reality, the same kind of autonomous structural being, that freedom had for Hegel, knowledge for Comte, and the family for Lewis Morgan.

We have seen Marx's insistence that the continuity of the law of motion for economic society cannot be broken by "bold leaps" or "legal enactments." From continuity it is but a short step to necessity, and we can scarcely be surprised, then, to find Marx referring to laws and tendencies "working with iron necessity towards inevitable results." The nation, he goes on, "that is more developed industrially only shows, to the less developed, the image of its own future." [24] As this passage suggests, Marx was willing to extend the idea of necessity of development from the constructed system that is his rendering of capitalism to the specific areas of historically formed nations. Such extension of the idea of necessity is, however, rare. Almost universally what was deemed necessary was the pattern of change presumed to be inherent within an institution or system, rather than in geographical areas. How important Marx's idea of necessity was in his larger scheme of the direction of economic change may be inferred from the quasi-theological debates among Marxists and other revolutionaries in Russia just before, and even during, the Revolution of 1917 concerning whether Russia could pass directly from its "feudal" stage to socialism, or must instead have an intervening neo-capitalist period.

For all the social evolutionists necessity was a cardinal element of what they deemed to be a scientific theory of change. Lewis Morgan, at the very beginning of his *Ancient Society*, stresses that all of the stages of development set forth in that book for society in general and for each of the three institutions he features—family, property, and government—are "necessary." They are necessary because they are natural, that is, natural to the entity involved.

So, too, in John Henry Newman's great treatise was necessity stressed. All that has happened in Christianity has been *necessary* according to Newman. He was replying to critics of Christianity somewhat as St. Augustine had replied to critics in the fifth century. But whereas Augustine's adversaries had the condition of Rome in mind, Newman's had the condition of Christianity before them. How, it was asked, could the vast, differentiated, complex, and affluent thing that Christianity was in the nineteenth century possibly be reconciled with the simplicity that Christianity manifests in the words of the early apostles? Through development, was Newman's answer; development as necessary as the growth of any living thing. From apostolic simplicity to the ecclesiastical differentiation of our own day, Newman declared, there has been a single line of development, an unfolding of latency into actuality, as necessary as it has been natural to Christian dogma.

Tocqueville whose obsession was democracy, its properties, and its development through time, wrote of the Revolution in France: "Chance played no part whatever in the outbreak of the Revolution; though it took the world by surprise, it was the inevitable outcome of a long period of gestation, the abrupt and violent conclusion of a process in which six generations had played intermittent part. Even if it had not taken place, the old social structure would nonetheless have been shattered everywhere sooner or later." [25] So, starting about 1918, were Marxists to write about the Revolution in Russia.

Change proceeds from uniform causes. The sixth and in many ways boldest of the conceptual elements of the theory of social evolution is the principle of uniformity. I mean by this, not any uniformity of evolutionary change from area to area, but rather the uniformity of *fundamental causes of the change* involved in evolution. This is the meaning of the word that reigned in the late eighteenth century and throughout most of the nineteenth century.

Like everything else that is basic in the nineteenth-century theory of social evolution, the principle of uniformity comes most directly from the theory of natural history. And specifically, it was James Hutton, himself one of the Scottish philosophers of natural history, who did more than anyone else to give the principle secure place. Hutton was a geologist—or more accurately a natural historian of the earth, just as Adam Ferguson was the natural historian of civil society—and it was his contention that the only *scientific* approach to the study of the history of the earth was through the study of present processes. [26] That is, on the assumption that "Nature must be consistent and uniform in her working," it could be further assumed that careful study of the processes of change now occurring in the earth would yield all necessary knowledge of the past, in other words, of the forces which had been involved in giving present shape to the surface of the earth and to its atmosphere. The possibility of great, unique, catastrophic events (which Cuvier and others in Hutton's day hypothesized) could be conveniently dismissed in favor of a principle that worked solely in terms of the manifest processes of the present. The present is the key to the past! This was the cornerstone on which Hutton and after him Playfair and then the great Charles

Lyell built their science of geology. Along with the principle of uniformity went the assumption of vast, almost endless expanses of time—geological time—in the past. For only thus could the minute and slow processes of the present—such processes as erosion—be reasonably held to have caused the differences of topography that observation revealed.

Even Lyell saw fundamental difficulties with the theory of uniformitarianism; the evidences of catastrophic events in the geological past were too pressing to be disregarded by a mind as fine as his. It is entirely possible that thoroughgoing uniformitarianism would have lost its monopolistic position in the physical sciences before it did in fact had it not been for two conditions. The first was the great attack that nineteenth-century agnosticism mounted against Christian fundamentalism; the second was the publication of Darwin's *The Origin of the Species*. Christian creationism was, in a manner of speaking, a "catastrophic" theory of the terrestrial past; and the principles of uniformitarianism laid down by Hutton and Playfair were admirably designed to cast doubt on catastrophism not merely of the Cuvier variety but also of the fundamentalist variety and, with it, the whole edifice of Christian dogma. Once the war on Christian fundamentalism began in earnest, and once the fundamentalists began to counter-attack the theory of uniformitarianism, it was inevitable no doubt that rationalists and secularists would rally for polemical reasons alone to advancement of a theory that, as Lyell realized, presented great difficulties.

The second and equally powerful reinforcement to uniformitarianism was Darwin's wholesale acceptance of the theory in conjunction with his doctrine of natural selection. For what was truly novel in *The Origin of the Species* was not the idea of biological evolution but the argument that biological evolution could be explained through a single uniform process—natural selection—that always has been in operation in the past, is now in operation, and will always be in operation in the future. In perfect accordance with Hutton's principle that the present contains the processes of the past, Darwin declared that the vast, complex, and differentiated assemblage of biological types to be seen now in the world was the consequence of a single process, natural selection, working through infinitesimally small, gradual, and continuous variations, also to be seen now working in the world. Any reliance upon the possibility of event-like mutations, of large, more or less unique changes in the past was, Darwin argued, unnecessary. Biological change in time has been the work of uniform processes.

I am not suggesting here that the principle of uniformity arose first in the physical sciences and then was passed to the social disciplines. This would be no more true than the assertion that the idea of evolution itself began first in the physical or biological sciences. Uniformitarianism is as residual an element historically in the theory of social evolution as any other. But there is no gainsaying the immense prestige that was given the whole idea of uniformitarianism in the biological and social sciences alike by its honored role in the works of such men as Lyell and Darwin— household names in Victorian England, virtually canonized names in the powerful secular movement that dominated so much of nineteenth-century thought.

It is hard today to realize the degree to which the attack on Christianity obsessed intellectuals of rationalist and utilitarian will. Christianity had much the same position that capitalism was to hold in the first half of the twentieth century. It was *the* enemy in the minds of most intellectuals. Uniformitarianism, above any other single element of the theory of evolution, was the perfect point of attack on a theory that made external manipulation its essence and a succession of "catastrophes" its plot. And the uniformitarianism that figured so prominently in Hutton, Playfair, Lyell, and Darwin figured with equal prominence in the works of the social evolutionists.

It had from the beginning. Even if we go back to those earliest philosophers of social growth, Aristotle, for instance, in his theory of the growth of society and the state, we find interest in the "efficient" or "motor" cause; the indwelling, persisting, cause that activates, as it were, the whole process by which *physis* manifests itself in time. What else was St. Augustine's convulsive conflict of the Two Cities but dramatization of the uniform conflict in human nature present since the Fall? After all, did not Augustine himself explain the marvellous progress that had been man's cultural history on earth through the efficient causes of "necessity" and "human inventiveness," both of them present throughout mankind's epic sojourn on earth?

The idea of uniformitarianism was a powerful one in eighteenth-century natural history. As I noted above, Hutton has been named a "geologist" only by our own present time. He was in fact, and regarded himself as, a natural historian, doing with the earth exactly what his contemporary Adam Smith was doing with the economic system and what, across the Channel, Rousseau was doing with human institutions generally—explaining their development through ongoing and uniform causes. For Adam Smith the uniform cause of development was competition. For Rousseau it was the ceaseless operation of men's vices—avarice, ambition, etc.— that explained the development of culture in time. Mandeville's immensely influential *Fable of the Bees* had given to "private vices, public benefits" the status of uniform cause in human history.

It was, however, Immanuel Kant who probably had most to do with putting the idea of endemic, uniform conflict in the form most usable to the study of developmental change. In his *Idea for a Universal History*, written in 1784, Kant set forth, in the form of a "fourth thesis" the following: "The means employed by Nature to bring about the development of all the capacities of men is their antagonism in society, so as this is, in the end, the cause of a lawful order among men."

By this antagonism Kant is referring to what he calls "the unsocial sociability" of men in association; that is, their desire to enter into association combined, however, with their desire to maintain the autonomy of egoism. It is the opposition between these two impulses, both of them grounded deeply in man's nature, that provides the uniform and timeless dynamic of mankind's ascent from primitive barbarism. "This opposition it is which awakens all his powers. . . . Thus are taken the first true steps from barbarism to culture." [27]

The emphasis on conflict that we find in Kant and in other German philosophers dealing with human development is not, as a myopic and parochial criticism once had it, a consequence of German love of force. Everywhere in eighteenth-century Europe, France, England, and Scotland alike, the demand for some endemic, uniform mechanism to give continuity and necessity to social development put a premium upon conflict or competition of one kind or other. How better than by some premised internal conflict to explain the course of mankind's advancement through time? [28]

From Kant and others in the eighteenth century it is an easy step to the concept of uniform processes that we find in the nineteenth-century theory of social evolution. Hegel, like Kant, found internal conflict to be the effective cause of the development he studied in terms of the idea of freedom. Through the dialectic, by which thesis and antithesis are resolved into synthesis, the spirit is "at war with itself." Whereas, Hegel tells us, development in the sphere of nature is a peaceful growth, it is "in the sphere of the spirit a severe, a mighty conflict with itself." [29] In light of the eminently *non*-peaceful process that Darwin would find the process of natural selection or "survival of the fittest" to be, Hegel's words on the sphere of nature have a certain charm.

The notion of endemic conflict or tension of internal elements as the motivating spring of social evolution was to remain a pervasive one in the nineteenth century. Marx, as we know, made such conflict an inherent process in economic society, one that took its origin from the rise of private property and, with it, social classes. Class struggle is a vital and constant element of all societies, Marxism declares, and will remain such until, through long-range development of the social order to the final phases of capitalism, both private property and social class have been abolished for once and all. After this, Marx and Engels argued, the motivation for change and indeed for all subsequent human history would lie in man's consciousness.

Tocqueville, too, gives a picture of endemic conflict as the motive power of the development of democracy: conflict between the values of equality and of achievement, the first a reflection of the democratic urge toward likeness of social condition, the second an equally irresistible reflection of the democratic urge toward improvement of one's economic and social status. Tocqueville saw the first as the triumphant one in the long run; hence his picture toward the end of *Democracy in America* of democracy having reached a final condition of standardization, homogeneity, and inertia, with all-embracing political power having risen out of the passion for social equality.

For Comte the continuing motivation toward change within the developmental process rises from the human psyche itself, with its limitless demands for satisfaction of human needs. Comte refers to "the individual impulsions which make up the progressive force of the human race" and to "that instinct which results from the concurrence of all our natural tendencies, and which urges man to develop the whole of his life, physical, moral, and intellectual, as far as his circumstances allow." [30] Given this manifestly inherent, timeless, and uniform urge to ambition in the human species, Comte saw no reason to look for any other source of social change. This human craving for knowledge, status, and power served Comte's theory just as class struggle served Marx, as the struggle for equality served Tocqueville, as "unsocial sociability" had served Kant—as a uniform mechanism of change, a mechanism built into the developing entity, one that rendered superfluous any dependence upon either a Providence above, or external and unique events below, to explain the course of human development.

Such, it would appear, are the central conceptual elements of the nineteenth-century theory of social evolution. The naturalness of change to each social institution or system, as well as to the whole of society; the directional or trend-like character of change; the emanation of change from forces internal; the genetic continuity of change; the necessity of change to each social system; and, finally, the dependence of natural change upon uniform, persisting forces throughout time.

These are the concepts fundamental to the theory of social evolution. And, as I shall indicate in the final two chapters of the book, they are equally fundamental in the contemporary study of social change.

Six

THE COMPARATIVE METHOD

By this method, the different stages of evolution
may all be observed at once. Though the
progression is single and uniform, in regard to the
whole race, some very considerable and very
various populations have, from causes which are
little understood, attained extremely unequal
degrees of development, so that the former states
of the most civilized nations are now to be seen,
amidst some partial differences.

> *Comte*

. . . the institutions of man are as distinctly
stratified as the earth on which he lives. They
succeed each other in series substantially uniform
over the globe, independent of what seem the
comparatively superficial differences of race and
language, but shaped by similar human nature
acting through successively changed conditions
in savage, barbaric, and civilized life.

> *Tylor*

1. ETHNOCENTRIC FOUNDATIONS

Closely related to the theory of social evolution, inseparable from
it indeed, is the system of culture classification known admiringly
in the nineteenth-century under the name of the Comparative
Method.

Few subjects, one is forced to conclude, have been more thoroughly and widely misunderstood than this one. The Comparative
Method is thought to be the consequence of the "scientific" anthropology of the late nineteenth century. It is not. Its roots and
basic framework are as old in Western thought as Greek and Roman interest in origins and cultural stages. It is thought to have
disappeared in the twentieth century along with the theories of

Spencer and Morgan. It has not. It remains the framework of countless "comparative" treatments of institutions and cultures. It is thought to provide evidence for the reality of the general line of social development put forth by the theory of social evolution. It does not, for fundamental to the Comparative Method and its assumed validity as a body of evidence are the very preconceptions —conclusions, too, actually—of the theory of social evolution that the Comparative Method purportedly verifies. It is one of the outstanding examples in all social thought of circular reasoning. It is thought, rather vaguely, to be part and parcel of the kind of comparison that goes into all genuinely scientific work; analogous, for instance, to the profoundly comparative studies of Frederick Le Play in the nineteenth century or to those of Max Weber in the field of religion. But it is not. Whatever the superficies of comparison which adorn the Comparative Method, it is not comparative in any vital sense whatsoever, and has no relation to the kind of work that lay behind Le Play's great study of family types in the world or Weber's comparative examination of religion and its relation to economic changes.

But the greatest misconception in terms of abstract theory, methodology, and purpose is of its asserted universalism. The Method is widely thought to mark the beginning of dispassionate and objective comparison of cultures and institutions in the world. It is frequently described as the instrument of Western scholarship's release from thralldom to its own past and as the vantage point from which new and more universalized criteria of history and development were gained. With the advent in the nineteenth century of the Comparative Method—so the familiar assertion goes—the history of Western Europe was placed in due perspective as but one of the innumerable histories in the annals of mankind.

In fact, however, the Comparative Method, as we find it in the writings of the nineteenth-century social evolutionists, and to a considerable degree at the present time, is hardly more than a shoring-up of the idea of progressive development generally and, more particularly, of the belief that the recent history of the West could be taken as evidence of the direction in which mankind as a whole *would* move and, flowing from this, *should* move. The specific set of cultural qualities that seemed to most rationalists in the nineteenth century to manifest the direction of Western history were adapted for comparative purposes to become the criteria of classification of the peoples and cultures of the world.[1]

Comte, Marx, Spencer, Tylor, Morgan, without exception, were convinced that the specific line of development which they thought they could see culminating in Western Europe was much more than Western development alone. They saw the West, and most especially England and France, as the vanguard in a mighty movement of historical development that would eventually encompass the rest of the world. What was so evident today in the most progressive parts of Western Europe would be evident tomorrow in the rest of Europe and the Americas and the next day in Asia and the day after that in Africa, Oceania, and other "primitive" parts of the world.

If we ask the question, what precisely *was* so evident in genetic-developmental terms in the West and what could be accepted as the attributes of the West's vanguard status, the answer is simple and clear: *modernity*. By this I mean, of course, such traits and ideas as technology, industrialism, democracy, secularism, individualism, equalitarianism, and, for some, socialism. Counterposed to these were the attributes of *traditionalism* or, as the case might be, of "backwardness" or "primitivism": kinship, the sacred or religious view of life, corporatism, hierarchy, localism, handicraft, ruralism, and the like. All of the social evolutionists (and for that matter all of the social scientists generally of the century) were obsessed by this contrast of values and traits. In one context the contrast could be the base of programs of reform, of revolution. In another context the identical contrast could be the perspective for marking the path of progress, of assessing the nearness or remoteness of a given people to what was not merely good and right but, far more important, *modern, developed, mature*. For Comte, Marx, Spencer—profoundly different as the ideas of these three men were in so many respects—were united in the belief that these two sets of values, give or take a value or two, could be taken as, not merely evidencing the general track of progress but as providing the necessary clues to arrangement of the cultures of the world in useful classification.. Whether a people was pronounced civilized or primitive depended upon the extent to which its culture corresponded with the values in the first set. Hence the interchangeability then as now of "civilized," "modern," and "developed."

2. HISTORICAL ROOTS

Like the larger perspective of developmentalism of which it is a part, the Comparative Method was not really new in the nineteenth century; an old approach was simply made more systematic in statement and more voluminous in content than it had been. In the preceding pages I have made occasional reference to the kinds of data on which scholars, from the Greeks onward, sought to prove their contentions respecting some early condition of mankind or some line of development. There are frequent manifestations of use of the Comparative Method in one degree of formality or other among the Greeks and Romans. Comparison of a sort followed directly from the idea of *physis*. As John Linton Myres writes:

> In order to distinguish "according to mode of growth and to describe actual status," it was necessary first to collect the facts. Hence, sooner or later, on the political side, collections of constitutions like those collected for Aristotle and Dicaearchus; in zoology, collections of animals and plants (these, for practical reasons, rather later than sooner); in geography, a "tramp around the world" like that of Hecataeus, one of the last and greatest explainers of growth; in physiology and medicine, collections of diseases, like the epidemics of Hippocrates.[2]

It should not be imagined, however, that the method Myres is describing—or, for that matter, the full-blown Comparative Method of the nineteenth century—was a mere comparison of types in terms of overt attributes. It was comparison, but *within a presumed order of growth and development* of the types. Myres's first words in the passage above emphasize this. "To distinguish according to mode of growth" was to distinguish in terms of the *physis* that each society or institution or other type contained. When Aristotle compared his own polity to that of the Cyclopes in Homer, and then adduced "barbarous" peoples living even in his time, he was pointing to a presumed line of development from kinship through the community to the *polis*. Contemporary barbaric peoples seemed to Aristotle fit evidence of what the Greeks themselves had once been like.

This comparative-developmental perspective is found in the early pages of Thucydides as well, where, as background for his account of the fifth-century Athenians, he delves into the earliest ways of Greek society as these might be inferred from records, from archaeological remains, from superstitions of the past persisting into his own time, and from the ways of coexisting peoples whom Thucydides chose to regard as examples of what earlier Athenians were like. Similarly, a few centuries later, when the Roman moralist-historian Tacitus wrote about the Germanic peoples then living on the borders of Rome, it was not only to hold the glass up to the Roman people in order that they might see in Germanic vigor and virtue their own debasement, but also to suggest further that as the Germans were in Tacitus' day, so were the Romans of long ago.

At no point in the history of European thought has this combination of comparison and developmentalism been really absent. Even in the seventeenth century, a period generally more interested in the abstract and structural than the developmental, we find Hobbes, Locke, Pufendorf, and many others drawing from accounts of contemporaneous savage peoples to illustrate their various propositions on what the state of nature must have been like. Accounts of explorers' and missionaries' visits to the remoter parts of the world—in such works as *Purchas His Pilgrimage* (1613) and then the same enterprising author's later and far more successful *Hakluyt's Voyages* (1625)—made exciting reading for the populace, which bought them avidly, and instructive reading for the social philosophers, who were able to make scientific or political capital out of one or other of the peoples described in these collections. For Hobbes's purposes, given his political values with respect to sovereignty and the need for uncompromising exertion of sovereign power, the Indians of eastern North America served admirably to illustrate his thesis that the state of nature is one of war and insecurity, for these Indians were among the more warlike of the hemisphere. Locke, writing a generation later, and with different political values in mind, found no difficulty, however, in pointing to other primitive peoples to illustrate a state of nature considerably more peaceful.[3]

In the eighteenth century, especially in France, this prototype of the Comparative Method attained immense popularity as a means of supporting the theory of the progress of civilization. All the existing cultures of the world, ranging from the simplest and rudest to the most civilized (Western Europe, naturally), could be arrayed, it was thought, in a conceptual panorama of human progress.

Looking at this panorama, Turgot declared that, through its infinitely varied hierarchy of differences, "the existing state of the universe, in presenting at once on the earth every shade of barbarism and refinement, shows us in a manner at a single glance the monuments, the vestiges, of every step taken by the human mind, the likeness of every stage through which it has passed, the history of all ages."[4]

Turgot's words were uttered in 1750. They are the most concise statement of what is fundamental in the Comparative Method that I have been able to find in the literature of the eighteenth century. In them we can see immediately the link between comparison and the theory of progressive development. But Turgot was far from alone in his admiration of this method. There were very few social philosophers in Western Europe in the eighteenth century who did not make use of the method in one way or other. What Rousseau, Condorcet, Adam Smith, and Adam Ferguson gave us in their natural histories involved reliance upon the point of view contained in Turgot's words.

3. THE THREE SERIES

Let us turn now to the essential elements, to the framework, of the Comparative Method.[5] It is a synchronization of three distinct orders of data. The first is that of *coexisting peoples and social organizations and artifacts arranged in logico-spatial fashion*. In this order we are given simple classification of cultural materials, in terms of a given theme or subject—kinship, war-making, modes of transportation, stratification, religion—drawn from all parts of the earth, and arranged essentially in terms of logical progression from the simple to the complex. At one end of the logico-spatial spectrum might fall, say, the Andaman Islanders' or the Tierra del Fuegians' mode of life and at the other, almost invariably, that of Western Europe. This, clearly, is simple taxonomy. But the matter does not rest there.

The second order of fact and concept involved in the Comparative Method is *temporal*. Here a time-series is brought into view, one drawn to the best of the methodologist's ability from the historical and archaeological records of the cultural history of the West particularly but also of other areas, such as Chinese, Mayan, Indian, where documents, artifacts, and fossils contribute some notion of temporal sequence. Obviously, there were limits to this purely temporal order of fact and concept. In the first place, even the best preserved of areas (in archaeological terms) had the kind of "imperfection" that Darwin complained about in the geological record, and did not go back far enough to satisfy those who were striving to uncover the very earliest condition of mankind. Ordinary historical records might take the investigator back three or four thousand years, archaeological remains another few thousand, and that was the end. Left unanswered was the question, what was the condition of mankind like even earlier? In the second place, archaeology was necessarily confined to material culture or to such tantalizing glimpses of non-material culture as sketches in stone or paintings on the walls of caves might occasionally supply. But what was earlier man's religious belief, his systems of kinship, his techniques of social control, his social organization in general?

It is here that we come to the third order of data and concept involved in the Comparative Method: *the developmental or evolutionary series*. This is a series abstracted from the concrete existences of actual peoples or historical periods and areas. It is the series constructed of those traits, ideas, and elements which might be supposed to have formed, for society as a whole, over the whole duration of total society's existence on earth, the successive stages of development. Or, instead of total society or culture, it might be *the* kinship system of man, *the* economic system, or *the* religious beliefs of man, each given a high degree of universalization, even reification, thus permitting actual, empirically given, types of kinship, economy, and religious belief to be employed in the fashioning of stages for *the* development of each system.

I can illustrate this with an example much favored by those for whom the Comparative Method demonstrates or even proves the progressive nature of change in time: transportation. In the beginning was walking; we see it now as a kind of persisting survival of mankind's earliest means of locomotion. Thus the developmental series begins. Today, however, man has learned to transport himself through supra-terrestrial space in rockets traveling distances in a split second that primitive man (that is, man on foot) would require days to travel. In between these two linear extremes falls the great bulk of the "data" yielded by the Comparative Method. All the diverse and variegated means of transportation ever encountered by explorer or ever set down by annalist are interposed between the two extremes as a series of developmental steps in the entity we call "man's transportation."

I say "developmental" steps. But development means change, at the very least. And change we have defined as a succession of differences in time in a persisting entity. Where in this series of asserted developmental steps is the process of change? The answer is plain. There is no change; only a succession of conditions and types of transportation drawn from all possible periods of history and all possible areas of the earth, and then arranged in a series bearing as much relationship as possible to the actual historical series in the West but synchronized also with the logico-spatial series that inevitably yields the widest variation. What we have, in fact, in the so-called developmental series is a finely-graded, logically continuous series of "stills" as in a movie film. It is the eye— or rather, in this instance, the disposition to believe—that creates the illusion of actual development, growth, or change.

It is all much like a museum exhibit. (It might be observed in passing that the principles of museum arrangement of cultural artifacts have not been without considerable influence on the principles of cultural evolution.) The last one I saw was an exhibit of "the development of warfare." At the beginning were shown examples of primitive war-making—spears, bows and arrows, and the like. At the far end of the exhibit were examples (constructed miniatures) of the latest and most awful forms of warfare. In between, constructed in fullest accord with the principles of logical continuity, was the whole spectrum or range of weapons that have been found or written about anywhere on the earth's surface at whatever time. All of this, observers were assured, represented the development of warfare. But the development of warfare where? Not, certainly, in the United States, or in Tasmania, or in China, or in Tierra del Fuego, or in any other concrete, geographically identifiable, historically delimited, area. What "develops" is in fact no substantive, empirical entity but a hypostatized, constructed entity that is called "the art of war."

Here let me make a point that I shall come back to in the final chapter, for it has something to do with the kind of problem that is involved in making the concept of development serve the needs of our understanding of empirical variation. I am referring to *variation.*

There are two quite different and equally important meanings that we assign to this word. There is first the meaning drawn from logic and taxonomy. Here we are referring to variations of type, variations that have reality only in terms of some common theme or principle of classification. Statistical variations fall within this meaning. We speak of one form of dance or eating utensil or kinship varying from another. There is, however, no change implied in this meaning of the word.

But "variation" also means change: actual substantive change. Here a single persisting entity moves or is moved from one condition to another. Manifestly there is something more than logical variation of type involved. There is in clear view *change*. Obviously the second meaning of the word carries with it much of the first. But—and here is the point I stress—the first meaning by no means implies the second.

One can almost pinpoint the difference between the theory of biological evolution in the nineteenth century and the theory of social evolution in these terms. The kind of variation that Darwin and Wallace were interested in explaining, and even more obviously Mendel, was *genetic* variation; that is variation in the sense of type, yes, when looked at taxonomically, but above all variation in the sense of change. But when we consider the theory of social evolution through looking at panoramas of it formed by the Comparative Method, we see *classificatory* variation, that is, variation in the sense simply of gradations of logical relationship.

Hence the fondness of the social evolutionist in the nineteenth century for dealing with total society or total culture. And when he went below this it was still to something large and capable of universalization—such as kinship, polity, law, means of transportation, warfare, etc. It was not the origin of any one of these in a specific area or people that interested him—save insofar as the practice or belief of a given people could be universalized into the origin of the institution or trait as a universal type—but rather the origin of the practice in the totality of space and time.

In all of this it was of utmost importance *how* one arranged his historical and ethnographic materials; *how* precisely one chose his example of the simplest, rudest, most archaic of existing peoples on earth. How else was one to prove that religion began in animism rather than totemism, that group marriage preceded the matriarchate, and so on? How, in short, was one to validate his preferred line of evolution for a given trait?

The answer was fashioned from one or other arrangement of the data drawn from the first and second orders of concept and fact I have mentioned. With the second—that is, the temporal series, incomplete but *known*—to guide him the evolutionist could go to the first order—the logico-spatial series—for all the materials necessary to fill out his particular theory of origins or stages of development.

Thus Auguste Comte could write—with respect to his own reified entity, human knowledge through the ages—that by virtue of the Comparative Method "the different stages of evolution" could be observed simultaneously in the world. "From the wretched inhabitants of Tierra del Fuego to the most advanced nations of Western Europe, there is no social grade which is not extant in some points of the globe, and usually in localities which are clearly apart." [6]

And here is Tylor: "[T]he institutions of man are as distinctly stratified as the earth on which he lives. They succeed each other in series substantially uniform over the globe, independent of what seem comparatively superficial differences of race and language, but shaped by similar human nature acting through successively changed conditions in savage, barbaric, and civilized life." [7]

What is Tylor specifically referring to with respect to his "series substantially uniform?" To *civilization*, a word he uses in exactly the same generic, abstract, reified sense in which it was used in the eighteenth century. It is this abstraction, civilization, that Tylor is referring to in the following passage:

> So far as the evidence goes, it seems that civilization has actually grown up in the world through these three stages, so that to look at a savage of the Brazilian forests, a barbarous New Zealander or Dahoman, and a civilized European, may be the student's best guide to understanding the progress of civilization, only he must be cautioned that the comparison is but a guide, not a full explanation.[8]

Guide or full explanation, the Comparative Method served the purposes of the theorists of social evolution in a way that Darwin must have envied. We will remember that Darwin, operating also from a theory of slow, gradual, and continuous change, had expected, or at least strongly hoped, that the geological record would exemplify this theory through its preservation of fossil types of all the intermediate species and types in the chain of being. Darwin, of course, did not find this continuous chain and accordingly declared the geological record "imperfect." But the social evolutionists, drawing from the materials of history, archaeology, and, above all, the seeming plenitude of ethnographic evidence, thought they were in precisely the position that Darwin had only dreamed of.

Herbert Spencer was by all odds the most elaborate and enthusiastic user of the Comparative Method. Everything he read was grist for his mill. (He did not really read books; he *mined* them.) The file drawers of his study (he describes the whole thing in his *Autobiography*) were neatly and hierarchically placed in terms of evolutionary stages for each of the major institutions of society. Whenever he came across a new trait in his reading, it was noted and filed away in the section of the drawer to which the trait had evolutionary relevance. When the time came to commence the writing of one or other of his evolutionary treatises, it was a matter, he tells us with utter and artless candor, of simply transferring to the pages of his manuscript the contents of the multitudinous slips of paper in the file drawers. Never, Spencer tells us, was there a moment's doubt. Given the prior discovery of each and every pattern of institutional development, it was child's work to fit to it the social and cultural traits unearthed in his reading.

Countless readers in our day have laughed at Spencer's artlessness, and his seemingly simple-minded pursuit of a method that was his own. But, candor and artlessness aside, it was the very method used by all the social evolutionists—then and now—and, given the objectives and premises of a theory of social evolution it was indispensable.

The identical Comparative Method is the framework of Morgan's *Ancient Society*. Here, through logical arrangement of material drawn from ethnography and the early history of Western Europe—notably of the Greeks down through the Cleisthenean reforms—Morgan presented the evolutionary panorama that we have described before. Like Tylor, no doubt, he intended that it be a guide rather than a full explanation. The materials of the Comparative Method illustrated the natural development of the three institutions (or, rather, of the *idea* of each): kinship, polity, and property.

Marx and Engels, as we know, were both fascinated by Morgan's book, seeing in it detailed exemplification of not merely the central role of property and its conflicts in social evolution but also rough approximation to their own claimed sequence of stages for mankind. Engels, in his *The Origin of Family, Private Property, and the State* (a volume that continues to have near-biblical status in Marxist anthropology), was, as he acknowledged freely, drawing heavily on Morgan's researches. There is no doubt whatever that Marx and Engels saw the taxonomic distribution of institutions in the world as being at one and the same time a developmental series, one reflected in that abstraction they called "society" or "economic society."

As I said at the beginning of this section, the Comparative Method was a means of substantiating not merely the progressive character of change in time—that is, its movement from the simple and undifferentiated to the complex and highly differentiated —but also the manifestly advanced position of the West. For whatever else critics of Western society might say of it, however necessary reform or revolution might be to its further advancement, no one could take away from the West its position at the top of the evolutionary hierarchy of cultures.

By the same token, one could categorize non-Western peoples as not simply exotic or different but as reflecting lower stages of an evolutionary advancement that was thought to be universal. Much therefore could be forgiven Western slave traders, missionaries, and colonial administrators in the "more primitive parts of the world." For however rapacious in the short run their acts might seem to the humanitarian conscience, these same acts, in the long run, could be the means of hastening the development of these peoples toward modernity; accelerants to modernization. Thus,

Marx, in some reflections on India, gave his blessing to the depredations there of the East India Company on the ground that, however repugnant they might be at first sight, they were nonetheless necessary to India's progress in the long run.

To those primarily interested in buttressing a Western nation's political position in Africa or in other spheres of "primitive" or "retarded" culture, the theory of social evolution was, of course, a marvellous justification for ascendancy of the West. If a given native people was indeed to be shown as holding a relatively low place in the evolutionary scale made manifest by the Comparative Method, then was there not a case to be made for paternalism, for saving such a people from the worst experiences of, and the lengths of time involved in, natural evolution? Under such Western paternalism native peoples could be shown the way to modernity. The literature of colonial administration, of Christian missions, and of commercial traders in the nineteenth century has a good deal in it about the stages of advancement involved in what was widely thought to be the course of social evolution to Western peaks.

But the Comparative Method served the purpose also of reassuring Western intellectuals about the developmental rightness of their own society—or, rather, *of those elements in their society that were "modern" in contrast to those elements held to be retrograde*. On this basis of comparison, large sections of social organization—even family and religion—could be contemptuously dismissed as archaic, as destined to be dissolved in the long run by the processes of development that had already elevated to ascendancy in the West technology, rationalism, equality, and related qualities. Nothing has mattered more to the modern rationalist intellectual than being thought on the track of historical development. Beliefs, attitudes, and actions must correspond with what is progressive rather than what is non-progressive. Elements of belief and behavior that did not have ready assimilation into the category of modernity could be rejected as "survivals," comparable to the arrowheads and shards of pottery found in midden heaps, and which similarly bespoke earlier stages of development, of primitivism or backwardness, instead of modernity.

The word "survival" took on very strategic significance, it might be pointed out, in the works of Tylor and Morgan, particularly Tylor. For, in the latter part of the nineteenth century, some rather shrewd, if sometimes fundamentalist, minds attacked the logic of the Comparative Method and of progressive developmentalism generally. How, it was asked, can we so easily conclude that the progressive order in which the world's peoples is arranged by the social evolutionist is the proper order? Why, on strictly logical and even empirical grounds, could not a very different order be contrived, one in which, say, China or India is placed at the top in the status of "developed" or "more developed" instead of England or France and Western Europe as a whole?

Still another and even more fundamental question was asked: On what logical and empirical ground do we assume that change in time tends to be progressive rather than regressive? (It will be remembered from a preceding chapter that there were prophets of decadence and degeneration as well as of progress in Western Europe in the nineteenth century.) Although, as is usually the case when questions are asked in science and philosophy that do not fit prevailing paradigms, these questions were officially disregarded, if not derided, as T. H. Huxley derided all critics of Darwinism, there is considerable evidence that they nevertheless hit their mark. The major social evolutionists were obliged to re-examine, one way or other, the major premises of their theory and to seek, if possible, reinforcement for the assumption that development is progressive, that is, in the direction of ever greater complexity, differentiation, and functional adaptation.

Here was where the doctrine of survivals came handily into use by the progressive evolutionists. As Margaret T. Hodgen has shown in an impressive piece of scholarly detection,[9] Tylor for one was so stung by the attacks on his cherished theory of developmental progress in time that he literally created the idea of survivals as a form of counter-attack. How he did it need not be dealt with in detail here. It suffices to say that he proceeded by elaborating precisely the distinction, so cherished by all the Victorian rationalists, between traditionalism and modernism in Western society, his own England included. Close inspection of some of the elements of traditionalism—to be found among the rural, the peasantry, the backward, even in children's games, as well as in the whole gamut of superstition—revealed, Tylor declared, very close similarity with elements of culture in one or other preliterate people, where such elements existed in perfect conformity with the consensus or social structure of that preliterate people. If this were the case, Tylor argued, could not the presence of these same traits among the "backward" sections of Western populations or within purely superstitious or ritualistic or ceremonial contexts be taken as proof that Western society had once known a stage in which these elements were also perfectly conjoined to the larger belief-system of the social order? Tylor, along with approving a good many other uses of the Comparative Method, thought the answer was a clear affirmative. Once the kind of beliefs represented today by, say, Hallowe'en observances were standard, were quite literally functional parts of the Western cultural order. Time, however, has passed them by. The processes of progressive development have, by elevating rationalism and other more progressive modes of belief, made Hallowe'en observances what they are today in the West—the sport of children, the belief of the backward elements in the population.

One would not wish to count up the elements of the self-fulfilling, the self-sealing, and the purely circular in this whole mode of analysis. It does not matter in any event. I am only concerned to indicate the importance of the idea of survivals in the framework of the Comparative Method. The voices of critics of progressive developmentalism were largely drowned out by those who found in the Comparative Method abundant justification for what the idea of progress had argued: that change is normally self-realizing, self-fulfilling, working always toward greater adaptation and differentiation of function and type, and that the native peoples of Africa, South Asia, Oceania, and the Americas, could be regarded, *had* to be regarded, therefore, as constituting a record of temporal succession. The simplest of such peoples became—with perfect logic, given the premises regarding growth which underlay the Comparative Method—"our contemporary ancestors," "our primitive contemporaries," or "fossilized societies."

All of the phrases I have just quoted come from fairly recent works, which would suggest that the Comparative Method is far from dead, even though it is most commonly referred to in the manner of something that died with Herbert Spencer. In point of fact classificatory systems widely used at the present time in the study of non-Western cultures derive straight from the nineteenth century's Comparative Method. To a very large extent these systems employ as their criteria for separation of the "progressive" from "non-progressive" peoples (or, as is much commoner at the present time, "modernized" from the "relatively modernized" or "non-modernized") the self-same qualities—technology, individualism, secularism, etc.—that the intellectuals of the Enlightenment in France discovered and that the social evolutionists in the nineteenth century conceptualized into a framework of evolutionary comparison. We continue to divide the societies of the world between the "developed" and the "non-developed," with one or more degrees of intermediate development intercalated to provide that continuity which is as cherished today as it was during any period in the past. We would not allow ourselves use of the words "savage," "barbarous," and "civilized" today, believing they might suggest ethnocentrism, although these words gave no offense to the impeccably rationalist and liberal mind of Edward Tylor.

But whatever the terms we may choose today, the blunter ones of Victorian-rationalist usage or the more neutralized and bland ones of current coinage, one and all they depend for their meaning upon the criteria I have mentioned—criteria which first rose to intellectual ascendancy a couple of centuries ago in the West when reformers and revolutionaries were seeking to emancipate Western culture from its medieval heritage and, in so doing, enlisted the mighty idea of progressive development in their behalf.

The most widespread, if often subtle, consequence of the

nineteenth-century evolutionary-comparative perspective is the way in which we continue to arrange cultural materials for cross-study and analysis even when there is no hint in a given work of interest in social evolution as such or even in social change. That all of the essential elements of the Comparative Method should be found in such a work as Talcott Parsons' recent *Societies: Evolutionary and Comparative Perspectives*,[10] with its arrangement of the peoples of the world, past and present, into three great and ascending levels of "primitive," "intermediate," and "modern," is a matter for no surprise, for Professor Parsons' intent is frankly and avowedly evolutionary. Granting, even stressing, its own unique theoretical sophistication and the greater abundance of materials on which he could base his work, his work falls clearly in the type of labor that in the nineteenth century produced the works of Spencer, Morgan, and Tylor. It is, in brief, a work that argues the slow, gradual, and continuous evolution of all mankind through the three great levels which form the structure of his book.

But there are many works which, dispensing altogether with any avowal of interest in change and development, nevertheless organize themselves, for comparative purposes, through the framework of the same Comparative Method. One of the most recent is Gerhard Lenski's important work on social stratification, *Power and Privilege*.[11] The book is so free of any evolutionary intent that the words "evolution," "development," and even "change" are altogether absent from the index. Professor Lenski's purpose is purely theoretical and analytical. He is concerned with reaching an understanding of the nature of social stratification and providing certain hypotheses about it. He is at no time suggesting that the panorama of social stratification laid before us in the book's chapters is a developmental or evolutionary one—least of all, anything unilinear.

But one need only inspect the table of contents to see instantly how powerful the hold of the Comparative Method continues to be in contemporary social science. We begin with the nature of man, just as every study of natural history in the eighteenth century began with precisely this subject. We pass to analysis of the several universal elements of society and culture, those which are indistinguishable from human society wherever it is to be found. Then come the "dynamics of distributive systems," and "the structure of distributive systems"; in short, the statics and dynamics of that part of society which is of major interest to Lenski— social stratification systems. On the basis of these preliminary analyses of the nature of man, of society, and of stratification, we then move to consideration of societies in the world to which Lenski carries, as it were, his hypotheses concerning the nature of social stratification.

How are these societies—of the entire past and present— arranged taxonomically for purposes of his investigation? In terms of what I referred to above as the two series; that is, the logical-spatial and the quasi-historical series. Since his book is not concerned with evolution, the third series, the evolutionary series, is omitted. If the reader desires to draw from Professor Lenski's panorama any evolutionary conclusions that is his business. It is not the expressed intent of the book.

Few readers, however, will be able to resist drawing such evolutionary conclusions. For what follows, and forms most of the book, is a series of chapters on, first, "hunting and gathering societies"; second, "simple horticultural societies"; third, "advanced horticultural societies"; fourth—in two degrees—"agrarian societies"; and, fifth and finally, those aspects of economic, political, and technological modernity which Professor Lenski puts under the heading of "industrial societies."

Admittedly, once one embarks upon the task of classification of whole societies or whole social systems, such as stratification, *some* system of taxonomy is required. But why this one? I daresay a host of reasons could be advanced to justify it—reasons analytical, theoretical, inductive, and deductive—but I would like to suggest that, despite these undoubtedly plausible reasons, it is highly unlikely that this system would recommend itself if either of the following considerations prevailed: (1) the author were not himself a representative of the modern, industrial, democratic civilization whose central elements provide the criteria for cross-cultural comparison; (2) the Comparative Method associated with the names of Comte, Spencer, and Tylor had never been brought into being.

One final point must be made about the nineteenth century Comparative Method: its circularity of reasoning. The grand intent of the Method was to prove, through comparison of peoples and periods, the validity of the idea of evolutionary development —of progressive differentiation of type and function through time, taking the whole of civilization as the fundamental subject. But, as will surely not have escaped the reader by this time, the value of the Comparative Method along these lines was dependent utterly upon prior acceptance of—the idea of progressive development!

PERSISTENCE AND CHANGE

SEVEN

THE PERSISTENCE OF METAPHOR

Every culture passes through the age-phases of
the individual man. Each has its childhood,
youth, manhood, and old age.

> *Spengler*

The whole history of man is thus comparable
to his individual life.

> *Reinhold Niebuhr*

We may liken the progress of mankind to that
of a man a hundred years old, who dawdles
through kindergarten for eighty-five years of his
life, takes ten years to go through the primary
grades, then rushes with lightning rapidity
through grammar school and college.

> *Robert H. Lowie*

1. CYCLE, EPIC, AND PROGRESS

For twenty-five hundred years a single metaphoric conception of
change has dominated Western thought. Drawn from the analogy
between society and the organism, more specifically between social
change and the life-cycle of the organism, this metaphor very early
introduced into Western European philosophy assumptions and
preconceptions regarding change in society that have at no time
been without profound influence on Western man's contemplation of past, present, and future. In its earliest formulation, in
Greece, the metaphor and analogy produced the idea of recurrent
cycles of development. It was an idea that went unchallenged for a
thousand years. Then in the fifth century A.D. St. Augustine, without abandoning the analogy, modified it; and from his modification came the momentous Christian envisagement of change that
we call the epic, which is cyclical like the Greek doctrine from

which it was drawn but without recurrence. Twelve hundred years passed, and in the seventeenth century the analogy, still popular, was again modified; this time to produce the modern idea of linear progress; the vision of mankind without old age and decline, with ever-increasing knowledge ahead.

These momentous perspectives, however, are but a part of the heritage of metaphor. Also proceeding from it, as we have seen, have been the conceptions of the *modus operandi* of social change. From the metaphor came the notion of change as a process *natural* to each and every living entity, social as well as biological, as something as much a part of its nature as structure and process. Second, social change—that is, natural change—was regarded as *immanent*, as proceeding from forces or provisions within the entity. Third, change, under this view, is *continuous*, which is to say that change may be conceived as manifesting itself in sequential stages which have genetic relation to one another; they are cumulative. Fourth, change is *directional*; it can be seen as a single process moving cumulatively *from* a given point in time *to* another point. Fifth, change is *necessary*; it is necessary because it is natural, because it is as much an attribute of a living thing as is form or substance. Sixth, change in society corresponds to *differentiation*; its characteristic pattern is from the homogeneous to the heterogeneous. Seventh, the change that is natural to an entity is the result of *uniform* processes; processes which inhere in the very structure of the institution of culture, and which may be assumed to have been the same yesterday as they are today.

From this set of assumptions came the theory we know as social development or social evolution. In its essentials, this theory is, as we have seen, a very old theory in Western thought; as much a part of the philosophy of Aristotle or Lucretius as of the social science of Comte, Marx, Spencer or Tylor. Stated succinctly, the theory of social evolution is a way of arranging the materials of the present—the materials of the documentary and archaeological present juxtaposed to the materials of existing cultures in scalar relation to one another—and endowing these materials with the set of attributes of slow, gradual, and continuous change that I summarized in the paragraph above.

Throughout the long history of the metaphor of growth there has been the conscious distinction between *growth* or *development* on the one hand and *history* on the other. For, with the possible exception of St. Augustine, who, with God in hand, so to speak, strove to fuse the Greek concept of growth and the record of historical events and actions that he took largely from the Hebrew writ, no major theorist of social development ever argued that the kind of change he was describing, whether cyclical or linear, encompassed the totality of actions, happenings, and occurrences in the history of mankind or of any of its parts. From Aristotle on, the distinction has been rigorous between development, conceived as a natural and self-contained process of change in some persisting entity, and history, conceived as a record of the unique, the fortuitous, and the external.

As we have seen, moreover, from the very beginning certain characteristic, more or less inevitable questions have formed the framework or methodology of the study of social change. Among them have been questions of *origin:* for to know the cycle or path of change that is natural to an entity, one must know the primal condition from which such change emerges; of *stages of development:* for, precisely as the physiologist or botanist must know these in organism or plant, in order to recognize the relationship of differences in conditions at any given moment, so must the sociologist or ethnologist know how to synchronize, through the Comparative Method, social and cultural differences with the stages of growth natural to family, religion, or state; and, finally, questions of *purpose* or *ultimate end:* for, given the existence of growth controlled by some kind of pattern of forces, assumed to be endogenous, given continuity, emergence, and cumulative direction, does it not follow that there is destiny? Men have thought so for a very long time. The question is, *what* destiny: beneficent or malign?

These are the assumptions and questions that have been with us for a very long time. And they are with us still. No new perspective, no new set of assumptions and questions regarding historical change, has replaced the old ones. If there is anything distinctive about the twentieth century it is simply that all three of the age-old perspectives—cycle, epic, and progress—are with us, and that no one of them has obvious ascendancy.

Consider the Greek doctrine of cycles. Here is Oswald Spengler, Prussian mystic-historian, whose *The Decline of the West* has so often been regarded as an original effusion of twentieth-century reaction to the idea of linear progress. Even Spengler, it should be mentioned, was persuaded of the novelty of his theory of recurrent cycles; he thought that he was the first, save possibly for hints from Nietzsche, to present an alternative to the vision of unitary civilization and unilinear progress in time. And, to add piquancy to the humor of it all, we have his solemn conviction that the Greeks knew nothing of change and development, of cycles, or of "the ancestor-series, the genealogical tree that is eternalized with all the marks of historical order in the family-vault of the West." We are told even that for such Greeks as Herodotus, Heraclitus, Aristotle, and others "the past is subtilized instantly into an impression that is timeless and changeless, polar and not periodic in structure."

All previous students of civilization, declares Spengler, have seen the past as either stationary (Greeks, Romans, Christians) or linear-progressive (the moderns since the seventeenth century). It is to offset all of this, to provide genuine alternative, that we are presented with a view of development in time that is, in fact, Greek to the core and that is premised upon each and every one of the central elements of the Greek philosophy of growth.

We are given in the past, argues Spengler, some eight major Cultures, "all of the same build, the same development, and the same duration." They differ in details, but these are but surface details, even as are the details from one human individual to another. The important point is that Cultures are organisms, and "organisms of the same genus possess structurally cognate life-histories." This means of course that each of the Cultures of the past (Egyptian, Chinese, Classical, Arabic, and others) goes through more or less identical stages of development, thus making possible, by Spengler's own variant of the Comparative Method, establishment of what he calls "contemporaneity"; that is, the present "stage" of Western culture is contemporary with an identical stage in the cycle of genesis and decay that all previous cultures have manifested in time. Spengler's cultures are living things; let us make no mistake about that. Cultures are "higher individualities whose coming, growth, decay constitute the real substance of history underlying the myriad colors and changes of the surface." And, Spengler frequently assures us, for everything organic "the notions of birth, death, youth, age, lifetime are fundamentals." We are therefore entitled to let "the words youth, growth, maturity, decay *be taken at last* as objective descriptions of organic states." (Italics added.)

> A culture is born in the moment when a great soul awakens out of the protospirituality of ever-childish humanity and detaches itself, a form from the formless, a bounded and mortal thing from the boundless and enduring. It blooms on the soil of an exactly definable landscape, to which, plant-wise, it remains bound. It dies when this soul has actualized the full sum of its possibilities in the shape of peoples, languages, dogmas, arts, states, sciences, and reverts into the protosoul. . . .
> Every culture passes through the age-phases of the individual man. Each has its childhood, youth, manhood, and old age.[1]

It is easy to laugh at much of this—the oracular style, the confusion of his own "intuition" with what had in fact been acquired through a conventional classical education, and then the source forgotten, the bombastic mysticism, the Teutonisms, etc.—but let us not, while laughing, overlook the fact that the substratum of Spengler's theory is the same metaphor of growth, the same analogy, that we have been dealing with in the preceding pages of this book.

Nor is Spengler an eccentric or oddity in the twentieth century, allowing only for the mysticisms and the style. The theory of cycles is more popular today than in any age since that of classical civilization. Repeatedly one finds it and the analogy on which it rests in the pages of contemporary thought, for the idea of genesis and decay, of cycles of youth, maturity, and old age, is an almost irresistible idea to many searching for dogma on which to pin the multiplicity and uncertainty of the age. In both Toynbee and Sorokin, who are along with Spengler—and far more learned than he—prophets of genesis and decay in the present century, the image of the cycle is powerful.

Toynbee, in his A *Study of History*, explicitly rejects the organismic analogy which, he tells us, underlies Spengler's vision of development. But, as one scans the table of contents alone of Toynbee's monumental work, it is evident that, while the analogy may be unacceptable, the proceeds of analogy are fully acceptable. For the very volumes of the book are organized around the themes of "genesis," "growth," "breakdown," "disintegration," and so on. The organismic analogy in the usual sense of structural analogy Toynbee rejects, as have many others in the present age. But analogy in the sense of the life-cycle of stages of growth is something else again. Without the framework formed by the derivations of *this* analogy, A *Study of History* would not even exist.

Toynbee's mind was formed by study of Greece and Greek thought; and that the analogy of the life-cycle and the whole metaphor of growth took deep root in his mind is amply attested, it seems to me, by the following passage, drawn from an essay written about the time he began his great work:

> The germ of Western society first developed in the body of Greek society, like a child in the womb. The Roman Empire was the period of pregnancy during which the new life was sheltered and nurtured by the old. The 'Dark Age' was the crisis of birth, in which the child broke away from its parent and emerged as a separate, though naked and helpless, individual. The Middle Ages were the period of childhood. . . . The fourteenth and fifteenth centuries . . . stand for puberty, and the centuries since the year 1500 for our prime.[2]

It is evident, I trust, that my objective in this chapter is not idle ransacking of contemporary writing for uses of a figure of speech. We are concerned with the much more important matters of the perspectives of civilization that men live by. It is impossible, however, to separate these perspectives from a very powerful metaphor.

The Augustinian view of history is not less in evidence in contemporary thought than the Greek-cyclical. The present age, with its two mighty World Wars, its horrors of Hitlerism and Stalinism, its seeming inability to find fulfillment in the more obvious secular accomplishments of the past century or two, is fertile ground for a view of history that finds redemption only in the transhistorical and the supramundane. It is the Augustinian epic that underlies nearly all of the dominant Christian philosophies of history in our age. I shall mention but two of them, Nicholas Berdyaev's and Reinhold Niebuhr's.

"When we examine the destinies of peoples, societies, cultures, we observe how they all pass through the clear-cut stages of birth, infancy, adolescence, maturity, efflorescence, old age, decay, and death." [3] So writes Berdyaev. But where a Spengler might find this pattern coterminous with full reality, Berdyaev, like St. Augustine, sees it as but the mundane appearance of reality. He does not, of course, follow the Bishop of Hippo in his chronology of the world, in his fundamentalist-literalism, any more than he does Augustine's conviction of the imminent ending of the world through holocaust. What is Augustinian, however, is the fundamental patterning of human history. From the very beginning, through God's will, a single direction for mankind as a whole was set. And this direction has been followed rigorously. The initial stage was characterized, Berdyaev tells us, by man's fall and his alienation from God. There followed the sequence of epochs and stages through which man, now plunged into the "uttermost depths of natural necessity," succeeded in raising himself step by step to his present material eminence over the earth.

Cultural values are themselves deathless, eternal, for culture itself, that is, mankind, contains a deathless principle. This principle comes from God. But individual nations, civilizations, and cultures are far from eternal; not even the West. All peoples, "considered as living organisms within the framework of history, are doomed to

wither, decay, and die as soon as their efflorescence is past." [4]
It could be St. Augustine himself writing the next passage:

> The fall of Rome and the ancient world teaches us two directly
> opposite things. It demonstrates the instability and fragility of all
> terrestrial things and cultural achievements; and it constantly re-
> minds us that all cultural achievements are corruptible and con-
> tain the seed of their own decay when opposed to eternity. But in
> the light of history this fall teaches us not only that culture has its
> stages of birth, flowering, and decay, but that it is based upon an
> eternal principle. [5]

The eternal principle is, as we know, transhistorical. The profound criticisms of the secular idea of progress which we find in
the neo-Augustinian literature of our century reflect in its entirety
Augustine's denunciation of the pagan-secular hopes and devices
of his day and his insistence that the City of God will be achieved
only in the realm beyond this one.

It is admittedly from an Augustinian point of view that Reinhold Niebuhr offers us the conception of history that underlies his
great *The Nature and Destiny of Man*. For Niebuhr, as for Berdyaev, there is no possible support for the principle of human
progress—that is, secular progress into the indefinite future. It is
not even possible, Niebuhr writes, to distinguish periods of
creative advancement from periods of decline. For "every civilization and culture, every empire and nation, reveals destructive elements in its periods of creativity, even as there are creative
elements in its period of decline." [6] So had Augustine written in
the very aftermath of Alaric's invasion of the city of Rome. To
consider the whole of history from the point of view of linear
progress is as meaningless, Niebuhr writes, as to consider this complex whole from the opposite point of view of linear decline.

> Whatever meaning there is in the rise and fall of civilizations
> can be known only "by faith"; for it must be viewed from the
> vantage point of an eternity above history, which no man has as a
> possession but only by faith. From such vantage point history is
> meaningful, even if it should be impossible to discern any unity in

its continuing processes. It is meaningful because eternal principles are vindicated in both the life which overcomes death in rising civilizations, and in the death which overtakes proud life in
dying ones.[7]

What Augustine said to the pagans in the fifth century,
Niebuhr says in our own century: History does not solve the
enigma of history. Mystery stands at the end of the whole pilgrimage of man just as mystery stands at the beginning. The clue to the
mystery is the *Agape* of Christ. It is the clue to the mystery of
Creation. "It is the clue to the mystery of the renewals and redemptions within history, since wherever the divine mercy is discerned as within and above the wrath, which destroys all forms of
self-seeking, life may be renewed individually and collectively." [8]
The antinomies of good and evil, far from decreasing with the advance of knowledge, only increase.

"The whole history of man is thus comparable to his individual
life." [9] It is precisely through his use of this Augustinian mode of
the analogy that Niebuhr extends the argument to even the self-
destructive elements that lie in human freedom. Freedom is the
means whereby man expands his creativity. But it is also the means
whereby man is tempted to deny his mortality. And "the evils in
history are the consequence of this pretension."

The Christian faith is the apprehension of the divine love and
power which bears the whole human pilgrimage, shines through
its enigmas and antinomies and is finally and definitely revealed in
a drama in which suffering love gains triumph over sin and death.
This revelation does not resolve all perplexities; but it does triumph over despair, and leads to the renewal of life from self-love
to love.[10]

And just as Augustine found it necessary to criticize classical-
pagan ideas of recurrent cycles, so does Niebuhr take to task the
cyclical theories of our own age. He singles out Toynbee and particularly Toynbee's two notions—both derived from his larger
cyclical perspective—of pluralism and recurrence. From Niebuhr's
point of view "Toynbee's pluralism obscures the empirical unity of

history as it is established by the interpenetration of cultures and civilizations. His twenty-one civilizations are not as discrete as he supposes. . . . The emphasis upon the classical idea of recurrence enables Toynbee to find many illuminating analogies in history which the modern idea of progress has obscured. On the other hand, Toynbee's method obscures the novelties and new emergents in history." [11]

There is no substitute, Niebuhr concludes, for the idea of a *universal* history. But such universality cannot be deduced empirically. "History is conceived as a unity because all historical destinies are under the dominion of a single divine sovereignty." [12]

So is the secular idea of progress ascendant in the twentieth century. It is occasionally said that the events of the century—two World Wars, Hitlerism, Stalinism, the defeat of many progressive-secular hopes that had flourished at the beginning of the century, the malaise to be found in so much writing—have rendered the faith in progress unacceptable to our time. This may be true for the short run, or in certain intellectual coteries. But it is only too evident that for the majority of Westerners—and perhaps by now of the literate world population generally—the idea of the progress of mankind, the linear progress through the present and into the indefinite future, is a vivid one, almost as much an article of dogmatic faith as it ever was in the eighteenth and nineteenth centuries. And if there are those for whom the idea is repugnant, so were there, as we saw, in those two centuries of optimism and secular faith.

If Aristotle may be said to have his Spengler in the twentieth century and Augustine his Niebuhr, so does Fontenelle have his assured spokesmen. Here is V. Gordon Childe, eminent historian and archaeologist: "Progress is real if discontinuous. The upward curve resolves itself into a series of troughs and crests. But in the domains that archaeology as well as written history can survey, no trough ever declines to the low level of the preceding one; each crest out-tops its last precursor." [13] So declared the champions of the moderns in the seventeenth-century quarrel that produced the modern idea of progress.

And here is Sir Charles G. Darwin, late physicist, distinguished grandson of the author of the *Origin:*

> . . . there will be vast stores of learning, far beyond anything that we can now imagine, and the intellectual stature of man will rise to ever higher levels. And sometimes new discoveries will for a time relieve the human race from its fears, and there will be golden ages, when many foi a time may be free to create wonderful flowerings in science, philosophy, and the arts.[14]

We should not omit mention of the writings of Pierre Teilhard de Chardin, Jesuit Father and paleontologist. Not perhaps since Herbert Spencer has there been anyone who has made the idea of progressive evolution so completely the shaping theme of an entire philosophy. For Teilhard de Chardin all modern knowledge demonstrates the reality of an internal, timeless, perfecting principle, one that has led to global unity in all the events in what he calls the biosphere—"a continuous adjustment coadapts them from without. A profound equilibrium gives them balance within."— and that is on the way to similar unity for human society. Like St. Augustine, Teilhard de Chardin looks out on a world of unease of spirit, and like Augustine he proffers relief in the form of faith: faith, however, not in the transhistorical character of redemption, not in rediscovery of the timeless individual soul, but rather faith in what he calls a collective consciousness, a "single thinking envelope," on this earth. Like Herbert Spencer, Teilhard de Chardin seeks to make the principle of progressive, purposive, and perfecting evolution the answer to man's doubts and fears, but unlike Spencer he takes refuge in a form of ultimate communality of thought in which the individual would appear to be virtually extinct. There are more than a few critics who find Teilhard de Chardin's philosophy a rather murky compound of modern evolution and ancient teleology. But my only intent here is to suggest that, behind the otherwise extraordinary, even incomprehensible appeal of his philosophical writing, lies a profound faith in cosmic and human progress. "Having once known the taste of a universal and durable progress, we can never banish it from our minds any more than our intelligence can escape from the space-time perspective it once has glimpsed." [15]

Lest it be thought that faith in the progress of mankind is an element of capitalist ideology alone, we need but turn to the Program of the Communist Party in the Soviet Union, published in draft form in 1961. Here we learn that "the epoch-making turn of mankind from capitalism to socialism, initiated by the October Revolution, is a natural result of the development of society." We further learn that "the highroad to Socialism has been paved. . . . Many peoples are already marching along it, and it will be taken sooner or later by all peoples." In the future men will achieve the perfect society, and "harmonious relations will be established between the individual and society. . . . Family relations will be freed from material considerations and will be based solely on mutual love and friendship." [16]

Thus, in the twentieth century, as in the eighteenth and nineteenth centuries, an idea of gradual, cumulative, perfecting change that had first been presented in terms of knowledge alone, that has its real meaning indeed with respect to knowledge alone, is made into a dogma of faith encompassing everything from unicellular organisms to relationships between individual and society.

Progress or Providence; God or Evolution. It used to be said— the refrain of a poem we learned in school runs through my mind as I write—that as moderns we must take our choice. No doubt there is a valid choice in some degree between history conceived as the outcome of a process instigated by God and, on the other hand, history conceived as simply process, with the First Cause removed. The choice is lessened considerably, however, when we realize the extent to which the substance of the second, as we find it in the literature of developmentalism from the eighteenth century down to the present, is formed by ideas which had their original justification solely on the premise of God—or else of metaphor that performed the same basic function to thought.

Comte was not the less religious for having explicitly made Civilization his *Grand Être*, nor Hegel and Marx for having secularized Augustinian conflict of opposites, with synthesis provided in transhistorical terms, into a dialectic that is not the less supernal for all its trappings of historicity. And Augustine was not the less sociological or anthropological for having insisted that the qualities of immanence, growth, development, progress, and differentiation which he found in human history were all derived from, *had* to be derived from, a cause no smaller than an omnipotent God.

To believe that the vast, plural, and infinitely particular history of mankind can somehow be worked into ordered frameworks of either cyclical or linear development, that somehow progress (or degeneration) can be made endemic processes, fixed parts of reality, calls plainly for a gigantic act of faith. More, it calls for gigantic acts of compression of diversity into unity, of reduction of incredible complexity into simplicity, and transposition of the moral into the existential.

But it is exceedingly doubtful that we could live, most of us, without such faith. I shall come back to this point in the next chapter. For the moment it is enough to be reminded that the idea of historical cycles, whether in Aristotle or Spengler, and the idea of the redemptive character of history, whether in Augustine or Niebuhr, and the idea of linear progress, whether in Fontenelle or the reigning theorists of the Soviet Union, are one and all dogmas as constitutive of human belief today as they were in the ages of their earliest appearance.

2. NEO-EVOLUTIONISM

Nor has the philosophy of social evolution seriously diminished in twentieth-century regard. Whatever may have been the waning of interest in the more panoramic aspects of the theory of evolution during the first half of the century—interest in universal origins and sequences of stages of development for mankind—there is no evidence that there was much if any waning of interest in the key concepts of evolutionary theory: immanence, directionality, continuity, uniformitarianism, etc. And within most recent years there have been clear signs of a resurgence of evolutionism in its more classic form.

This is not to say that the theory of evolution has been exempted from attack. Around the beginning of the century a veritable barrage commenced against the theories of Spencer, Tylor, Morgan, and the others. Not all participants in the attack went as far as Berthold Laufer, who wrote: "the theory of cultural evolution (is) to my mind the most inane, sterile, and pernicious theory in the whole theory of science." [17] But in the writings of the American school—Franz Boas, A. L. Kroeber, Robert H. Lowie, foremost among anthropologists—and in Europe in the writings of those who took their inspiration from Durkheim's *Elementary Forms of Religious Life*, a conspicuous and even crusading type of reaction to social evolutionism is to be seen. All of a sudden the air is filled with indictments of "unilinear schemes," of "necessity," of "violations of cultural context," and of "universal patterns." No one outdid in all of this the late Robert H. Lowie, whose special object of attack was the work of Lewis H. Morgan. Morgan, one would conclude from reading Professor Lowie, was ignorant of the fact that areas vary in their actual cultural histories, that peoples impinge upon, and thereby influence, each other, that diffusionary processes are to be seen, that the history of the family (or of government or property) may be very different in Brazil from what it was in India—and so on.

Had any of the classical social evolutionists been around to defend themselves, they would have had no difficulty, I think, in making plain two very important facts: the first in defense and clarification of their own works; the second, and to me more interesting, in counter-attack upon their critics.

They would have been able to say, first, that they were well aware indeed of the inapplicability of their evolutionary sequences to all the areas and peoples on the earth's surface, and would have been able to point chapter and verse to their knowledge of differences and divergences of history in these areas and peoples. What they could have said—Comte, Spencer, Morgan, Tylor, and the others—was that they were not pretending to deal with these concrete areas and peoples; that the sole object of their labors, for better or worse, was to identify the natural line of development of, first, civilization as a whole, as civilization reaches from the remote past down to the present, and, second, of one or more of the generalized institutions which in their aggregate form human society. Criticisms based upon the concrete histories of the Crow Indians, the Melanesians, the modern Europeans, and other peoples were therefore irrelevant to the express purpose of their labors.

Proceeding from this, and in direct attack upon the attackers—that is, the self-styled critics of social evolutionism—the classical evolutionists could have noted this rather striking aspect of the critics' work: that, although they were denouncing schemes of social evolution, they were accepting at full value the concepts of change that underlay the theory of social evolution. Worse, it could have been said by the classical evolutionists, these concepts of change—immanence, continuity, uniformitarianism, etc.—were being applied to bodies of data for which they were manifestly unsuited: that is, to specific and concrete cultures, to discrete geographic areas, and even to behavior patterns of individuals within the short run of history. For, as Morgan made clear in his *Ancient Society*, the notion of slow, gradual, and continuous change, of development natural and necessary, of sequential stages, applied to, *and only to*, what he expressly labeled *the idea* of the family, of property, and government: emphatically not to the localizable history of even the Iroquois, much less to Americans, British, Chinese, and other peoples.

There is a certain wry humor in the fact that when Professor Lowie himself came to write a little book called *The Origin of the State*, he seemed wholly unaware of the irony involved in his two uses of the word "the" and, of greater importance here, of what he declared the objective of his book to be. This objective is, he writes, that of "vindicating the principle of continuity in the sphere of political history." Not even Morgan or Spencer could have improved upon this or upon the next sentence: "What we have tried to do is simply prove that the germs of all possible political development are latent but demonstrable in the ruder cultures." And, Professor Lowie writes, in a sentence that could only have elicited huzzahs from the classical evolutionists, his objective was that of seeking "to bridge the gap between a tiny Andamanese settlement and the Roman Empire." [18] And this, though Professor Lowie showed no sign of realizing it, was closer to the heart of classic evolutionism than the sequences of stages he so relentlessly attacked in Morgan.

At the present time in the social sciences, including functional sociology, there is a revival of evolutionism in the grand manner. What distinguishes the "new" from the "old" evolutionism is supposedly an awareness of divergences of development and of radiations of adaptation that the nineteenth-century evolutionists failed to allow for. So, at least, we are repeatedly told.

But as Leslie White, for many years, and more recently other, younger students of the subject have emphasized, the "old" social evolutionism had its full share of recognition of such divergences and adaptations. Professor Sahlins gives us this passage from Herbert Spencer to illustrate the point:

> Like other kinds of progress, social progress is not linear but divergent and re-divergent. Each differentiated product gives origin to a new set of differentiated products. While spreading over the earth mankind have found environments of various characters, and in each case the social life fallen into, partly determined by the social life previously led, has been partly determined by the influences of the new environment; so that the multiplying groups have tended ever to acquire differences, now major, now minor; there have arisen genera and species of societies.[19]

I do not really think any contemporary cultural or social evolutionist, dealing with the totality of human society, would state the matter very differently from the words just quoted from Herbert Spencer. Granted that Leslie White, Julian Steward, Marshall Sahlins, Elman Service, and other leading cultural evolutionists of the present day have found or have emphasized mechanisms of innovation, of adaptation, and of modification not necessarily found in the writings of the classic evolutionists of the last century, the vista that is presented, the panoramic distribution we find in the assessment of cultural types, remains substantially the same.

There is also an emphasis on multilinear evolution that was not present, at least in the same degree, in the writings of Morgan, Tylor, and the others. But this, as I have stressed, is solely the consequence of the fact that the older evolutionists were dealing with either mankind as a whole or with some universalized institutional type. They were not interested in areas as such. Had they been, it is hardly likely that they would have missed the all too manifest variation of patterns of change in the areas.

A good many of the methodological and theoretical problems of the contemporary social evolutionists would seem to derive from efforts to make the preconceptions of classic evolutionism serve the demands of concrete, geographically distinct areas. This is a point I shall come back to in some detail in the next chapter. It is enough to say here that when a contemporary critic of classic unilinear evolutionism does direct attention to some universalized social type, as Professor Lowie did with respect to the state, he winds up with substantially what a Maine or Morgan did in the last century. And, turning to more recent work, when Professor Parsons turns to what he calls "total society," he too gives us as unilinear a panorama of evolutionary change as did any of those evolutionists of the nineteenth century whom Parsons has often criticized for their monistic, necessary, and universal schemes.[20]

Despite the careful distinction today made in the literature of social science between the "old" and the "new" social evolutionary theory, I confess that I cannot find the substantive difference. Given the direction of attention to the same problem—that is, mankind or total society as it is conceived to have existed for countless millennia—we come out with the same result, which is a sequence of stages that is by its very nature unilinear. When a contemporary social evolutionist selects for his subject kinship or religion through the ages, he too comes out with a series of stages through which his subject has passed, all the while, of course, protesting that there have been divergences, that multilinearity must be recognized, and that it would be unscientific to insist that the pattern discerned is a necessary one for all areas.

The differences between contemporary *biological* evolutionary theory and the biological evolutionary theory of Darwin are immense. The differences between contemporary *social* evolutionary theory and the theory of Herbert Spencer do not seem very large or very significant.

I do not, however, wish to imply that persistence is the whole story. Admitting the existence of contemporary theories of social evolution in the more or less classic mold, it remains true that one of the signal features of this century has been the so-called revolt against the idea of evolution in the social sciences. As I said, it began toward the early part of the present century, featured the attacks by such men as Boas, Kroeber, and Lowie in this country, by the diffusionists, Perry and G. Eliot Smith in England, and along with these the sharp criticisms of the functionalist school of anthropology and sociology. It is the latter that I want now to turn to, for it represents the most persisting line of attack on the whole perspective of evolutionism.

That is, and the distinction here is a vital one, it represents the most persisting line of attack on the whole perspective of *macro*-evolution, the perspective of universality in dealing with institutional types, or with human culture as a whole. But the essential point I wish to make in the remainder of this section is that functionalism is anything but an attack on the *micro*-evolutionary theory of the nineteenth-century.

Functionalism is, without any doubt, the single most significant body of theory in the social sciences in the present century. It is often thought to be essentially a theory of order, of stability, of how society is possible. It has been frequently criticized for being devoid of a theory of change. But such criticisms are without merit. For functionalism is as surely built around a conception of change as was any evolutionary theory in the nineteenth century. The whole objective of functionalism, one can scarcely avoid concluding as he reads the principal works in this body of theory from Durkheim down to Talcott Parsons, is to present a unified theory of order *and* change. To be able to draw the motivational mechanisms of change from the same conditions from which are drawn the concepts of social order, this is the main and overriding objective of functionalism.

In the same way that so much of contemporary biological evolutionary theory is about the micro-mechanisms of change, so is this (in intent at least) the case in the social sciences. As the canvas of interest has narrowed from total society to a specific culture or social system, so has the interest in change tended to narrow to such matters as tensions, strains, and disharmonies within cultures and systems which are, it is thought, the motivational mechanisms.

Modern functionalism was given its main start in Durkheim's *The Elementary Forms of Religious Life,* published in 1912, the last of his major works to be published within his lifetime. I noted earlier that Durkheim's first major work was his *Division of Labor* and that this book was designed in the classic pattern of nineteenth-century social evolutionism. It was, in principal aim at least, an effort to descry the stages of development of social solidarity within human society at large, an aim that places the book within the same realm occupied by, say, Comte on human knowledge, Marx on economic society, Morgan on kinship, and Tylor on religion.

But with this book Durkheim's interest in the *larger* pattern of social evolution ended. Never again did he pick up the themes of mechanical and organic solidarity—the two major stages of development in that work—even though, as I have elsewhere indicated, a great deal of empirical and theoretical consequence in his work followed from his reflections upon the two types of social order represented by these stages.

And yet, despite some fairly widespread misconception, Durkheim did not really drop his interest in social evolution. He merely altered its focus. From evolution in the grand manner he passed to evolution of a more microcosmic kind—to preoccupation with the forms and elements of social change that, he argues, lie within the social group, within the social system.

Far from dropping interest in social change, Durkheim sought to make the study of social change a phase of the larger study of social order and, more important to our present concern, an added demonstration of his notable insistence upon the priority of social facts in the study of social behavior. In an age dominated by analytical individualism and by biologism, not to mention other forms of determinism—geographic, economic, etc.—it was Durkheim's achievement to insist upon *social* explanations of *social behavior;* to go straight to the structure and the functions of social systems for explanations of such matters as suicide and crime, and also of education, kinship, and religion. No single figure of the turn of the century contributed more to the study of social order than Durkheim and, as we know, his ideas worked a veritable transformation of inquiry in a number of social disciplines, beginning with sociology and social anthropology. But, to repeat, Durkheim did not, in all of this, really abandon interest in social change; he simply moved from the macroscopic emphasis of his *Division of Labor* to the microscopic emphasis that we find in both *The Rules* and *The Elementary Forms.*

In the former work we find Durkheim stating flatly: *"The first origins of all social processes of any importance should be sought in the internal constitution of the social group."* [21] (Italics in the original.) Now this is one of the most significant sentences in modern social theory from the point of view of its impact on subsequent thought regarding social change. I believe that Durkheim's primary objective in the statement is simply that of declaring independence from explanations that are drawn from individual psychology, or physiological instinct, or geography, or any other domain outside the social system itself. But, irrespective of larger objective, the statement also had the effect of concentrating attention, in the decades that followed, upon the social system's internal processes in the study of social change. And the kind of processes that tended to be emphasized were precisely those of the theory of social evolution—those of immanence, continuity, cumulative accretion, uniformitarianism, and the like—but removed from the large canvases of Comte, Spencer, and Tylor to the smaller canvas illustrated so well by Durkheim's own great study of religion.

In passing it is of some interest to note that much the same kind of transition of focus had occurred in Marx's work. Marx, like Durkheim, never lost his interest in social evolution as such. But as

Capital suggests, the work on which Marx spent the last part of his life, his interest shifted from the panoramic stages of evolution to the internal mechanisms within capitalism, considered as a single, developmentally arrived at, social system. These were, in Marx's view, mechanisms of change, the mechanisms that would, through their incessant operation within the capitalist system, lead at once to its destruction and to the emergence of the next stage, socialism. And for Marx the central mechanisms of change within capitalism were those of conflict: conflict of proletariat and bourgeoisie, yes, but also the subtler and more basic conflicts that were tied up with the structural contradictions of capitalism, as Marx thought that he perceived these in his studies of wages, capital, value, etc.

To return to Durkheim, whose influence on contemporary functionalism is direct: In his *Elementary Forms of Religious Life* he wrote:

> Everytime we undertake to explain something human, taken at a given moment in history—be it a religious belief, a moral precept, a legal principle, an esthetic style, or an economic system— *it is necessary to go back to its most primitive and simple form,* to try to account for the characterization by which it was marked at that time, *and then to show how it developed and became complicated little by little,* and how it became that which it is at the moment in question.[22] (Italics added.)

Several things may be said about this vital passage. First, it described with admirable succinctness what Durkheim's *Elementary Forms* is about. In choosing the religion of the Australian Aborigines Durkheim was selecting for study and analysis religion in "its most primitive and simple form," and he makes it plain throughout that work that in treating of the molecular elements of Australian religion—the cult, rites, etc.—he is treating of the elements of *all* religion. And by avoiding the ethnographic "table-hopping" so common in his day—traits drawn from scores, even hundreds of religions to form a stage of development—Durkheim succeeded in presenting the religion of a preliterate people in terms of the functional unity of parts that he so prized.

Second, this passage seems to me to embody all that is fundamental in neo-evolutionism: concentration upon *one culture*, with
full awareness, however, of its implications to other cultures in the
evolutionary scale, rather than upon either civilization as a whole
at one extreme, or a single universalized social system, such as
knowledge, religion, or kinship, at the other. After Durkheim
(though I am far from suggesting that his was the only influence
in this regard) there would be fewer and fewer ethnological studies of the kind we find in the works of the Morgans and Tylors of
the nineteenth century and in the works of men like Hob-
house, Westermarck, and Briffault in our own century. Increasingly in ethnology and social anthropology the emphasis would be
on some one primitive culture, approached more or less as Durkheim approached the materials of the Australian Aborigines.

Third, this passage seems to me the essential point of departure
for the theory of change that is to be found in contemporary functionalism. Precisely as Durkheim confined his interest to the *single
social system*, that is, Australian religion, never turning his eyes
away from the elements of this system, finding in it alone all necessary elements of social integration and change alike, so, generally, have functionalists proceeded since.

In a nutshell, the objective of functionalism is to achieve a theory
that at one and the same time serves the problem of order and the
problem of change. As Talcott Parsons has written: "If theory is
good theory, whichever type of problem it tackles most directly,
there is no reason whatever to believe that it will not be *equally*
applicable to the problems of change and to those of process
within a stabilized system." [23]

It was A. R. Radcliffe-Brown—who did more than any other
single social scientist in this century to communicate the essence
of Durkheim to the larger areas of social anthropology and
sociology—who first laid out the pattern of theoretical consideration of change in these neo-evolutionist terms. In his A *Natural
Science of Society*, Radcliffe-Brown made very plain indeed what
he considered to be the theoretical articulation of what he called
problems, on the one hand, of classification and of persistence of

social systems, and, on the other, of how societies and systems change their type.[24] He referred to the first as "synchronic" problems and the second as "diachronic," and, very much in the manner of Auguste Comte a full century earlier, Radcliffe-Brown stressed the degree to which both sets of problems flow from identical premises. True, he made a sharp distinction between changes *within* a social system and changes *of* the social system—that is, of the structure of the system. He also made very clear that the problem of social change, of whichever of these two types, demanded consideration rather different from that which would go to "synchronic" problems of classification and persistence.

But the fact remains that, like any classical evolutionist, Radcliffe-Brown put the problem of change *within* his over-all theory, his *natural* theory, of the social system. And the inference is plainly to be drawn, I believe, that while he does indeed distinguish between the two types of change—changes within and change of the system—and suggests the clear possibility that the latter may be the result of external forces, it was the possible connection of the two types, the genetic cumulation of the first into the second, that tantalized him as the "natural scientist" of society. Certainly, there is no evidence that for Radcliffe-Brown, any more than for Comte or Tylor, the external *historical* record has more than perhaps catalytic significance in assessment of the dynamics of change. For—and it is the question that has haunted the theory of development from its beginnings in the Western tradition—how could this record be made congruent with a *natural* science of society and with those processes that are, as it were, *natural* to the social system?

Let me emphasize one point here. I am not implying that either Radcliffe-Brown or Talcott Parsons or any of the other functionalists are unaware of the historical record. All are learned in historical scholarship; some, such as Robert Merton, have written in exemplary fashion of what is involved historically in a major social change, such as the rise of systematic physical science in the seventeenth century. But then neither were the classical evolutionists, least of all Spencer and Morgan, unaware of the historical record, with its incessant and multifold impacts upon human behavior in the forms of war, invasion, catastrophe, great men, and the like. As I noted above, the evolutionists never denied this record. Their objective, however, was to discern the provisions for change, natural change, that lie within society or culture and that do not depend for their existence upon the myriad random events and actions of the historical record.

And this is equally true, I suggest, of functionalism. No one has more lucidly and succinctly described the functionalist theory of change than has Robert Merton. As Professor Merton writes, functional analysis is usually directed toward "the statics of social structure" rather than to the "dynamics of social change." But, as he emphasizes, this is in no sense intrinsic to functional analysis.

"By focusing on *dysfunctions* as well as functions, this approach can assess not only the bases of social stability but the potential sources of change. . . . *The stresses and strains in a social structure which accumulate as dysfunctional consequences of existing elements* . . . will in due course lead to institutional breakdown and basic social change. When this change has passed beyond a given and not easily identifiable point, it is customary to say that a new social system has emerged." [25] (Italics added.)

In this important passage it will be observed that Merton has, in effect, abandoned the rather sharp distinction that Radcliffe-Brown made between changes within and changes of the social system. What Merton is saying, certainly by implication, is that the dysfunctional elements that tend normally to be a part of any social system, to lie within it, may themselves, in their accumulation, result in the more overt types of change that affect the structure itself.

As I say, Robert Merton needs no instruction, since he is a historian as well as sociologist, on the external and fortuitous impacts that can profoundly modify a given social system, or at least its setting. He is not pretending to deal, in the passage quoted, with the totality of human experience. He is dealing, as a theorist, with the *social system*, with the elements in the system that may in one form lead to stability and in some other form to change. And, giving ingenious reinforcement to his contention that functionalism is as much a theory of change as it is of order, he supplies us with, in parallel columns, the key elements of Marxism and the key elements of functionalism. I can think of no better demonstration anywhere in the literature of social theory of the affinity between the classical theory of evolutionary change and the theory of change that is embedded in functionalism.

Talcott Parsons distinguishes between what he calls "endogenous" and "exogenous" changes affecting the social system, the first being those that arise from within the articulation of roles and norms that form the system, the second arising from outside the system. But how strictly Parsons defines his social system may be gathered from the fact that he specifically describes as exogenous those changes that originate in "the personalities of the members of the social system, the behavioral organisms 'underlying' these, or the cultural system." [26] One may hazard the guess that most if not all of the classical evolutionists, also concerned with the distinction between endogenous and exogenous changes, would have accepted such "exogenous" sources as these as being quite sufficiently endogenous for their purposes. And despite his distinction between the two types, one can scarcely avoid concluding that Professor Parsons' clear preference—theoretical preference at any rate—is for the endogenous.

This is almost equally true, it would appear, of other major theorists. What we discover is that all of the central premises of the classical evolutionary theory of change—immanence, genetic continuity, differentiation, directionality, and uniformitarianism—figure prominently in functional analysis. No functionalist denies the existence of the historical record or is blind to the incessant impact of random events upon social systems. The fundamental assumption of the functionalist is, however, that independent of all this, there are sources of change within social systems, more or less natural sources, and that from these there flow patterns of change that are as congruent to the social system as growth is within the living organism. The affinity between functionalism and organicism is one that has frequently been noted with respect to functional analysis of structure; but the affinity is as close with respect to analysis of change. Functionalist premises in the study of change are precisely those we have observed under the metaphor of growth.

Hence the incessant search by the functionalist for the specific types of strain and stress that tend naturally to inhere in a given social system. Wilbert Moore, in what is without any question the best single book on the theory of change yet to emerge from functionalists, asks the question: Is there a source or are there sources of changes in systems that are universal and not merely repetitive, trivial, or essentially unpredictable accidents? His answer is an affirmative one. "The affirmative answer lies in a universal feature of human societies which in its most general form may be stated as the *lack of close correspondence between the 'ideal' and the 'actual'* in many and pervasive contexts of social behavior." [27]

Matters are not very different in anthropology. Following the heavy blows delivered a half-century and more ago to the nineteenth-century social evolutionists, much of the study of preliterate cultures took refuge, as it were, in detailed, monographic works on single cultures. Inevitably, most especially given the quasi-organic, functionalist, contemplation of these cultures, there was a major stress on problems of order, stability, and adjustment. The equilibrial aspects of functionalism were given theoretical emphasis by ethnologists. Coexisting with functionalist concentration upon the single culture and functionalist disdain for taxonomic sequences of cultural traits drawn from a great variety of cultures was the theory of diffusion which, though never united in any way with the work of the functionalists, delivered its own barrage at the theory of evolution.

It would appear, however, that anthropologists today are seeing in their primitive or individual cultures the same kinds of endogenous processes that sociologists find in their social systems. And the anthropologists have one immense advantage over the sociologists. When they are trying to reconstruct the line of development for a given preliterate culture out of the remote past, and do this through analysis of present processes, they cannot be charged with ignoring the historical record. For, except with respect to the record of possible recent historical contacts of the culture with, say, Europeans, there is no historical record. The anthropologist has no alternative to trying to read the past, to making judgments on processes of social change, to reconstructing lineal sequences on the basis of ongoing processes and relationships he may find in the present.

The point, however, is that functional anthropologists, like functional sociologists, are dealing with their materials in terms of preconceptions regarding the nature of change that are drawn from the theory of social evolution. Thus Raymond Firth writes: "A theoretical framework for the analysis of social change must be concerned largely with what happens to social structures." [28] This is clear enough, and perfectly acceptable. But it is characteristic of the functionalist in Firth that he also tells us, "The dynamic picture demands recognition of the possibility that the operation of a social system, however simple, involves continual tendencies to change." [29] And it is equally characteristic that he should look to some uniform, ever-present feature of the social structure or system for the source of this continual tendency to change—just as did the nineteenth-century evolutionist. And Firth finds this in the individual psyche. "The essence of the dynamic process lies in the continuous operation of the individual psyche, with its potential of unsatisfied desires—for more security, more knowledge, more status, more power, more approval—within the universe of its social system." [30] It is reflection upon this type of internal, continuous, and directional process, actuated by a uniform process, that encourages Firth to look hopefully toward what he calls "autonomous change."

Thus George Murdock, in his *Social Structure*, working from the same fundamental assumptions as other functionalists, suggests that the study of human behavior can be put in terms of study of social systems; that "social organization is a semi-independent system comparable in many respects to language, and similarly characterized by an internal dynamics of its own." [31] The analogy to language—conceived as a more or less autonomous system, exhibiting philological laws of change and development—is a frequent one in functionalist appraisals of social behavior and social systems. Murdock writes that the "phenomenon of linguistic drift exhibits numerous close parallels to the evolution of social organization." All of which encourages Murdock to declare that the "search for the sources of change must be shifted from the external factors to the social structure itself." [32]

And this declaration serves as well as any other in print to define the over-all objective of contemporary functionalism. I repeat, no functionalist, either in sociology or anthropology, denies the existence of a historical record, of influences engendered by random events, contacts, unique occurrences, and the purely fortuitous. But, it is asked in effect, how is one to construct a *theory* of the random, the fortuitous, and the unique? If there is to be a theory of social change, must it not be drawn from the same elements, though perhaps in different patterns of interaction, which comprise our theory of social organization, of order?

Putting the matter differently, granted that if we had the total historical record for, say, the Andamanese or some other relatively isolated, essentially recordless primitive people, we could present a narrative account of all that has happened to them just as we now do, with abundance of records, for the English or French. But we don't have the record for the Andamanese. So why should we not seek to deduce the past, more or less, from present processes: structural imbalances built into the surrounding social organization; role-tensions, status-anxieties, endemic conflicts of function, status, or value, and so on? And, second, if we did have the full historical record on, say, the Andamanese for a thousand or more years back, as we do on the English or Japanese, we should still not be able to derive from it the kind of unified *theory* of structure and change that is our goal.

So runs the argument of contemporary functionalism in the social sciences. It is plausible and, given the passion for theory and for perspective among contemporary data-gatherers, it is very nearly irresistible. So also, however, ran the argument of the theorists of natural history in the eighteenth century who were similarly occupied in searching for the laws of development most in accord with rational concept, with the nature of man and social organization. And so too ran the argument of the classic evolutionists of the nineteenth century who also, with Comte as their leading theorist, sought to unite the principles of order and change.

There is, it seems to me, a certain poetic satisfaction in the realization that Talcott Parsons, on any count the pre-eminent functionalist and social theorist in contemporary sociology, has come full circle in his theory, so far as the study of change is concerned.[33] I mean that just as Durkheim, in his study of religion, was the first to effect the transition from the panoramic, macrocosmic type of evolution to the social systems, microcosmic type so Professor Parsons may be said to be the first of the contemporary functionalists (I am referring here solely to sociology) to lead the way back to thoroughgoing, classical, large-scale evolutionism—from which, of course, functionalism was derived in the first place.

EIGHT

REFLECTIONS ON A METAPHOR

1. THE USES OF METAPHOR

What, finally, are we to say of a metaphor that has persisted through all of the changes of setting in Western European history through the last twenty-five hundred years? We shall ask first, what are the functions served by this metaphor in our culture? second, what are the more obvious abuses of the metaphor in social science? and third, what are the areas of behavior in which the metaphor is patently irrelevant?

First, the functions or uses of metaphor. I will begin with a general proposition. The usefulness of the metaphor of growth is determined by the *cognitive distance* of the object to which the metaphor is applied. The larger, the more general, abstract, and distant in experience the object of our interest, the greater the utility of the metaphor. Conversely, the smaller, more concrete, finite, and empirical our object, the less the metaphor's utility. Now let me expand briefly on this.

History in any substantive sense is plural. It is diverse, multiple, and particular. There have been innumerable histories since the first history of the first human group began, wherever and whenever that was. Such plurality is, however, but a part of the problem, though admittedly the major part. Even within a single area or people there is a plurality of histories: technological, economic, political, religious, educational, artistic, moral, and so on. To suppose that any one of these histories is literally confined within the single area or people of our interest—that is, separable from histories of technology, economy, art, thought elsewhere—is, of course, absurd.

Not only are there many histories; there are many chronologies, many *times*, if I may put into accurate plurality here what is usually thought of in terms of single, homogeneous flow. It is essentially Western "time" that we have in our minds when we ruminate upon past, present, and future for mankind generally. By a gigantic act of faith we assume that the chronology in which we fit (with difficulty and distortion enough!) the events and changes of that tiny part of the earth that is the promontory of Eurasia which we call Western Europe is also the chronology of mankind.

Many histories, many areas, many times! The mind boggles at the task of encapsulating such diversity within any empirically drawn formula or synthesis. It cannot be done; not empirically, not pragmatically. So we turn to metaphor and analogy. *If* the multiple is assumed to be the unitary, the distant as the near, and the random as the ordered; *if* we can but assume, following the happy precedent of the medieval ontological proof of God's existence, that by virtue of our being able to conceive a unified civilization, such civilization must have actuality for purposes of law and principle; and *if* we can assume that even as each biological entity in nature grows and develops, so must that vast entity to which we give the name civilization or mankind or society; *if* we can assume all of this, then we are in a fair way to achieving the impossible. All the rest—immanence, continuity, progress, purpose, etc.—are of no special order of difficulty.

Achieving the impossible is what metaphor is all about. From it spring religions, prophecies, and dogmas. From it also, as we have seen, spring world-views of the kind that stretch from Hesiod to contemporary Marxism. We could not well do without metaphor. Man, as I have repeatedly emphasized, does not live by the finite and the particular alone.

Metaphor we shall always have with us. It is what we do with metaphor, in what areas of thought we allow it to prevail, that matters. Our world of perceived experience presents itself in diverse ways, a consequence of the mind's powers of conceptualization and abstraction. The power to conceptualize is also the power to hypostasize, to reify. And what we have brought into conceptual existence, we are prone to believe has actual existence. Logical positivists may declare meaningless such abstractions or wholes as Civilization, Destiny, Purpose, and their linguistic relatives in thought. And, clearly, there is not much we can do with any of these in pragmatic or scientific terms.

But on the evidence of several thousand years of religion and philosophy, nothing is likely to prevent human beings from speculating, believing, brooding, and philosophizing about them. The same impulse that winds up in a conception of the Godhead in one person will wind up in a conception of the historical dialectic in another. The power of metaphor is indispensable to both.

I said at the beginning that in actual empirical observation we do not see processes of unfolding, of genetic continuity, of the latent evolving through resident forces into the manifest, and so on. We see assorted patterns of persistence and change in our data; we see fixity punctuated now and then by modification or change; we see all manner of shapes, designs, and meanings in these data, the result of one or other esthetic, moral, political or religious bent. But we do not see, not in any literal way, processes of growth and decay. Not in the immediate present or in the short run.

It is, however, a very different matter when we turn to the large wholes of human preoccupation, to such wholes as civilization or mankind. It is as inevitable in modern Western consciousness (perhaps in all human consciousness) to ask the question, whither Civilization (or any of its generic cognates)? as it is to ask the question, what is the meaning of life? Not the most resolutely empirical or pragmatic mind, surely, can resist the occasional allure of such questions.

And when we raise the question of the origin, history, and future of some such abstract entity as civilization considered as a whole, it is inevitable that we will endow it with more or less vitalistic qualities such as growth and development.

Once we have created in our minds an entity such as this, one constituted by the familiar set of material and non-material elements with which we give body to the *idea* of civilization—an idea compounded of the intellectual, moral, and esthetic, as well as technological traits of greatest relevance to the contemporary West— then, clearly, the various attributes of the idea of growth and development in time take on vivid meaning. For, unless one proceeds from a strictly fundamentalist-religious view, with a divine being willing each and every thing that happens, how else can one think of so vast and abstract an entity as civilization save in terms of immanent forces of change, of continuity, of differentiation, of necessity, and so on?

What I noted above with respect to the Comparative Method and its uses is eminently pertinent here. If we take, for example, transportation through the ages, or warfare, or technology generally, we have no difficulty at all in arranging all the manifestations of each which are presented by historical record and by the contemporary gradations among the peoples of the world into a single, continuous series; a series in which the *properties* of growth—even if not the dynamic actuality of growth—are clearly evident. What better metaphoric generalization than growth to summarize all that lies between the most primitive type of transportation and our most recent missile? And the metaphor is even more strikingly relevant when we are considering civilization as a whole.

True, there are many instances to be seen in past and present that suggest not growth and progress but the very reverse. We see cultures that are, so to speak, mere wreckage and spoilage; peoples fixed in rudimentary simplicity for centuries and even millennia, where nothing seems to change either for better or worse; ages and periods characterized by intellectual aridity and cultural drought, even with civilizations that over the long term evince the attributes of progress.

But no philosopher of social growth ever pretended to the contrary. Whether proponent of human progress or theorist of social evolution, what was asserted had nothing to do with the empirical flux of circumstances in concrete areas and periods; only with *the total picture*. It might be the totality of knowledge, which was the initial concern of the idea of progress; the totality of civilization, which fascinated the eighteenth and nineteenth centuries; or the totality of culture or society. Even when a Lewis Morgan used the perspective of growth to explain specific institutions, it was, as he made explicit, the *idea* of each that he saw unfolding through time: the *idea* of the family, of property, of government. Universality and also abstractness were built in, despite the apparent specificity of his illustrative data. The same with others. Beyond stating what should or must *normally* or *naturally* happen, no theorist of either social progress or social evolution ever made so bold as to certify or predict what would happen in a given area or short-run period.

Of the evolutionists in the nineteenth century it has been well said that for them there was an unlimited bank of time to which they felt free to take any amount of scientific paper for discount. Time, save in the picket-fence sense of before and after, was meaningless. Similarly with area. Evidences and illustrations were drawn, of course, from concrete, living peoples. But their significance lay in what they could do to support a theory of evolution that took universals and wholes for its province, not concrete geographically delimited, temporally finite areas.

What I am saying of the theory of social evolution is equally applicable, I believe, to the so-called histories of civilization, the genre of which the late Professor Lynn Thorndike's one-volume *History of Civilization* remains classic.[1] Great historian that Thorndike was, we would expect, and we find, something as graceful in design as it is learned. It is in essence a biographical study of the entity we call Civilization. I am not implying that it is supernal. The pages teem with Egyptians, Chaldeans, Indians, Greeks, Romans, and so on. Real events, changes, personal identities are the stuff of the book. It is in its type a masterpiece.

It will be said that for a work of this sort the difficulties are insuperable. How, for example, to fuse the different time-orders of all the concrete peoples and civilizations that have existed into the *single* time-order demanded by any history of civilization, whether it be in one volume or in twenty or fifty volumes. Here, at the beginning, the Egyptians are introduced, their accomplishments three thousand years ago described; then they are abandoned. We never know what happened to the Egyptians after, say, 1000 B.C., for we have moved in the next chapter to some other people, the Chaldeans, who also are limned at the moment of their greatness and then dropped, as it were. Thence to the Hellenic peoples, with Israelites, Chinese, Hindus, and assorted other peoples somehow sandwiched in, and after the greatness that was Greece, on to the grandeur that was Rome. From which we move (taking up a substantial part of the book) to the Medieval period (whose medieval period? Inevitably that of a small part of what we know as Western Europe; certainly *not* the "medieval" periods of China, India, and other concrete civilizations), the Age of Reason, the Enlightenment, and on down to the twentieth century, in which once again we encounter some of the peoples we were compelled to abandon early on in the interests of the narrative. But this time we meet them in the context solely of the West's impact on them, whether peaceful or aggressive.

Ostensibly such a book is about the whole of civilization, a word that one might confuse with the sum total of all that has happened to all peoples, or at least all civilized peoples. Such a treatment—if it were possible—would fill us in, so to speak, on *what* ever happened afterward to the Egyptians, Greeks, Chinese, and the other peoples we examined briefly at a given moment in time and then discarded. But here, too, the difficulties would be enormous; conquerable only, one can suppose, through the device of parallel columns of individual histories. It is difficult, however, to imagine the format of such a work and even more difficult to imagine its uses.

The point is, in such a work as Lynn Thorndike's *History of Civilization* we are not, nor is there any pretence to this effect, dealing with civilization in the mechanical sense of all that has happened to all civilized peoples in their diverse time-orders. We are dealing with—Civilization! We are dealing with an abstract entity given body by attributes drawn from a score of civilizations —technology, arts, agriculture, writing, philosophy, fine arts, etc.— and the historically concrete civilizations are used only as periodic incarnations, as it were, of the single entity, Civilization. We are not studying, not really, despite appearances, the Egyptians, Greeks, Chinese, Romans, and other peoples. We are studying *Civilization* in its successive and fleeting resting-places in Egypt, Greece, China, and elsewhere. That Thorndike, as a Westerner, makes the meaning of Civilization—that is, its attributed substance

—flow from what we in the West since about the eighteenth century have meant by the word, rather than what Moslems, Chinese,
or Hindus might mean, is beside the point. So is the fact that, just
as in the pages of Condorcet and of Comte, all the diverse and
complex time-orders in history are somehow fused, before the
book is far underway, into the single time-order of the West that
we traditionally divide up into "ancient," "medieval," and "modern." All of this can be charged up to precisely the same kind of
ethnocentrism and parochial selectiveness that the Chinese or
Hindu or Moslem would be guilty of were *he* writing a work called
The History of Civilization.

As I say, the difficulties of such an enterprise are immense. But,
then, so are the difficulties in any perspective that seeks to unify
conceptually all that is involved in the astronomical number of
events, changes, persons, acts, values, and structures that has gone
into the myriad histories of all the peoples who ever have inhabited or now inhabit the earth.

Difficulties notwithstanding, it is safe to say that as long as human thought is capable of abstraction, as long as human beings are
lost in wonder at what has happened in the almost infinite vistas
of the past and what will, or is likely to, happen in the infinite
vistas of the future, just so long will the metaphor of growth and
all its derivatives be used. For the metaphor serves what might
well be called a dogmatic or prophetic function in man's life. We
cannot do without dogma and prophecy; each is a part of the very
framework of a social order. Belief in Providence is a dogma; so is
belief in Progress—or, if we prefer, belief in cyclical recurrence or
in the transhistorical nature of redemption. Prophecy, in its temporal as well as moral connotation, is probably an inalienable part
of the human condition and of human aspiration.

Who will deny the function of the metaphor? As one looks at
the immense difference between what was known by human
beings fifty thousand years ago and what is known—known at least
by the scientists, scholars, and professionals—at the present time,
it is almost impossible *not* to reify what we call human knowledge
into an entity that has had a life and development independent of

the astronomical number of "human knowledges" involved in all the clans, tribes, peoples, and nations that have, in their aggregate, made up the empirical referent of what we particularize as Human Knowledge. And from the conception of knowledge growing and developing in time it is an easy step to the conception of culture, society, and mankind growing in time—each with its inevitable nuances or implications of morality, esthetics, government, religion, wisdom, and the like—that goes far beyond what seems so obvious when we confine the matter to knowledge alone.

Logical and structural difficulties or no, an interest in, a sense of wonder about, a fascination with, these great wholes, *Civilization*, *Mankind*, *Society*, and *Culture*, is an abiding feature of the Western mind, one likely to be as manifest in future generations is in past ones. Who, nurtured in our tradition, can refrain from asking about the past, present, and future of one or other of these abstract, reified collectivities? And to say that, in any empirical and logical sense demanded by contemporary science, none exists is beside the point. Like a good many other persisting questions of metaphysical and moral significance, questions pertaining to these entities will not be banished from our consciousness.

Once we have asked ourselves the question, what has happened in time, what is now happening, and what will happen in the future to Mankind or Civilization, what alternative is there to a metaphoric answer? We begin with an abstraction that is itself metaphoric in structure and must perforce pass to metaphor when we seek to answer the question of its change in time. What better solution to the problem could we come up with than one or other of the variants of cycle, epic, and progress? What better image of the whole process, from primitive beginning to complex present, than the life-cycle of the organism—in whatever form we choose its representations in metaphor, with or without any final stage of death?

Nor is the use of the metaphor restricted to Civilization in its abstract entirety. Is not the idea of genesis and decay equally appropriate when we turn to some *single* great civilization of the past, or, for that matter, to our own civilization—Western or

American, as we like—in its relation to time? Offhand, it is difficult to think of any substitute for the metaphor, once we commence reflecting upon an entity that we call Greek civilization, or Roman civilization—or Egyptian, Babylonian, or Mayan.

Consider the case of Rome, by far the most storied of all civilizations in terms of the epic drama of rise and fall, of genesis and decay. If we choose to look merely at the empirical data provided, it would be hard to come up with anything beyond simple, mechanical narrative of human generations succeeding one another in the several geographic areas that served, singly and severally, as the setting for Roman life. The records make plain that a great deal happened in the period beginning, say, 500 B.C. and ending, if we insist, 500 A.D. Of course human life was lived in Italy and its environs before—long before—the earlier date, and, very plainly, lives were lived by countless people in these areas after the latter date. But let us, for the sake of heightening our illustration, deal only with the thousand-year period that is commonly assigned to Rome—republic and empire. Monarchy was succeeded by republic, by principate, by empire, and by Christian political ascendancy. All manner of styles of polity, economy, religion, language, philosophy, work and play may be discerned and chronicled. That there were profound changes is a proposition that permits no doubt. The change from, say, Etruscan culture to Roman culture was assuredly an important one; equally important was the change from pagan-Roman to Christian-Roman culture. In between these two great changes fall, of course, a vast number of other changes, events, migrations, invasions, wars, impacts of one sort or another from civilizations as far distant as China. In between the two terminal changes fall also quite extraordinary persistences of belief, behavior, and value that characterize the lives of Romans during our thousand-year period. It can all be summarized accurately, empirically, and concisely by saying: A people known as the Romans existed for approximately a thousand years. During most of that period they successfully withstood all potential invaders and even expanded the limits of their state beyond anything that had ever existed before, so far as we know. Then, defenses failing, the political and economic unity of Rome changed, to become the diversity of peoples, tribes, and, then, nations that is, and has been for some fifteen hundred years, Western Europe.

This is accurate enough. But even fleshed-out by details of all that concretely happened during that thousand-year period, the account would no doubt be inadequate for most persons. We should feel lost, most of us, without the accustomed image in our minds of Rome, conceived as an autonomous civilization—one of Spengler's eight, one of Toynbee's twenty-one civilizations—that came into being (genesis), that matured to fullness (development or growth), that in time suffered decay through forces endemic in Roman polity and culture, and then withered and perished, fit consequence for Rome's never having cured itself of the diseases to which it fell heir in middle age.

That "diseases," decadence, and decay notwithstanding, Rome would very probably have gone on just as China and Japan did for at least another millennium, had it not been for some very concrete changes taking place, events occurring, in regions utterly outside Roman boundaries, does not often enter our minds. Or, if it does, we say that these could never have affected Rome, had it not been for weakness generated by diseases or poisons (or cancers or tumors—the variations are many) within Rome itself.

Such is the impress that words like "decadent," "senescent," and their analogues make on our consciousness that we sometimes slip into thinking that not only did Roman institutions become aged and corrupt in their being but that even later generations of Romans, *physical* generations, suffered the same aging of innate fiber, the same degeneration of instinct and natural valor. The cultural, social, and political dimensions of decay are thus subtly fused with those of a physical and biological sort, and we have the single image of, not merely a culture, but a people passing from youth to maturity to old age and death.

Not only is the metaphor of growth integrative in the purely historical sense; it is integrative in its social and psychological effects upon groups—national, ethnic, and other. To believe that one's identity as a nation, for example, is the consequence of ages-

old growth, slow, gradual, and continuous growth, the whole process self-contained and the result or immanent factors, with the
external and fortuitous retreated to the background, with a sense
of purpose or destiny unfolding throughout, is to endow one's own
nation with a degree of majesty it could hardly have otherwise.
Witness the school-texts on American (or French or Russian or
German or English) history. How viable would national unity be,
how deep would the springs of patriotism be, if the whole matter
were made more or less incidental to the actions and interactions
of random events, to the purposes and destinies of *other* nations
and peoples?

As I write, it is possible to see this same integrative-prophetic
function of the metaphor of growth serving the cause of Negro nationalism, of so-called Black Power, in the United States. Events
in the past, such as the Nat Turner revolt,[2] heretofore regarded as
fortuitous or random suddenly take on prophetic significance as
manifestations of the slow, gradual, and continuous growth of
the Negro nation within the United States. There is the familiar
shift of emphasis from persons and forces *external* to the Negro
people—such as early White abolitionism, the spread of constitu-
tionalism, technology, and the like—to persons and forces *internal*
to the Negro people. The whole history of Negro nationalism in
the United States is made consequent upon a kind of manifest
destiny within the Negro minority, upon processes of growth
which have been present from the outset, requiring only time for
their unfolding and manifestation, and upon persisting, uniform,
struggle against oppression as the mainspring of the whole process
of growth. External contributions, external impacts, external
causes in general fade to the background, leaving internal contributions, impacts, and causes as the principal manifestations of
growth. No matter what we may think of the Black Power rendering of the history of Negro civil rights from the point of view of
strict historical analysis, no one familiar with the ways modern nations became nations can take serious exception to current Negro
use of the metaphor of self-contained growth. It has integrative
and prophetic function.

It would be as difficult to live and think without the metaphor of growth as it would without metaphor generally. In a host of ways the image of genesis and decay serves to give meaning to action. For the devout contemporary Marxist, belief in the necessary decay of the capitalist system, and in the consequent liberation of the working class, is as vital to daily existence as is the Christian's belief in the redemptive character of the next world. In both instances metaphor serves to maintain hope and faith. Whatever may be the empirical, logical, and moral difficulties with belief in the idea of progress, and its implicit image of society becoming, through internal and inexorable forces, ever better, its prophetic function to the multitudes who have perhaps lost faith in Providence can scarcely be exaggerated. The metaphor serves today, as it served in the time of Greek and Roman and in the time of St. Augustine, as a synthesis of past, present, and future.

2. THE ABUSES OF METAPHOR

If the metaphor of growth and its various corollaries of immanent causation, continuity, differentiation, necessity, and uniformitarianism were confined to the cognitively distant, to the abstractions and wholes of classic evolutionary interest, no serious difficulties would plague its use. And, as I have said, the metaphor, in its several forms of cycle, epic, progress, and evolutionary development, does have its dogmatic-prophetic function, as well as its large-scale descriptive function.

It is a very different matter, however, when these same derivations of the metaphor of growth are given literal relevance, not just to abstractions and wholes, but to the concrete stuff of history, to the highly empirical problems of change which are the substance of contemporary social science.

It is impossible to argue with the contention that *civilization* has developed through processes internal to itself, slowly, gradually, and continuously, under the stimulus of forces which have been uniform and constant throughout. It is not merely possible but necessary to argue with the contention that these attributes of growth have much to do with observable processes of *the behavior of concrete human beings in specific areas in finite periods of time.* In the former, classic, type of developmental subject, the particularity of history can be disregarded, can be swept under the anthropologist's rug of culture or the sociologist's blanket of social systems. In the latter, and today more common, type of problem in the social sciences, the particularity of history cannot be disregarded or swept under any rugs and blankets. Not, that is, without trouble.

As I indicated in an earlier chapter, it does not do to liken the labors of the social evolutionist and those of the biological evolutionist. The latter is able, more or less successfully, to synchronize the results of laboratory and field study of genetic variations with the demands of the larger theory of evolution. For these variations are drawn from what is essentially a timeless world, a normless world, a world that has no other real existence save in the biologist's population-thought. For the social evolutionist, however, or, rather, the student of social change, any effort to deal with the problem of change *except* in terms of time and particularity courts disaster—or banality. Propositions drawn from the terminology and rhetoric of classic evolutionary theory to account for changes in, say, Negro-white relations in the South, caste in modern India, the extended family in modern France, or some equally finite subject, usually end up on a spectrum with manifest error at one extreme and description so general as to be bland at the other.

Rare indeed is the social scientist who today studies the totality of culture, society, or civilization. Who today studies Comte's Knowledge, Spencer's Society, Marx's Capitalism, Morgan's Kinship (*idea* of Kinship, that is), Tylor's Culture? Far more likely is the subject to be not Knowledge but attitudes of a given time and place; not Society but specified social systems in a neighborhood or city; not Capitalism but the behavior of consumers and producers; not Kinship-through-the-ages but family-patterns in East London; not Culture but the culture of the Andaman Islanders. I would not wish to imply that the older type of interest is gone; indeed it isn't; and, as we noted earlier, there are signs that evolutionism in the classic and grand manner is undergoing a revival at the present moment. One is tempted to say that so powerful, so irresistible, are the twenty-five-hundred-year-old concepts of growth in even contemporary consciousness that an appropriate subject or setting for them will be found even if this involves reverting to classic abstractions and wholes. Nevertheless, the difference I have just described between the common interests of nineteenth-century social science and those of today would appear to be generally accurate.

Thus, to pass to a few illustrations of my point in this section, if W. W. Rostow had contented himself in his *The Stages of Economic Growth*,[3] as Marx did a century earlier, with outlining alleged stages of development for all mankind in the realm of economic production, who could have put him down? But instead of mankind through the ages the subject in Rostow's book is the nation in modern Western European history. He subtitles his book "A Non-Communist Manifesto," and there is certainly no mistaking the non-Marxist political orientation of Rostow's widely read book. Nor is there any mistaking the often very shrewd criticisms of Marxian developmentalism and the assumptions concerning economic behavior on which Marx came in time to rest his early-adopted scheme of developmental stages. Nor would I suggest that there are not occasional insights of great value in Rostow's little volume so far as the study of what we call economic modernization is involved. If I happen to dissent rather strongly from the *political* argument of the book—which is in the clear direction of an almost despotic form of political centralization—this dissent has nothing to do with my chief objection to the book, which is entirely methodological. My objection is directed solely at Rostow's effort to make concepts of growth fit phenomena of a type for which the concepts of growth were never intended when they were fashioned in the long history of Western thought.

What Rostow calls his "stages-of-growth" analysis hardly differs, it seems to me, from the developmental essence of the Marxism he attacks in his book. Granted that in Rostow there is a more sophisticated, more diversified, and complex conception of man the actor in human history; granted that Rostow's conception of the nature of economic behavior, its principal incentives, motivations, and ends, differs from Marx's; and granted that, with the advantage of a century of economic history between the two men, Rostow can deal retrospectively with economic changes that Marx was forced to consider, if at all, prophetically. Granted all of this and more, the fact remains that, as Rostow himself indicates, there are several broad similarities between his approach to the problem of change and Marx's. I shall confine myself to the two most relevant to the whole matter: the nature of the entity for which development is asserted and, second, the nature of the development itself.

For Marx the essential subject of his laws of evolution was mankind. True, he sought to show the relation between this generalized development and the more specific development of a given nation, such as England, which he selected for its "maturity" of development. He dealt in extraordinary detail with the economic history of England. But while he searched British archives as no one before him had with respect to economic matters, his subject was not England, was not English economic behavior. It was, quite simply, *capitalism:* capitalism as it might be expected to be found anywhere at any time, its universal laws, processes, and structures. English data were useful for the reason given above: capitalism in England was assumed by Marx to be in its most advanced or mature phase; hence, as Marx pointed out to his readers, what could today be seen so vividly in English capitalism would be no less evident wherever capitalism in its mature stage of development might be tommorow. The development of capitalism was through internal processes or forces which worked continuously, uniformly, and necessarily. Out of the operation of these processes and forces would come, in time, the breakdown of capitalism and the birth of socialism. And, as Marx never forgot, even though his emphasis shifted in later years, capitalism itself was but a stage in an equally continuous series that was the evolution of the means of production for mankind—from antique slavery as the first stage through feudalism as the second, and then capitalism itself.

The point is Marx was dealing with, first, the larger entity of mankind and, second, the equally abstract, if smaller, entity, capitalism. Both are constructed entities, systems if we like, and to these alone did Marx's laws of development have relevance. We may find Marx's conclusions rather useless when it comes to the concrete study of economic behavior, in the present or in the past, but it is well to remember that what alone had reality to Marx was the succession of constructed social systems which he called "slavery," "feudalism," and "capitalism."

What Rostow has done, it would appear, is take the essential premises of developmentalism and seek to apply these, not to abstract social systems, but to those very concrete, historically formed aggregates that are the nations of modern Europe. Rostow gives a great deal of attention, just as Marx did, to England. But whereas Marx simply extracted data from English history to support a theory of capitalism, what Rostow is after is a theory of change that will account for what has happened economically in England during the past two hundred or so years. He seeks to endow England with the same kind of self-containment, the same conceptual autonomy, and the same internal mechanisms of dynamism with which Marx had endowed, not any historical nation, but capitalism.

But this, all too plainly, simply will not hold water. For it is utterly impossible to extract from the myriad events, forces, impacts, and historical contacts of modern economic history, of which those in the British Isles are but an aspect, any self-contained national entity with its own dynamisms, its principles of development, and its "stages of growth." I am not at all suggesting that it is impossible to ascertain the conditions or "causes" of the remarkable explosion of British industrialism in the late eighteenth and the nineteenth centuries. I am suggesting only that, as the innumerable criticisms of Rostow's developmental approach make clear, it is impossible to ascertain these conditions and causes when one is working from, first, the assumed existence of a self-contained, more or less autonomous national entity and, second, from premises regarding growth, and stages of growth, themselves the products of application of the idea of development to abstractions from which the concrete particularity of history has been excluded.

One may do this excluding, or at least get away with it, when the subject is civilization in its entirety and one is seeking general laws of its asserted advancement. But it is very difficult—I should say impossible—to exclude the concrete particularity of history when one is dealing with, say, modern England. Making all allowance for the vivid meaning that England, or any other nation, has to its citizens, and for the continuing political and cultural identity that it may be seen to have had for some centuries, it is not possible to deal with any of the major changes of England save in terms of incessant historical interaction of the English—traders, merchants, artisans, scholars, artists, as well as statesmen—with peoples and ideas and forces of one kind or other which cannot conceivably be localized in England.

Let us turn now to another and different type of study: Marion Levy's *The Family Revolution in Modern China*.[4] One must admire this book for the light it throws on the complex structures and processes of order, integration, and cohesion. Professor Levy is one of the leading American functionalists, and in his hands functionalism proves to be an extremely useful approach to the understanding of roles, statuses, and patterns of authority, function, and allegiance within the traditional Chinese family. Armed with functionalist insights he is able to demonstrate conclusively *why* certain types of role- and status-strain are embedded in this ancient and long-lasting system of kinship. He disabuses us forever of any possible notion that the traditional family in China was a thing of perpetual love and harmony, all compact. Structure means equilibrium, but it also means, as Levy shows, disequilibrium.

Disequilibrium, however, is not necessarily the same thing as change. Changes within the family system do not necessarily accumulate genetically to become changes *of* the system. A demonstration of the existence of role- and status-strains, of social dysfunctions within the system, is far from being a demonstration of the actual empirical sources of change of that system. For, functionalist theory or no, the actual historical record simply cannot be omitted from consideration—not at least in an area and period as well recorded and documented as China in the nineteenth and twentieth centuries.

Professor Levy is well aware of the historical record and what it says about Western economic, political, and intellectual invasion. But Levy is fundamentally interested in a theory of change, a theory that is broadly deducible from the premises of functionalism. Given these premises and given his theoretical objective, Levy is compelled to turn his back on the historical record. He makes us aware of his knowledge of that record, but he also makes us aware of his immunity to its content so far as his conception of the sources of change in kinship are concerned.

Precisely as Auguste Comte found the sources of change *in* the structure of knowledge, considered abstractly from the play of historical circumstance, so does Professor Levy find the sources of change in Chinese kinship *in* the structure of the family. True, he would concede immediately that external conditions and events leave their mark on the family, affect perhaps the rate of change of the kinship system. But, theorist that he is, Levy is concerned with locating the *structural*, the *lasting*, and the *uniform* sources of the change that has taken place in the Chinese family, and to do this he must obviously abandon something as kaleidoscopic, as mercurial, as the historical record and focus his attention upon the very elements which, in his previous analyses, have proved so wonderfully clarifying to our knowledge of the stability and equilibrium of the traditional family.

For we discover that despite the appearance of fixity in the long history of the family down to the end of the nineteenth century, despite the fact that on the evidence of all available records the essential structure of the family persisted unaltered, save in insignificant ways, for two thousand or more years, all the while it was being worked on from within by role-tensions involving the generations and sexes, by strains resulting from status-conflicts within the family, and by lack of correspondence between the "ideal" and the "actual." And as the consequence of these persisting and uniform strains and conflicts, there were changes taking place—changes within the structure of the family and, eventually, changes of the structure.

But when did the latter changes, the really significant ones, become manifest? Not until toward the end of the nineteenth century. Not until, by a remarkable coincidence, the full impact of the West's technological, economic, political, and cultural resources was transmitted through the coastal cities to the hinterland of China. For a very long period of time the Chinese family kept its essentially unaltered framework. Then, beginning with the momentous impact of the West on China in the nineteenth century, clear changes of structure began to be evident in the traditional family. From this one might conclude that the determining cause of the changes lay in the historical events associated with this impact. But to conclude thusly would be to deny the long-run effect of accumulating *internal* changes, assertedly the result of the uniform and incessant conflicts of role and status within the family. And this would in turn demolish the functionalist theory of change—at least so far as the Chinese family is concerned.

We thus find Professor Levy asserting—in full awareness of the momentous events connected with the West's penetration of China in the nineteenth century, in full awareness of the fact that structural change did not become manifest until this penetration, that "the motivation for change in China lay *primarily* in the stresses and strains created by, but contained within the 'traditional' structure. *The contact with the industrialized West increased those stresses and strains.*" [5] (Italics added.)

Let no one doubt that throughout its long history the Chinese family was indeed freighted with stresses and strains which resulted from persisting relationships of roles and statuses. It is highly unlikely that any pattern of social behavior, large or small, has ever existed, or could exist, apart from such stresses and strains. The question is, however, what *demonstrable* functions do such perturbations perform in the actual initiation of change as structurally significant as that which we find in China in the late nineteenth century? If this initiation of change could today be looked back on in a nineteenth-century China that was *not* subjected to Western invasion and cultural crisis, we might have the materials present for a functionalist, endogenous theory of change—a theory based perhaps demonstrably upon the role- and status-conflicts. But we, obviously, do not have such materials, for the historical record will not be denied. Nor does Professor Levy deny the historical record. He is well informed on it. It is simply that in the interests of fashioning a theory of development founded upon internal and structural elements, he, in effect, ignores it. So did Comte, Hegel, Marx, and Spencer. But they, wisely, did not choose to deal with entities smaller than total societies.

Both Rostow's and Levy's works point up, it is only too clear, the perils of trying to make the corollaries of the metaphor of growth serve subjects as finite and inextricably historical as the ones they have chosen. Each, more or less in defiance of history, has tried to locate *within* the structure chosen, British nation or Chinese family, uniform forces which through genetic continuity become converted into changes within the system and then, eventually, of the system.

Turn to Neil Smelser's *Social Change in the Industrial Revolution.*[6] This is a study that Professor Smelser subtitles: *An Application of Theory to the British Cotton Industry.* The period dealt with is the late eighteenth and early nineteenth century, without any question an age of very real social change in Britain. From this work, as from Levy's book on the Chinese family, we learn a great deal about matters that have either been ignored or else minimized by other scholars. A better book on the *descriptive* aspects of social change connected with the cotton industry would be hard to imagine. Nor is the book without valuable analytical insights concerning both structural process and social change.

But the book insists, as the title suggests, on being more than simply an excellent study of the industrial revolution. It is "an application of theory." And the theory is functionalism. Professor Smelser, let it be emphasized, is not concerned with trying to prove that changes in kinship during the period were all endogenous. Historian that he is, he is well aware of historical impact—

the impact of technological change upon social structures. Smelser's theoretical interests follow a different track from those of Professor Levy, though they are equally grounded in functionalism. He is concerned with the dimensions of *complexity* and *differentiation*, both of them manifest attributes of organic growth, both of them central concepts in the classical theory of social evolution. But the fact that increasing complexity and structural differentiation are obvious aspects of the history of human civilization, taken in the broad and abstract, in no way qualifies them as useful explanations of the kind of changes that may be found in a seventy-year period within a single industry in one country.

Putting the matter differently, it is surely true that something akin to these processes may be found in both industry and family during the period indicated. The question is, however, what analytical function is served by their utilization; what light is thrown upon key processes of persistence and modification by their transfer from schemes of classical evolution to very finite and concrete subject matter? The answer is far from clear. And it is made less clear by the easy transition from the process of differentiation to certain central concepts of functionalist theory which are, rather subtly, made into affinities of differentiation when in fact there is little evidence that they are affinities.

The objective of Professor Smelser's book, we have to remind ourselves continually as we read it, is not really "social change in the industrial revolution." It is instead the explicit application of an intact body of theory, functionalist theory, to the study of social change. He does not derive a theory or set of propositions concerning change from the materials of the cotton industry in a seventy-year period. He takes to this industry and period the propositions and theory of what I have called neo-evolutionism. Smelser is perfectly candid about all of this. His prime purpose, he writes, is "to apply the model of structural differentiation to several changes in the family and community life of the British working classes in the early nineteenth century." [7] This model, we are told, is applicable to many types of structure. "Separate models are not required for analysing changes in the economy, the family, the class system, etc." Moreover, the change that is produced has a high degree of uniformity. "Even though unique conditions naturally govern the behavior of different social units, the growth *pattern* of each should follow the same model." We find also the characteristic evolutionary effort to synthesize time and genesis. "Because structural differentiation is a *sequence*, its components appear in temporal relation to each other. For instance symptoms of disturbance erupt when the obsolescence of the old structure is apparent but before the mobilization of resources to overhaul this structure begins." [8]

The last point suggests something that is, as we have seen frequently, close to the very heart of the evolutionary theory: the assumption that obsolescence, or at any rate *premised* obsolescence, *itself* gives rise to perturbations within the social system of roles, statuses, values, collectivities, etc., and that these more or less self-contained perturbations arising from obsolescence are the cause of, or at least precede, "mobilization of resources to overhaul this structure."

A mighty effort indeed is required of Professor Smelser to keep juggling in one hand the key elements of functionalism united with the historic premises of developmentalism and, in the other hand, the myriad data educed by his historical scholarship. For consider the scope of his problem: "to apply in two separate structural contexts—the industry and the family—a model of differentiation which posits a typical sequence of events which occurs when the system increases in complexity." [9] Nor is this all. The sequence must, for reasons arising from social systems theory, be shown to begin "when members of the system in question (*or some larger system*) express *dissatisfaction* with some aspect of the system's functioning. This dissatisfaction may concern role-performance in the system, the utilization of its resources, or both." [10] I have myself italicized the words in the parenthesis above, for it points up, it seems to me, the chronic problem faced by functionalism and other variants of evolutionism when the question at issue is the source of the change. To bring in "some larger system" when the search is on for beginnings and sources is in effect to cancel just about all that is implied in the functionalist's search for causes and motivations of change that stem from tensions, dissatisfactions, and strains within his announced system —be this the Chinese family or the British cotton industry.

I repeat, there is much of value in Smelser's and Levy's books: value in the study of the conditions of order chiefly, but also in the understanding of how social change can become filtered, so to speak, and sometimes even neutralized, by the roles and statuses in which human beings do in fact live. The difficulty of each book comes, however, from the effort to make concepts regarding change seem analytically useful within finite, concrete, and historical circumstances when these concepts are the products of developmental ways of thinking that were meticulously defined by their principal makers and users as non-finite, non-concrete, and, above all, non-historical. That to the abstract, the substantively large, and the very long run, such concepts as continuity, differentiation, and progressive complexity may have relevance and even some explanatory value is one thing; it is something else to apply them to the short-run, geographically finite, and concrete behavior of human beings.

We are justified in saying, I believe, that all that gives the concepts even the limited and mostly apparent relevance they do possess in such studies as those by Marion Levy and Neil Smelser is the all-important theoretical context provided by the social system. Without a premised *system*—whether as small as kinship or as large as civilization—the theory of social evolution has little application to the facts of social change in time.

Something of this kind of reflection may well be involved in the recent redirection of Talcott Parsons' interests. Professor Parsons, without ceasing to be the pre-eminent functionalist that he is, has enlarged the canvas from the social system to what he frankly calls the "total society." Again I refer to his *Societies: Evolutionary and Comparative Perspectives*.[11] It is a work to respect, for in its very breadth there lies hope that the social sciences may once again turn their attention from the small and immediate to the large and historically more distant. And, within limits, Professor Parsons handles his materials skillfully.

The book is nevertheless steeped in the essential ideas and premises of classic social evolutionary theory. And its framework is as surely the Comparative Method as is anything ever written by Spencer or Tylor. That the materials used are up to date in their scholarship and fresh in their utilization does not affect the truth of what I have just said about the book. It is in essence nineteenth-century social evolutionism.

We have in a sense come full circle. The concepts of change drawn by the functionalist from classic social evolutionism, applied for a generation to single peoples, short-term social systems, isolated cultures or institutions, are now returned, as it were, to the bank from which they were borrowed. Changing the figure, the vital concepts of continuity, directionality, differentiation, increasing structural complexity, which were always threatening to fall out of the nest that is the social system, can, within the context of "total societies," be given escape-proof security.

Even the theory of more or less universal stages is resurrected for the total societies—though in full awareness that divergences can, do, and will take place from time to time. It is, nevertheless, Professor Parsons' argument that human society, over a very long period of time, has passed generally through the stages represented by his terms "primitive," "intermediate," and "modern." And although no effort is made or could be made in the compass of a single book to place all societies of past and present in one or other of these three great stages, the implication is clear that all societies could be so placed.

Parsons does not shy away from the implication of the title of his book. It is a work in evolution. Others have been, in recent times, gun-shy when it came to asseverations of change and development, when they have classified peoples and societies. Hence the so-called cross-cultural data banks. But it is not logical classification that interests Parsons any more than it did Morgan or Tylor. Not for its own sake. Not taxonomy but what he calls "socio-cultural evolution" is what interests him. And this, we are told, has, like organic evolution, "proceeded by variation and differentiation, from simple to progressively more complex forms."

But Parsons has told us at the very beginning of his work that in it he is interested in "*total society*," a phrase that he properly italicizes. And, as he well realizes, it is only with respect to the entity, the hypostatized entity, "total society," that the contents of the book can by any stretch of reasoning be made relevant to "stages" of evolution. For what we are given in the book's contents to form the three great stages—primitive, intermediate, modern—are, as it were, snapshots of an immense range of cultures and civilization, past and present. In the single stage of "intermediate," for example, are placed such widely separated and contrasting civilizations as the Chinese Empire, the Indian caste system, and the Islamic and Roman Empires, among others.

Now, if we look carefully at Professor Parsons' book we discover that the variation and differentiation which form, as he has told us above, the fundamental processes of evolutionary development, social as well as organic, are in no sense given embodiment *in the sense of change*, but only in the sense of classificatory distribution. That there is a "progression" of type, in terms of variation and differentiation, from Australian primitivism to Western modernism permits no doubt whatever. That it is continuous (in a footnote Parsons pays his own respect to the Leibnizian law of continuity by declaring his intent to "fill the gap of continuity") permits no doubt either. But by no possible stretch of the imagination can these attributes—variation, differentiation, continuity—here be said to be attributes of *change*. They are attributes of classification which, unfortunately, Professor Parsons confuses with change through his adoption of the entity "total society." For it is only in the sense of substantive reality belonging to "total society" that one can transfer the logical gradations of classification that are laid out before us in the forms of cultures, societies, and institutions into what they are held to be—gradations or stages of developmental change.

Consider the following instance. Parsons is describing the primitive societies of the Australians. In these societies "the core structure of the societal community as a whole is the affinal system regulated by the prescriptive marriage rules." At this point we are told that "we would expect structural change to become evident," whatever the causes. Further, a most important "source of change" arises when the strict status equivalence of the intermarrying kinship groups "breaks down." A "potential for evolutionary advance" exists, and, finally, "the long run evolutionary tendency is clearly toward the attenuation and elimination of *developmentally restrictive* regulations, which inherently *favor* the generalized equality of categorical collaterals." [12] (Italics added.)

Now, where precisely do we *find* the foreshadowed "structural change," the "source of change," the "potential for evolutionary advance," and "the long run evolutionary tendency toward attenuation and elimination of developmentally restrictive regulations"? This is the core question so far as anything properly pertaining to *change* is concerned. Do we find all of these sources, potentials, and tendencies toward attenuation *among the Australians*, which we should in fact expect to do if we were actually dealing with change as an empirical process? We do not. No matter how "unstable" the prescriptive system may seem to Professor Parsons, the fact remains that for evidence of its breaking down or elimination we have to go, not to the Australian primitives themselves, *but to the next higher level of social types in the classificatory series*.[13] In this level, which is, as it must be, a selected level, we find, sure enough, that the "restrictive" elements—the elements Parsons has called restrictive to development in the Australian system—have been sloughed off, and a higher stage of "evolution" has been achieved. In short, what is implied by Parsons to be change is not change at all, but variation of classificatory type.

I say "not change at all." But, of course, it *is* change in the reified entity "total society." The trouble is, we are led to suppose —and this is no more true of Parsons' presentation than it is of any other presentation of social evolution—that each variation of classificatory type, each jump from, say, Australian primitive to the Shilluk of the upper Nile Sudan, is more than a classificatory device. We are told that it is a "developmental breakthrough" and, further, that the process of innovation will "always approximate our paradigm of evolutionary change." [14]

That Parsons is himself aware of the tenuous relation between his evolutionary panorama and the actual process of *change* is made clear toward the end of the volume. He writes: "Emphatically, I am not saying that contributions to the analysis of process and change would not improve evolutionary theory enormously. But I am saying that the use of available sociological, anthropological, archaeological, and historical evidence to order structural types and relate them sequentially is a *first* order of business which cannot be by-passed." [15]

It is hard to see, however, what can be learned about *change* from the kind of arrangement of materials that we find in Parsons' book or, for that matter, in any book organized around the nineteenth-century Comparative Method. For, as the example just given of the use of Australian and Shilluk makes only too clear, it is not change in any empirical sense that is involved there but only simple classificatory variation.

Admittedly, observation of differences is the beginning of the study of change. But the differences must be within a persisting identity and in a finite time-series. What we have in Australian and Shilluk are two cultures quite unconnected, save in Parsons' taxonomy, not in a finite time-series, and without persisting identity. The nearest we can come to the latter is by employment of an entity—total society, civilization, mankind—so vast, so abstract, so empirically meaningless as to make impossible any conclusions of a substantive sort regarding change.

Professor Parsons suggests that the theory of social evolution is in substantially the same position in this respect as the theory of biological evolution where "morphology, including comparative anatomy, is the 'backbone' of evolutionary theory." [16] But this leaves a good deal out. Morphology and comparative anatomy may set the stage for evolutionary theory in biology, but the real "backbone" of the theory is a highly specific process of change—natural selection—that is clearly and incontestably rooted in what biologists know about variations and mutations in the short run, in the data which provide subject matter for modern genetics.

When we turn to the study of social behavior, however, no such correspondence is to be found. Neither the panorama of so-called evolutionary structures that is the Comparative Method nor the processes of evolutionary change implied by this panorama—such processes as genetic continuity, directionality, endogenous causation, and uniformitarianism—are supported by what the whole range of empirical studies of change in modern social science suggests in the way of crucial processes involved.

3. THE IRRELEVANCE OF METAPHOR

At the beginning of the chapter I suggested that the relevance and utility of the metaphor of growth are in direct proportion to the cognitive distance of the subject to which the metaphor is applied. The larger, more distant, or more abstract the subject, the greater the utility of such metaphor-derived attributes as immanence, continuity, differentiation, and the others we have dealt with from the Greeks down to the present.

We may now state the proposition in reverse. The less the cognitive distance, the less the relevance and utility of the metaphor. In other words, the more concrete, empirical, and behavioral our subject matter, the less the applicability to it of the theory of development and its several conceptual elements.

It is tempting enough to apply these elements to the constructed entities which abound in Western social thought: to civilization as a whole, to mankind, to total society; to such entities as capitalism, democracy, and culture; to social systems as functionalists and others conceive them; and to so-called evolutionary universals. Having endowed one or other of these with life through the familiar process of reification, it is but a short step to further endowment with growth—with internal mechanisms of growth and development around which laws of progress and evolution are constructed. Such, as we have seen, has in very large measure been the history of social thought in the West since the time of Aristotle.

It is something else entirely, however, when we try, as much social theory at present is trying, to impose these concepts of developmentalism upon, *not* constructed entities, but the kind of subject matter that has become basic in the social sciences today: *the social behavior of human beings in specific areas and within finite limits of time.* Efforts to extract this further utility from the metaphor of growth are, as we have just seen, wholly unsuccessful. The methodological reason for this lack of success, as we have also seen, lies in the utter lack of appositeness of concept to subject matter. Whereas the concepts involved stem from a line of inquiry, the purpose of which, from Aristotle to the social evolutionists of the nineteenth century, was to ascertain the *natural* path of change in time—the path that change would follow apart from interferences of random events—they are today used, as by Rostow, Levy, Smelser, and others, to try to deal with precisely the area of phenomena that the classical evolutionists avoided, and knew for good reason they *had* to avoid.

The difficulties encountered by those involved in this practice could have been foretold by any of the theorists of natural history and of social evolution during the past two centuries. In a sense, they did foretell. For one and all they made plain that whatever might be the value of the theory of progressive development in the study of mankind in the large, for the study of history it was valueless: history in the sense of the concrete, the particular, and the temporal.

But "history" is what the contemporary social sciences are all about. I do not mean, obviously, simple narration, for that, after all, is not basic to the craft of historiography any more than is any one of its other techniques. The methodology of history lies in its concern with the concrete and particular, and its strict observance of the limits of time. It is in this sense that the social sciences have become increasingly historical. At the beginning of the century when the great F. W. Maitland said, "By and by anthropology will have the choice between being history and being nothing," [17] he was, in the first place, referring to all the social sciences and, in the second place, by "history" he meant concern with time and particularity, not the common framework of narration.

Since Maitland's day a veritable revolution has taken place in the social sciences. Nearly gone is preoccupation with the vistas and abstractions, evolutionary wholes and universals, of the Comtes, Marxes, Spencers, and Morgans. To a high degree *comparison*—actual comparison of comparable modes of behavior —has replaced the venerable Comparative Method with its framework of levels into which cultural data were parked like so many automobiles. It is today not so much the long-run patterns of evolution that social scientists are interested in—though, as we have just seen, there can be revivals in social science as well as in religion—but the processes of change in the short run: in Detroit, in Muncie, in the Deep South, in the English Midlands, in East Africa among the Bantu, in Latin America, and so on. In short, history in the sense of an understanding of the concrete in time and in place.

Note that I am referring to empirical or what might be called monographic social science. As our present day social theory—or at least what looms up as conventional wisdom in social theory— makes only too plain, nothing like the same distance here has been traversed since the day of Maitland's warning to the social sciences. We are fond of referring to the great distances we have moved in our social theory since the heyday of evolutionism in the nineteenth century, but careful inspection suggests that these distances are largely illusory, and nowhere so evidently illusory as in our theory of change. Our advancement as social scientists has been almost wholly in the realm of empirical study: of social behavior in kinship, religion, education, social stratification, organizations, communities, processes of learning, communicating, and thinking, in ethnic groups, economic groups, political parties, and so on.

From such studies we have learned a great deal about what is involved in social order and also *social change*. True, what we have learned in both major areas of study is not without brilliant foretelling, in at least a general way, in some of the more neglected works of the recent past: in single essays of Hume and Turgot in the eighteenth century, in the works of such minds as Frederick Le Play, George Cornewall Lewis, and Max Weber in the nineteenth, in the studies of such scholars as F. J. Teggart, Carl Sauer, A. L.

Kroeber, W. I. Thomas, and others in this century whose studies in comparative history and historical geography light up the problem of change in ways we are just beginning to appreciate today.

And what we have learned from these empirical studies, old and new, adds up to one cardinal conclusion: the theory of change embodied in both the classical theory of social evolution and the contemporary theories of neo-evolutionism and of functionalism is singularly without merit when it comes to our understanding of the nature of change, the conditions under which change takes place, and the effects of change upon social behavior.

What I now want to do, in the remainder of this section, is contrast what might be called the conventional wisdom regarding social change which we find at every hand in our so-called social theory and the results regarding the nature of change which we find in literally scores of studies, hundreds indeed, of *social behavior*, as we find such behavior in empirical circumstances, in specified time and place.[18]

The priority of fixity. I begin with the very opposite of that most basic of all premises in the theory of social development, and indeed in most other theories of change which are current, the premise which tells us that change is "natural" to institutions and all other forms of social behavior.

Change is, however, *not* "natural," *not* normal, much less ubiquitous and constant. Fixity is. If we abandon metaphor and the constructed social systems to which metaphor is applied, and if we look at actual social behavior, in place and in time, we find over and over that persistence in time is the far more common condition of things. If we were Newtonians we could say with Newton that "every body continues in its state of rest, or of uniform motion in a straight line, unless it is compelled to change that state by forces impressed upon it." If we were writing in the vein of the eighteenth-century natural historians, we could say that, apart from all interferences and external impacts, social behavior tends to remain fixed and unchanging. Let us content ourselves, however, with the simple observation that, on the empirical record, fixity, not change, is the required point of departure for the study of *not merely social order but social change.*

Conventional wisdom differs, of course. From the ancient Greek apothegm, "change is king," down to the latest sociological incantation, "change is ubiquitous," the constancy of change, as well as the conceptual priority of change, have been among the most persistent of intellectual assumptions.

Why should this be? In the realm of simple observation and common sense, nothing is more obvious than the *conservative* bent of human behavior, the manifest desire to preserve, hold, fix, and keep stable. Common sense tells us that, given the immense sway of habit in individual behavior and of custom, tradition, and the sacred in collective behavior, change could hardly be a constant, could hardly be ubiquitous. One need but look at the actual history of any given way of behavior in a group or society—the way of behavior we call the monogamous family in the West, for example, or the Christian religion, or the university—and while changes in these are indeed aspects of the historical record, such changes can only be understood against the background of persistence that must, if we are to understand change, be our point of departure.

For the ancient Greek—and for philosophers ever since, down to contemporary functionalists—the fact of *manifest* fixity is unquestioned. What is questioned, as we have observed, is the constitutive reality of such fixity. It is declared that since, in time, even the most persistent of persisting things does occasionally reveal change, the *manifestation* of fixity conceals indwelling or latent forces which are in fact leading toward change. Hence, it is triumphantly concluded, change is intrinsic to social behavior, just as growth is in the organism. The difficulties with this point of view do not, however, need restatement. I am concerned only with setting forth the conventional wisdom of social thought and contrasting it with what straightforward observation reveals.

There is also the common confusion of change with mere motion, activity, movement, interaction. *These*, beyond any doubt, are constant and ubiquitous. But none of them, as a moment's thought tells us, is synonomous with change. They may be aspects of any given change, but they are not in themselves change.

Beyond these two timeworn sources of conventional wisdom regarding the constancy of change is common failure to specify *what* it is that is assertedly changing.[19] If it is the whole of mankind, the whole of any single civilization, or even of the somewhat smaller units within which people live, such as nations, regions, and cities, it would be hard to dispute the statement that somewhere something is changing at just about any moment in time. But this is hardly rigorous reasoning about change. Change, when it exists, is change of something with specific identity—whether this be a norm, a custom, a relationship, or an entire culture or nation. Failure to specify the identity of *what* it is for which change is claimed, from which study of actual change can proceed, is a frequent source of confusion.

But once we abandon metaphoric premise, as well as confusion of change with mere motion and activity, and once we make plain what it is we are studying precisely, there can hardly be any question, it would seem, of the reality of persistence and of the necessity of beginning with this reality when our object is analysis of change.

"When it is not *necessary* to change it is necessary *not* to change." This famous aphorism of political conservatism is actually as cogent a principle as one can think of in the comparative study of social behavior: it is attested to by the vast literature on human custom and tradition, by comparative study of social groups and organizations, by specific histories of localities and regions, and by what we have learned from social psychology about human habits and attitudes. It is a well-known fact that isolation from cultural contact—the type of isolation so often revealed in primitive, folk, peasant, and religious cultures and also in enclaves within even the most active of societies—coexists with cultural fixity and conservatism. This would hardly be the case were there, as the theory of social development and conventional sociological wisdom stoutly maintain, processes of change built into human interaction. For surely the members of these isolated cultures interact with one another—exploit, hate, fight with, as well as protect, love, and cherish. But there is no degree of internal conflict, internal stress, of human misery and degradation, not compatible with extraordinary persistence of types of social behavior. Whether it is caste in India or the traditional pattern of Negro-white relations in the Deep South, the existence of fierce, underlying conflicts may be taken for granted. The roots which such patterns of behavior have in over-all human acceptance—acceptance in turn rooted in inertia, tradition, fear of change—are, however, only too well known.

The principal case for the ubiquity and constancy of change (and particularly developmental, cumulative change) lies with human knowledge. Does not, it is asked, the panorama of what lies between us and those proto-historical beings who lived in caves prove the slow, gradual, and continuous development of knowledge? Does not the spectacle today of intellectuals and scientists in ceaseless search for new dimensions of reality and new technological aids to living prove that in the quest for knowledge there is an inherent dynamism that leads to change? Alas, they do not. We can acquire the *sense* of developmental growth, of continouous motion, through use of the same Comparative Method that we have seen applied to kinship, class, and religion. But, as with these, it is not actual change that is revealed; only logical, classificatory variations made possible to our eyes by the familiar device of putting all possible gradations in a single series.

That a long time has been occupied by man's intellectual existence is no more in doubt than the time of his physical or social or economic existence. That many thousands of years intervene between some primordial individual's first conceptual awareness of energy and contemporary awareness of nuclear energy is not in doubt either. Nor is the fact in doubt of relationships in knowledge, of the dependence of one thing upon another.

If, again however, we turn our gaze from the unmanageable wholeness of things to what concretely happens when we take a single idea in historical time, or examine the intellectual behavior of a given people or group or cultural in historical time, we do not find change to be a constant, much less progressive development. As but a moment's reflection tells us, there is nothing that persists like an idea! Think only of the idea with which this book is concerned, the idea of the growth-like nature of social change, and of the two and a half millennia during which it has been unfailingly directive in social thought.

So, as we have learned, do systems and patterns of ideas persist.[20] Even in the arts—some would say especially in the arts—where individual creativity and directness of reaction to environment are central, conventionalization of response for long periods is a very familiar phenomenon. What John Livingston Lowes so perceptively described in his notable study of English poetry is not less evident in other areas of the creative arts.[21]

And also in science. Surely, if there were any area of knowledge and creative expression where processes of fixity and of sheer conservatism would seem to be negligible it is modern science—actuated solely, as we like to think, by incessant desire to advance in accretional, cumulative fashion. But, as some recent studies have re-emphasized for us, the power of a single paradigm in the physical sciences can often be as great as the power of a dogma in religion.[22] And the vast bulk of the actual work of science is, in any event, mimetic, supportive, concerned with additional demonstration of the already known. Not only does science reveal infrequent changes of fundamental ideas or paradigms, it reveals frequent hostility to such changes when they occur.

There is no need to prolong discussion of a point that, as I stated at the start, was obvious once clearly stated. Despite the testimony of conventional wisdom in social theory, despite the first and abiding premise of the theory of social development, it is not change but persistence that is the "natural" or "normal" condition of any given form of social behavior. Such fixity is combinable with all manner of internal conflicts and tensions, all degrees of misery and degradation, and, as the historical record makes very plain indeed, can prove stoutly resistant to even shattering impacts from the outside.

Change and event. And yet, paraphrasing what Galileo is said to have muttered, there is change nevertheless. Fixity unpunctuated by change is as unlikely in the world of actuality as is change unpunctuated by fixity. The question is, how do we go about discovering the sources of change, the conditions under which change manifestly takes place? We may do as the classical theory of development has done—assume change as a constant, as something embedded within social reality, and seek merely to describe it, to chart its assumed rhythms and oscillations. We may do as contemporary functionalism—and much other social theory—does: seek to account for the sources of change through exploration of the properties of abstract social systems—the assertedly timeless, continuous, and uniform sources of change.

Or we may approach the problem of change *historically*. Instead of assuming, charting, graphing, and searching for timeless structural constants that are supposedly involved in all modes of change, we may ask the question, what are the conditions under which actual social change takes place in the history of a given institution or given mode of social behavior or cultural area? And if we do this, we cannot possibly make that distinction, so cherished by all social theorists since Aristotle, between "natural change" and the changes that are bound up with such non-developmental and strictly historical matters as *events*.

By an event I mean not simply an occurrence or happening, which is the commonest meaning given the word. I mean this too, of course, but from the point of view of the study of change, the most relevant meaning of "event" is some impact or intrusion from outside the domain of the form of social behavior, or cultural area, that is under study. What F. J. Teggart wrote on the subject is worth quoting here in full.

> The identification of "events" as "intrusions" is a matter of some importance. To reach an understanding of "how things work" in the course of time, we may envisage the facts of experience as arranged conceptually in a series of concentric circles. Outermost, we would have the stellar universe; within this, the

physical earth; within this, the world of organic life; within this, again, the world of human activities; within this, the larger group or nation; within this, the local community; and, finally, within this, the individual. In such a series, it is obvious that change in any outer circle will affect all that lies within it. We may, then, define an "event" as an intrusion, from any wider circle, into any circle or condition which may be the object of present interest.[23]

With one qualification that statement seems to me to say more about the actual nature of change than anything that can easily be derived from the theory of development, with its central concepts of immanence, continuity, and uniformitarianism. My qualification pertains simply to Teggart's statement that "it is obvious that change in any outer circle will affect all that lies within it." It is no disservice to the larger importance of the passage to observe that, given the tenacity of ways of belief, behavior, and of customs and institutions generally, it does not at all follow that changes in an outer circle must be visited upon what lies within an inner circle. They may; they may not. Like anything else reasonably connected with the study of social change, such conclusions are for investigation rather than assumption.

There is no better or more important example of the kind of study described in theoretical terms by Teggart than Max Weber's famous study of the rise of capitalism in the West.[24] We usually think of this work as an ingenious demonstration of the noneconomic foundations of the modern economy, which it is. But it is more. It is a brilliant refutation of the evolutionist—specifically, the Marxist-evolutionist—thesis of the internal source of change in the set of circumstances which produced modern capitalism.

For Marx, as we know, the source lay in the economy itself, with capitalism, the new form of economic society, "maturing in the womb of the old society." But Weber, taking his departure, not from the assumed existence of a reified whole, capitalism, but rather from the facts of the social behavior of business men, merchants, divines, and others, reached the very different conclusion that the sources of capitalism are to be found in the impact upon business men of certain ideas and incentives which lay *outside* the economy as such: the ideas and incentives which form the essence of Puritanism. It was, argued Weber, the prior change of values in Western religion that provided the precipitating event for the changes of an economic nature which were to lead to modern capitalism. That there are certain errors in Weber's demonstration need not detain us here. What is of importance is the method: a genuinely historical method, one which proceeds from social behavior, from events, from concrete circumstances, rather than from the abstract categories in which, as Marx put the matter in *Capital*, "individuals are dealt with only insofar as they are the personifications of economic categories, embodiments of particular class relations and class interests." As Marx himself noted, in the sentence immediately following the one I have just quoted, his treatment of capitalism is one "from which the evolution of the economic formation of society is viewed as a *process of natural history*. . . ." [25] (Italics added.) Weber, however, was no more interested in natural history than he was in the "emanationism" that he correctly saw as the essence of the evolutionary stress on internal causation of change.

It might also be noted in passing that for Weber the larger study of the origins of capitalist behavior—capitalist values, capitalist techniques, and capitalist ideas—was bound up with a genuinely comparative study of history; one as different from the Comparative Method, with its fixed hierarchy of levels and its culture-hopping and its trait-snatching, as any method could possibly be. Equally important is the fact that Weber, far from seeking simply to arrange the world's cultures in terms of greater or less approximation of the modern West, and striving in the process to uncover some "law" based on evolutionary universals, approached his materials—*historical* materials—armed with a specific question. The question was: What are the conditions under which rationalized economic behavior makes its appearance? So armed, it was possible, in the first place, to deal with a body of actual historical data and, in the second place, to formulate a *bona fide* hypothesis.[26]

I do not wish to imply here that all changes, of whatever kind and degree, are external in their sources. We should make the same distinction that Radcliffe-Brown did, to which I referred above: the distinction between changes *within* a given pattern of behavior—which, as Radcliffe-Brown observes, are more nearly in the character of readjustments—and changes *of* the pattern. The latter are the larger and more visible changes of type or structure. As Radcliffe-Brown made very emphatic indeed, the difference between the two types of change is very great.[27]

Unfortunately, under the continuing influence of eighteenth-century ideas of genetic continuity and of causal uniformitarianism, there is a strong tendency in social theory to seek to make change of structure the cumulative and linear consequence of the other type of change—the smaller, internal, more or less uniform changes which are to be seen in ordinary existence. Only by so doing, it is argued, can there be a genuine science of change. In this respect, however, social theory is taking a very different road from modern genetics. Darwin, as we saw, tried to hang the entire theory of evolution from the hook of variation—uniform, infinitesimally small, continuous variation—and to argue that large changes are but the accumulation of the small variations. Modern genetics, Darwinian variation notwithstanding, has, however, made very clear the role in biological evolution of random events, of mutations, and of changes which cannot be explained by simple cumulative variation.[28]

There are indeed changes engendered from within social structures. Even after we have discounted the all too common confusion of change with mere activity, interaction, and motion, with ordinary tensions and conflicts, there are changes which are beyond any question internal, arising from self-contained sources. On the evidence of history, however, such changes are small and frequently cancel themselves out in the course of time. The important point, in any event, is that of making the distinction between such changes and changes of larger, structural significance.

Let me say again, I am far from denying the appeal—metaphysical, religious, political—of metaphors of growth in which what is crucial and causative for change is drawn from within some aggregate or entity. Try to imagine the charismatic appeal of Marxism without the key cause lodged within capitalism and, more especially, within the proletariat. Try to imagine the cause of black nationalism at the present time—or of any of the older nationalisms. Theories of the "rise and fall" of the Roman empire which rest their weight on endemic processes, present from the start in Rome, clearly have philosophic and poetic superiority over those which deal with the whole matter in terms of the visible record of Rome's relationships with peoples as far distant as the Chinese. They seem profounder, possessed of some of the element of tragedy that dramatists reserve for individuals. Witness the appeal of Spengler and Toynbee!

We are concerned, however, not with matters of metaphysical and poetic profundity, but with the nature of social change considered as an empirical process in social behavior through historical time. And if from any *bona fide* historian's point of view [29] it is impossible to deal even with entities so vast as Greece or Rome or Western Europe or the United States in terms of endogenous forces, that is, apart from the relationships of each of these to literally scores of other peoples, to intrusions stemming from political, military, economic forces, to such matters as trade routes, wars, invasions, migrations, importation of alien values, and so on, it is the less likely that a plausible theory of change concerned with institutions can be constructed in the absence of explicit reference to such relationships, intrusions, and impacts.

Events, in the sense in which I use the word here are, then, indispensable to understanding social change—at least when it is above the level of the minor modifications which are common enough but which, as I have argued, do not leave any record of cumulative culmination in the large changes of institutions. If, as is so often argued today—as it was argued by Aristotle and all philosophers of growth who followed—events, "unique events," as they are called, are not amenable to the systematic needs of social theory, so much the worse for the theory. The objective, after all, is not illumination of concept and theory. It is illumination of reality as mind and sense reveal this reality. And the distinction between appearance and reality is as intellectually vacuous—and pragmatically dangerous—as it was in the days of the Pythagoreans.

Hence the high correlation, one frequently noted by historians, between periods of pronounced change in customs and institutions and the impacts of such events as invasions, migrations, new trade routes opened, wars, explorations—in short, of those forces most likely to effect cracks in what Walter Bagehot called the cake of custom. As isolation tends to intensify the forces of conservatism, so does contact of peoples, ideas, and values tend, for the most part, to create conditions of change.[30]

I am not suggesting that the historical record confirms simply a "great man" theory of history or a theory founded solely on the role of accident and caprice. This is far from my intent. I am suggesting that when we come down in our analysis from the abstract wholes such as mankind and civilization, within which, by definition, all change *must* be internally based, to the social behavior of human beings, considered in time and in place, significant change is overwhelmingly the result of non-developmental factors; that is to say, factors inseparable from external events and intrusions.

Again let us be reminded that none of the great proponents of the evolutionary view of society ever denied the existence of external events, of adventitious impacts. What they said was that while these plainly exist at every hand, responsible indeed for the specific and actual existences of things, the task of philosophy (and then, in time, of *science*) was to find out the true *nature* of things, a word, as we have seen, which the social philosophers interpreted in the sense of how things *naturally* grow—progress, develop, evolve —apart from the order of reality revealed by mere observation.

This, however, is hardly the objective or task of the contemporary behavioral sciences. Yet, with no particular exaggeration involved, it can be said that countless efforts are being made today, through laboratory experiment and systematic theorizing, to do what an Adam Smith or Rousseau did single-handed and without fuss: locate the source and pattern of change within the essentially non-historical realm of psychology or group dynamics.

I noted above, in the paragraphs on persistence and fixity, that isolation is one of the commonest of all contexts of cultural and social inertia. To this we may now add the further observation that the type of event we call intrusion or invasion *into this isolation* is one of the commonest of all sources of change—of visible, significant change, of change in institutions, customs, beliefs, values, and ideas.[31] Repeatedly this mode of invasion appears in history, and it has many types of manifestation as well as degrees of importance. It may be the set of processes of intrusion, impact, and mixture which lies behind that greatest of all Western cultural and social efflorescences, the fifth century B.C. in Greece (imagine dealing with *that* in the terms of simple, cumulative development of Attican institutions!) [32] or it may be so relatively simple a matter as the "invasion" of a ghetto or poverty-culture by Federal administrator or civil rights militant.

The theorists of natural progress in the seventeenth and eighteenth centuries saw wars as among the chief enemies of that natural progress of knowledge they worshipped. But the great David Hume and, in France, Turgot saw the matter very differently. Without in any way approving of war, they nonetheless saw the *kinds of contact*—social, cultural, psychological—generally involved in war as among the indispensable processes in history for breaking inertia, for liberating from iron custom and dogma, for the mixture of peoples which these two philosophers both saw clearly (in other respects, as we have seen, they were men of their age) to be the necessary conditions of genuine advancement of knowledge, of escape from the routine and traditional.[33]

Plainly, wars are not today, nor intrinsically were they in the past, essential to such advancement. There are, and always have been, other means of cultural contact, fusion, and mixture. What is essential to the understanding of change is no single type of event. It is the event as such: the intrusion, the impact, the impingement upon a given mode of social behavior of some force that cannot, by its nature, be deduced from that mode of behavior.

Change in any degree of notable significance is intermittent rather than continuous, mutational, even explosive, rather than the simple accumulation of internal variations. No computer could count and classify the number of role-tensions, status-tensions, and generational conflicts in the Western monogamous family. Its changes, however, the kinds of visible, explicit changes which the *history* of the structures of the family in the West reveals, have been relatively few, and they have been, without exception connected with events—political, economic, religious, *et al.*—emanating from areas outside kinship.[34]

What is true of the family is, by the very nature of the matter, infinitely more true of such a relationship as that of caste in India or the traditional pattern of relation of black and white in the Deep South in this country. I take nothing away from the internal conflicts which are generated by either system; I will stipulate indeed that such conflicts are as pervasive as they are endemic. No one but a functionalist would seek, however (except for metaphoric-political purposes), to encapsulate the extraordinary changes which have taken place in both of these institutionalized relationships during the past century within any timeless, uniform, and internal processes.

Change and crisis. Change involves crisis, as W. I. Thomas wrote, and made memorably evident in his great study *The Polish Peasant in Europe and America*.[35] The very tendency of social behavior to persist, to hold fast to values and convenience, makes a degree of crisis inevitable in all but the most minor of changes. A given way of behaving tends to persist as long as circumstances permit. Then, as Thomas points out, the way of behaving ceases to be possible, as the result of some intrusion, some difficulty which is the consequence of event or impact, and a period of crisis ensues. The crisis, with all its social and psychological accompaniments of conflict and tension, which have been occasioned by the shattering of old ways, continues until some new form of adaptation is reached; one in which elements of the old—usually a good many of these—are fused with new elements drawn in part from the precipitating intrusion.

It is impossible for me to think of any empirical study of change in contemporary social science—change of political, economic, ethnic, rural, urban, or other type of social behavior—in which the element that Thomas called crisis is not clearly present: mute evidence both of the power of persistence in social behavior, the strain for what Sumner called consistence, and of the external source of change.[36]

Change and persistence. All of this makes understanding of persistence and fixity vital to understanding of change. To deny the fundamental fact of such persistence, to take refuge in concepts premised on the unreality of persistence and on the sole reality of constitutive change is to make impossible any understanding of change as a concrete, historical process.

I do not, therefore, repudiate functionalism categorically. For all its mistaken emphasis on social systems, rather than social behavior, and for all its mistaken predication of change as an immanent process, there is nonetheless much to be learned from *functionalist studies of cultures, groups, and customs.*[37] From them we can learn a good deal, I believe, about the phenomenon I have mentioned several times: the phenomenon of continuing persistence and inertia even when a given way of behavior is subjected to events and intrusions which at other times, or in other places, plainly lead to change. The best of functionalism lies exactly in what critics have mistakenly condemned it for—its emphasis upon those processes which are involved in equilibrium and stability. For these are real processes and powerful processes in human behavior. Unhappily, as we have seen, functionalists have too often been unwilling to leave matters as they properly are. Stung by criticisms that functionalism possesses no theory of, no recognition of, change, functional theorists in all areas of the social sciences have tried to construct a theory of change out of the materials of their social systems. And this, as I have tried to make evident, simply will not do.

A more correct view of the matter is that social *change*, by the very nature of the social reality so well illuminated by functionalists in their empirical studies of social stability and fixity (I overlook the functionalists' *theoretical* use of these illuminations) is inextricably involved in the *historical* processes of event and external impact rather than the assumed processes of immanent developmentalism.

Is change directional? Beyond being able to specify the character of the *differentness* that prevails between the earlier and later conditions of whatever it is that has changed, it would not appear possible to find in historical circumstance the kinds of linear directionality so prized by the theory of social evolution. The late H. A. L. Fisher, distinguished and erudite historian, wrote of his lifelong study of European history: "One intellectual excitement has . . . been denied me. Men wiser and more learned than I have discovered in history a plot, a rhythm, a predetermined pattern. These harmonies are concealed from me. I can see only one emergency following upon another, as wave follows upon wave, only one great fact with respect to which, since it is unique, there can be no generalizations . . . the play of the contingent and the unforeseen." [38]

I would not myself draw from this statement any conclusion that history is therefore unamenable to scientific study, that a scientific study of change is impossible. And I doubt that Professor Fisher did. But the conclusion one may properly draw is that, philosophers of history and social evolutionists to the contrary, long-run directionality tends to be in the beholder's eye, not in the materials themselves.

Fascination with directionality, we saw, arose with Greek interest in the growth of things. Plainly, growth has direction that is inseparable from the type of change that is growth. Anything that grows does indeed possess directionality, and it was, of course, on the basis of the historic assumption of growth in social structures and institutions that the philosophers of social evolution, from Aristotle on, constructed the trends for which they are known. Whether Aristotle on the state, Marx on the means of production, Comte on knowledge, or Morgan on the idea of the family, each philosopher derived direction from what he deemed to be the character of the entity itself.

But here as with the other attributes of developmentalism we have so far considered, the validity of directionality of change depends upon the type of reality it is related to. When we deal with the social behavior of a given area we are, it seems clear, in much the same position that the historian Fisher found himself in with respect to Europe. Patterns, rhythms, trends, are inescapably subjective. There is no inherent relation to the data. However persuasive a given "direction" may be to our acquired interests or values, it has no independent or objective validity. A mind as profound as Marx's could see intensification of classes and class struggle as the trend of European history. A mind as profound as Tocqueville's could see the disappearance of classes and class struggle. Durkheim, in his first major work, declared the development of social solidarity to be from the "mechanical" to the "organic." But irrespective of the precise meaning we ascribe to each of these terms there would appear to be no great difficulty in substantiating the reverse trend. Herbert Spencer saw the direction of all development in the universe, physical and social alike, as being from the homogeneous to the heterogeneous. So persuasive today is the idea of differentiation of growth that, as we have noted, it is even applied to a seventy-year period in the economic and social history of modern England—where, quite evidently, it fails of substantiation. The reason is clear. Spencer saw differentiation as a trend in the growth of—things that grow! Or are assumed to grow! But when we look at the actual social behavior of an area, we see not growth but history; history that refuses to be cut to Procrustean beds. Parsons sees the direction of change in terms of several ends, all drawn from values which happen today to be central in Western society.[39] But substantiation, as we have seen, rests upon use of the Comparative Method, in which, not actual comparison but ranking prevails, ranking in terms of a logico-spatial series. That a *logical* order is revealed is not here in dispute. What is in dispute is whether a logical order, so revealed, has any relevance to *direc-*

tionality of change. The model of Western Europe and its seeming direction of social change during the past half-dozen centuries —*Gemeinschaft* to *Gesellschaft* is, of course, the most popular of directions claimed by sociologists—is made the trend of social change for all human civilization and, as countless studies of the so-called modernizing nations suggest, the stereotype for their individual analysis—and also their reconstruction! [40]

It is the assumed directionality of social change that accounts for the widespread confusion today between scientific prediction and prophecy. In science, to predict means simply to be able, on the basis of either deductive reason or comparative empirical observation, to supply a missing variable. If we know that under a specified condition, elements A, B, C, and D recurrently go together, with element D commonly appearing somewhat later in time than the others, and if we find elements A, B, and C present under the specified condition, we are justified in predicting that element D (which may be violence, crime, a fire, a war) will appear unless measures are taken to prevent it. But what is crucial here is, quite plainly, not time, not linkages of events or changes, but simply a causal association of elements; an association that repeated observation and rigorous reason prove is beyond the merely fortuitous.

Prediction is indeed the highest aim of a science, for to predict is to confirm that analysis has been sound. But prediction is not the same as prophecy, which is quite literally "to look into the future as far as one can see." It was prophecy, not prediction in the scientific sense of this word, that Comte employed, having ascertained to his own satisfaction the direction of all human development, when he foretold the society he described in such lush and occasionally ludicrous detail in his *The Positive Polity*. And it was prophecy, not prediction, when Marx foretold the demise of capitalism and its replacement by socialism. True, there are naïve, untutored, or merely superstitious prophecies, and there are prophecies based upon shrewd insight, upon profound intuition— prophecies which sometimes show themselves by later events to have been extraordinarily well founded in shrewdness and intuition.

But unless there is in fact the kind of natural, rooted directionality of change in a society or institution that is so evident in organic growth, prophecy, rather than prediction, must be the character of all efforts to foretell the future. These efforts today are to be found in abundance among us and, given the array of computers that lends the guise of quantitative rigor, they will become ever more abundant. (I am prophesying here, not predicting!) In the act of prophesying in time there is undoubtedly the same metaphoric-integrative function that can be found, as I have stressed, in metaphysical-political emphases on the internal character of change. A civilization that did not have prophets, in both the moral and temporal senses of this word, would no doubt be as bereft as if it did not have magicians. There is, on the evidence, as pervasive a need in modern populations to believe in magic and in charisma as in ancient or in primitive populations. Both serve to meet those uncertainties of life which, in whatever form they manifest themselves, will presumably always be with us. The art of temporal prophecy also serves in this wise. But prophecy should not, anymore than magic or charisma, be confused with scientific or pragmatic reason. After all, as Malinowski has emphasized for us, primitive man did not confuse them.

To go back once more to directionality as claimed process, there is certainly no doubt that two ages which are separated by a substantial period of time within a common area reveal *differentness*. It may indeed be possible to contrast the twentieth century with the twelfth in terms of the familiar *logical* continuum of *Gemeinschaft* and *Gesellschaft*, which we find in one form or other in all of the major sociologists. But differentness does not argue the existence of a uniting *process*, endemic, constitutive, genetic, and uniform, called differentiation.

Continuity and discontinuity. That change is continuous, in the genetic sense of growth, is, plainly, one of the more sacred principles of Western social thought. Without the crucial assumption of continuity of change, all laws, all principles, all cycles and trajectories would be valueless, in the judgment of every philosopher of social growth from Aristotle to Marx, and from Marx to the latest functionalist or neo-evolutionist in our day. Either change is cumulative, with small changes becoming larger changes, with the merely latent becoming the actual and the manifest, or else a genuine science of change is impossible. So declared the social evolutionists. Not even for Marx, philosopher of revolution, did nature, that is, social nature, make leaps. And, as we observed, the endorsement that Darwin gave—needlessly gave, in the judgment of such followers as even Huxley—to the Leibnizian principle of continuity was all that was necessary to give it the sacrosanct status that it enjoys throughout the social sciences today.

When we look at the actual history of any area, however, or the actual history of any institutionalized, persisting, form of social behavior, we no more find continuity of change than we do such claimed properties as immanence and directionality. And for precisely the same reason! It is needless to do more than briefly restate here what has already been referred to in several contexts: *There is no historical evidence that macro-changes in time are the cumulative results of small-scale, linear micro-changes.* There are those who regard such a statement, such a denial of historical continuity, as the virtual abdication of reason, for, so it is asserted, any rejection of the continuity of history is a necessary rejection of real causality and of the utility of history itself. But causality, as this word is used today in scientific discourse, and as it has been known since at least the works of Hume, has no more to do with the continuity of history than with its discontinuity. Causality as a principle says no more than that for every effect there is a cause. It does not declare that causes and effects are strung out in time in the fashion of the "begats" of the Old Testament.

One of the reasons for the widespread *sense* of the continuity of history (apart from the sheer historic hold of metaphor on our minds) is the ease with which continuity is confused with mere persistence. That things continue in time, persist, hold stable, is not to be doubted. Given such persistence, changes, however far apart, however random, discrete, and disconnected they may be in themselves, are nonetheless given the semblance of a continuity by the persisting identity itself—by the persisting kinship system, social class, religion, or whatever it may be. But, as a moment's reflection tells us, there is no continuity of *change* here; only continuity in the sense of persistence, punctuated, however, by the changes which occur from time to time.

There is also, plainly enough, *logical* or *classificatory* continuity. But the fact that phenomena may be arranged, without gaps in logical continuity, into some systematic hierarchy does not, in itself, argue for the continuity of change. This, as we have seen, was the most fundamental error of the whole mode of reasoning about change that is associated with the Comparative Method. The continuity of *change* was deduced from the logical continuity of instances in a classificatory series. Even that redoubtable opponent of evolutionism, the late Robert Lowie, could not resist, as I noted above, making out a case for the principle of continuity, "vindicating" it, as he declared. And he constructed his case precisely in terms of the arrangement of ethnographic materials that is the real substance of the evolutionary Comparative Method. So, at the present time, does Professor Parsons seek to demonstrate continuity of change by what he calls "filling in the gaps" of continuity in the classificatory system that is the Comparative Method.[41]

But neither continuity in the sense of persistence nor continuity of classificatory series is continuity of *change*. Much of the support for the assumption of continuity of change rests upon use of constructed systems such as evolutionary universals. Once we assume the existential reality of any "evolutionary universal," it is child's play to arrange data in a classification that is as continuous as it is symmetrical.

To the above-mentioned bases of the principle of continuity I should add one more: the continuity of time. As the distinguished cultural historian, Siegfried Kracauer, observed: "Chronological time is a homogeneous medium which indiscriminately comprises all events imaginable." And, let us add, all changes, all differences, all similarities, imaginable. Under "the spell of the homogeneity and irreversible direction of chronological time," continued Kracauer, "we tend to focus on what we believe to be more or less continuous sequences of events and to follow their course through the centuries."

But, Kracauer concluded, "we are not justified in identifying history as a process in homogeneous chronological time. Actually history consists of events whose chronology tells us but little about their relationships and meanings. Since simultaneous events are more often than not intrinsically asynchronous, it makes no sense indeed to conceive of the historical process as a homogeneous flow. *The image of that flow only veils the divergent times in which substantial sequences of historical events materialize.*" (Italics added.) [42]

As one thinks about it, the notion of continuity is rather amusing when applied to the historical record of any given area, for the record itself—I am now referring to the documentary record—tends overwhelmingly to be filled with events and changes which were recorded in the first place because of their very *lack* of "continuity," their break with the routine and persisting.

The cardinal maxim of the social evolutionists and of Darwinian biological evolutionists, too, was the Leibnizian principle: Nature never makes leaps. Today, in biology and other spheres of the physical sciences, it has been made clear that nature does indeed make leaps. Accounts of discontinuities and of random events are, it must be confessed, more frequent in contemporary genetics than in contemporary social science, where the principle of continuity holds a degree of prestige that one would have to go back to Darwin to find equaled in biology.

The real objection is not so much to continuity in the sense of the linear series, with gaps filled by cultures and cultural traits wherever a gap seems to exist. The real objection is to *genetic continuity*: to the fixed notion within the conventional wisdom of social science that one change necessarily engenders another, that one "stage" of developmental change *produces* the next stage, just as one stage of growth does in the organism.

There is not the slightest empirical evidence for this when we confine attention to the concrete area and to finite time. There are certainly changes over a period of time and they may certainly be arrayed in linear fashion. But from this to the next conceptual step, *genetic continuity*, is one that has been more often taken in the dark than in the full light of empirical study. That all changes have conditions, have contexts and sources, is not, of course, in dispute. That the study of such conditions, contexts, and sources is the proper business of social science is not in dispute either. What is in dispute is simply the assumption, drawn first by the Greeks under the influence of the doctrine of *physis*, that the task of the student of change is that of discovering genetic linkages of change. But there aren't any—except in our retrospective imaginations. All that holds true of the relation of event and change makes the fact of *dis*continuity in change paramount.

Durkheim wrote tellingly on this point. Admittedly, Durkheim was at first an evolutionist, and then a neo-evolutionist in the successive episodes of his life's work. But this notwithstanding, in his notable *The Rules of Sociological Method* we find a treatment of the study of change that goes right to the heart of the matter of continuity. It is one of the most trenchant criticisms of developmental, genetic continuity to be found anywhere in the literature of social science.[43]

We find the sources of social change, Durkheim tells us, in the *social milieu*, in the assembled circumstances and conditions and events which form the time and place within which the specified change has taken place. The social milieu is our point of departure, and it remains our effective context of investigation. All the data necessary to account for the change are to be found in the social milieu. Granted that this milieu is itself a consequence of history—of varied processes of persistence, stabilization, as well as of the impacts and intrusions of changes in the past—the social milieu is nonetheless the context of the study of any given change.

What we must not do, Durkheim declared, is try to derive the change in question from some preceding change and it from a change still earlier, and so on. "The antecedent state does not produce the subsequent one, but the relation between them is exclusively chronological." [44] Now the really fundamental point of this is not the conclusion Durkheim immediately draws: that "all scientific prevision is impossible." It is the distinguishable one that all *genetic derivation* is impossible. It is not impossible to find conditions and also causes of change. What is impossible is to fix causality into the linear succession of events and changes with which the historian or social scientist deals. For, as Durkheim makes very plain, it is the social milieu, not the antecedent change in a linear succession, that is the background of the causes. "*The stages that humanity successively traverses do not engender one another.*" [45] (Italics added.) In that one brief statement is the crux of the matter. Whether for mankind as a whole or for some smaller and more empirical pattern of behavior, the distinction between mere succession and causal continuity is a vital one.

The idea of continuity as an explanatory concept has by no means been limited to the developmental tradition in Western thought. Different as this tradition is from historiography, the two traditions nonetheless have in common the assumption of genetic continuity. For many centuries historians have dealt with the past as a "seamless web," to use a favorite phrase. To see events as begetting events in unbroken genealogy has been, for the historian, an enterprise comparable to the social evolutionist's envisagement of changes begetting changes. Siegfried Kracauer, whom I quoted above, noted in this connection: "What the philosophers impose from above, the historians try to achieve from below." [46] That is, historians try to picture historical reality as a seamless web of events, motives, actions, and thoughts.

One of the most striking characteristics of the present generation of historians is, however, its critical re-examination of the doctrine of continuity. The doctrine of continuity, writes the English historian, Geoffrey Barraclough, "is serviceable, provided it is not pressed too far. . . ." It is one thing, Barraclough notes, to remain aware of the persisting and the continuing in the historical scene. It is something else to pass from this to a belief in the "central fallacy of historicism," that continuity is "the most conspicuous feature of history." More and more historians, Barraclough observes of his contemporaries today, find themselves feeling

> renewed sympathy with all those historians who . . . have been more impressed by the cataclysmic than by the continuous in human affairs.
>
> Nor is it easy, any longer, to believe that the "nature of anything is entirely comprehended in its development." This plausible view leaves too little room for the impact of the fortuitous and the unforeseen, for the new, the dynamic and the revolutionary, which breaks through . . . untrammeled by the past at every great turning point in history.[47]

We find the same doubts of causal continuity in time in the masterful article on historiography written for the *International Encyclopedia of Social Sciences* by the American historian, J. H. Hexter. Professor Hexter uses the ingenious and charming illustration of the succession of events in 1951 by which the New York Giants, rather than the Brooklyn Dodgers, won the National League pennant after a down-to-the-wire race in which the Giants overcame a thirteen game deficit within the final month and a half of the season. Here, beyond doubt, is drama. Here also is history—in just as sure a sense as if we were dealing with Germany and Russia, or America and Britain, in the realm of international politics. And here also is as well-documented a succession of happenings as one would be likely to find anywhere. For no one else handles records with the scrupulous, not to say worshipful, care of baseball statisticians and sports writers.

Here, if anywhere, given the day-by-day succession of acts and events so well recorded, continuity, in the sense of implicit causal relatedness, should be found. Alas, it cannot be found. Neither by Professor Hexter himself nor by the reader of his account, which is not lacking in the charts and graphs and all the other quantitative data which are so favored in the social sciences.

The materials and problems presented by this single set of events, culminating in a Giant victory after the famous play-off, make it clear, writes Hexter, "that offering an answer in the form of a narrative explanation which is structurally determined by the logic of causal ascription is not an appropriate response to the difficulties or an adequate solution to them. *Within the bounds of the logic of causal ascription there is no solution.*" [48] (Italics added.)

Does such a conclusion mean that useful explanations cannot therefore be found by the historian or social scientist? Certainly not. It means only that we dare not confuse a proposition by which we *account* for an aspect of reality with the nature of reality. This was David Hume's famous point about causality in general and human history specifically. And this was Émile Durkheim's point about so-called genetic change in society. Continuity of change lies in our constructions; not in history.

Is there necessity in change? I will be very brief here, for the essence of the answer has been given in the preceding sections. Plainly, there is no necessity in any pattern of change if our attention is fixed, not upon the wholes and universals of social evolutionary theoretical interest, but instead upon the social behavior of human beings in time and place. Marx saw necessity in the successive phases of the development of the means of production, stating explicitly that other nations could look to England for their own future, and adding that no nation could be expected to clear its necessary stages of development. This, however, was a utilization of the idea of social evolution that most of the social evolutionists stayed carefully away from. And, witnessing the rather ludicrous efforts of Marxists since to make the Marxian theory of social development apply to this area or that, they stayed away with the best of reason! Other social evolutionists of the century were more careful. When Lewis Morgan referred to the development of family, government, and property, in the specific succession of stages which he described as both natural and *necessary*, he was referring solely to the "idea" of each of these. It is natural and necessary that the *idea of the family* proceed from Consanguine to Punaluan to Monogamian to the Syndiasmian and to the Modern stage. It is natural and necessary, Morgan makes emphatic, because of the way in which the different types of family-system to be found in the world may be logically arranged. The necessity lies only in the abstract system that is Morgan's "idea of the family." Would Morgan have suggested that necessity lay in the concrete history of the family for any given locality or period of time? If so, there is no evidence of it; and it is highly unlikely that he would have even thought in these terms, for he was not interested, as an evolutionist, in such matters. He was interested solely in what could be deduced about the nature of development from the logico-spatial framework of the Comparative Method.

Today there is much less said in social theory about "necessity" than there is about "irreversibility," which is closely related. So, let us ask, are there sequences of change which may be labeled "irreversible" in any approximation of the sense of this word when it is applied to organic growth, or to physical processes in the universe? Any affirmative answer would seem dubious in the study of social behavior. As with the metaphor of growth itself, the utility of any concept of irreversibility applied to human society would appear to be in direct proportion to the size and abstractness of subject matter. Granted that there are very real elements of contemporary science and technology which would be unintelligible save in terms of certain historically prior achievements which formed the "necessary" base of these elements, we are still far from anything that might properly be called an *irreversible process of change*. In the conceptual world of the social evolutionist there were indeed sequences of change as irreversible, by definition, as they were natural and necessary. The Law of Three States was, for Comte, an irreversible law. The Marxian law of motion by which society was seen as moving from slavery through feudalism to capitalism to socialism was, obviously, an irreversible law. Both Comte and Marx were, however, dealing with constructed systems, with universals, not with social behavior in specified historical areas.

Efforts to convert from the one to the other, as by Communist "theoreticians" in the Russia of 1917, have a faintly comic note. When it became clear that the long-awaited revolution, through which socialism would be inaugurated, was to take place not in a country of "developed" or "mature" capitalism but in a country which was, by Marxist definition, still generally feudal, theoretical necessity called for quick response. Out of Marxist disputation came Trotsky's ponderous *Law of Combined Development* through which two stages could be had, so to speak, for the price of one! Faintly comic it may be, but hardly a matter for astonishment. If Marxist dogmatics could then, as it still does today, achieve the intellectual feat of making the Revolution of 1917 the outcome of forces internal to Russia, forces contained indeed within the "womb" of Russian feudalism, so called, and thereby omitting most of what non-Marxist historians feel compelled by the evidence to regard as central, no great difficulty should attach to laws of combined or even re-combined development. Cutting to the requirements of Procrustean beds has ever been the vocation of those who seek to transfer laws of development to the historical scene.

In sum, let us say simply that in the realm of social behavior in historical time there appear to be no changes or processes of change which could properly answer to the requirements of the concept of irreversibility.

Uniformitarianism. Given the persisting character of human beings—physiological and psychological—and the persisting requirements of a social organization, there are undoubted uniformities of behavior and interaction. More doubtful is the degree to which such uniformities throw light on the problem of change in time. Constants are ordinarily of little help in accounting for variables. Comte thought that the uniform instinct for bettering one's condition was sufficient to explain mankind's progressive development. Kant thought it was the "unsocial sociability" of the human species that was the fixed and persisting cause. Marx and Engels saw class struggle as the endemic process by which mankind has been moved forward. The conventional wisdom of much social theory today is still occupied by the tensions, imbalances, unfilled needs, dysfunctions, and conflicts which, it is said, exist naturally and uniformly in social structures and social systems and thus provide the motive force for change in time. Uniformitarianism, in short, still has much appeal to social theory at least.

Interestingly, it does not have such appeal today in those realms —geology and biology—where, in the nineteenth century, under the impress of such names as Lyell and Darwin, it achieved its highest glory. Lyell, as we have seen, drawing from the great Hutton, believed that a *science* of geology had no alternative but to rest upon the premise that "the present is the key to the past." Even Lyell, however, did not go as far as Darwin did in dedication to the principle of uniform process in accounting for the countless changes by which the species in their present form have come into existence.

Today the principle has little more than historical or antiquarian interest in a field such as geology. Plainly, the contemporary science of geology does not rest, Sir Charles Lyell's views notwithstanding, on the notion that the past is contained in the present, that the present is the key to the past—however it is phrased. Every beginning student of geology knows that to account for the configuration of the earth's surface it is necessary to go beyond processes operating timelessly and uniformly throughout all geological time and to take into consideration events of sometimes cataclysmic proportion; events which are different only in their content from the events that are bound up in the historical study of social behavior.

As the geologist Nelson Goodman has put the matter, the principle of uniformity served valuably in its day to help put to rest the idea that all geological change was the consequence of specific interventions by God. For this it must be honored. But, Goodman goes on, the principle of uniformity must not be confused with the principle of simplicity of theory. We all prize simplicity and compactness of theory, not because we think nature is simple and compact, as did the eighteenth-century natural historians, but because for rhetorical reasons alone a theory that is simple is preferable to a complex one, *only provided the simple theory accounts for the data involved.*[49] Uniformitarianism, in the form set forth by Lyell and Darwin, does not account for the kind of data with which geology and biology alike deal.

No more do uniformitarian concepts aid appreciably in the

study of social change. Again let us emphasize that there can be no doubt of the existence of uniform processes wherever human beings interact with one another. Greed, lust, ambition, covetousness, like love, altruism, charity, and compassion have always been with us in one degree or other. So have the functionalist's prized tensions and conflicts and processes of disequilibrium. They are not unlike such processes in geology as erosion. They are assuredly real, they cannot help but have some effect upon the shape of things. But to try to make them serve, as Lyell and Darwin once tried to make such uniform processes do in their disciplines, as the principal causes of change in time is, it would seem evident, at least as futile as such processes are today deemed to be in geology and biology.

Not surprisingly, the stronghold of uniformitarianism in the social sciences lies in the efforts—of ethnologists chiefly—to deduce patterns of change in the past from ongoing processes in preliterate cultures. After all, the historical record for such cultures goes back but a very short time, and it is often of little worth even for the short time in which there is a record. What alternative, then, is there to the traditional practice of trying to infer social change in time from the continuity of the structural pattern of goals, motivations, and tensions which is to be found in the present? What Raymond Firth writes on this matter is highly pertinent:

> The social anthropoligist is faced by a constant problem, an apparent dilemma—to account for this continuity, and at the same time to account for social change. Continuity is expressed in the social structure, the sets of relations which make for firmness of expectation, for validation of past experience in terms of similar experience in the future. . . . At the same time there must be room for variance and for the explanation of variance.
> *This is found in the social organization, the systematic ordering of social relations by acts of choice and decision.* . . . In the aspect of social structure is to be found the continuity principle of society; in the aspect of organization is to be found *the variation or change principle—by allowing evaluation of situations and entry of individual choice.*[50]

Elsewhere Professor Firth tells us that "the dynamic picture" demands our recognition that the "operation of a social system, however simple, involves continual tendencies to change." [51] Or, more accurately, the *assumption* of such continual tendencies of change. But of the empirical existence of such tendencies—that is, uniform, cumulative tendencies—apart from the impact of historical events we are given not the slightest hint. Professor Firth is certainly aware of the presumptive character of what he writes regarding uniform processes. Writing of the field anthropologist, he says:

> He usually sees his community for only a year or two at a time. Rarely does he return later to measure interim changes. He lacks the long series of documents which give the historian a sequence of contemporary or near-contemporary pictures of events. So, to give depth to his analysis, the anthropologist has to make many assumptions. He relies upon ideas about social homogeneity or the continuity of the social process, or about the historical meaning of traditions. Sometimes he translates differences in contemporary social conditions in related communities into differences in stage of development. He turns space into time. He can fairly assume something about the continuity of the society he studies—he knows it will not vanish like a fairy castle when he leaves. *But what he assumes about the past and what he estimates about the future will depend very much on his theories about the nature of society in general.*[52] (Italics added in all the quoted passages.)

Exactly. No one could possibly fault Professor Firth, it would seem, in what he has told us about the difficulties of studying nonliterate cultures. What alternative is there to assumption, deduction, and presumption when it comes to matters of social change over long periods in such cultures? Obviously, none.

Let us, however, note two points in passing. First, whatever the necessity of dependence upon such uniform processes when the problem is that of accounting for long-term change in the absence of records, the evidence is very clear that when social anthropologists deal with processes of change in preliterate cultures *within historical time*—as, for example, in the now multitudinous studies of the impact of Western civilization during the past century or so upon native cultures of the world—they emerge with processes of change, with causes and conditions, which bear little relation to those of the kind Professor Firth has just detailed for us.

Second, while clearly there is no alternative to use of "the present is the key to the past" principle when the subject is a pre-literate culture, it hardly follows that the conclusions so derived should become—as they so plainly have in much contemporary social theory—a part of the theory by which we seek to account for change in peoples which *do* have historical records. Over and over in what I have called the conventional wisdom of the theory of change, we find utilizations of concepts derived from study of peoples without historical record. There is nothing wrong with this when our objective is that of understanding mechanisms of order and stability. But of change? Offhand it would make more sense, I cannot help thinking, to reverse the process, and to carry what we have learned about the processes of change in historical peoples to study of the preliterate or non-historical peoples.

This, however, is rarely done; the reasons proffered being commonly that historical records are concerned only with "unique events" and hence not subject, it is thought, to theoretical assimilation, and, second, that in the simple cultures we have easier and more objective opportunities of study.

Let me conclude this section by reference to that area of cultural reality most often used as a model by those whose search is for uniform mechanisms of change in social organization. I am referring to language. Here, for example, is the anthropologist George Murdock, whom we noted above in terms of contemporary functionalist theory: "The forms and structure of language are known to constitute a relatively independent body within culture as a whole, changing according to a dynamics of their own in response to causative factors that are exceedingly difficult to relate to social events or the environing culture itself." [53] Murdock, as we saw above, is convinced that social organization is also a semi-independent system "comparable in many respects to language and similarly characterized by an internal dynamics of its own."

To be sure, social organization is not quite the closed system that language is, writes Murdock, and it does change in response to external events. Nonetheless, the model of language is an imposing one, and one is left with the clear impression that, for this distinguished functional theorist, the proper study of social organization is along the same line that has been followed by philology.

But *is* language so difficult to relate to social events, to historical intrusions? Granted that there are internal and persisting—that is, uniform—processes at work in language. To deny it would be to fly in the face of a philological tradition that stretches from eighteenth-century natural histories of language down to the remarkable works of Noam Chomsky and others in our own day. What is described in, say, Grimm's Law of consonant shift is assuredly change: it is change of a degree of substantive reality, let it be conceded immediately, rarely found in the so-called comparative studies of social evolutionists. There are clearly processes of modification at work in language without manifest relation to external events; processes which would appear to have a higher degree of "autonomy" and, therefore, uniformity than what is yielded by explorations of kinship, religion, political behavior, and the like.

Even in language, however, such processes are far from the whole story. If we deal with language, not as a system of vowels, consonants, and other "atoms" in their numberless patterns, but rather in the same terms in which we have been considering other forms of behavior in this section, we gain a picture that is anything but free of the effects of historical events. If we consider a specified language in time in a given area we find that it reveals much the same properties that are to be found when the subject is religion, kinship, or any other institution: long periods of relative persistence of form; processes of very minor modification; and, rarely, bursts of extraordinary change directly relatable to the impacts of external events.

Consider the English language—or, more precisely, the language spoken as the common language in England during the past one thousand years. Could all that we now know, or might ever know about the structure of language and its uniform, endemic processes ever be sufficient to account for the totality of changes which have taken place in the spoken language during this long period? Plainly not. How, for example, could we hope to understand the source of the greatest single change that took place during this thousand-year period: the shift from Anglo-Saxon to the amalgam of Anglo-Saxon and Norman French that became the base of the language as written and spoken by Chaucer? We could never explain it if we excluded the Conquest in 1066. And if we seek to account for the changes that took place between Chaucer's time and our own time we shall find, of course, that historical events, impacts from areas outside language as such, not to emphasize the immense influence of a few writers such as Shakespeare, Milton, and the authors of the King James version of the English Bible, all had vital and indispensable influence.

There is no need to press the point. No philologist would dispute it. Quite evidently, in the example just given, a different kind of question is involved from any of those dealt with in the areas of philology where language is considered to be, much as the eighteenth-century considered it and every other institution, an autonomous, natural system with its own processes of growth in time. Not being a philologist I will not stop to do more than wonder whether the two types of question pertaining to change have the same uneasy relation in philology they so plainly do in social theory. Language is, in any event, by its unique nature a rather deceptive model for those seeking to account for change in such institutions as religion, kinship, social class, and politics.

Here, obviously, we turn to history and only to history if what we are seeking are the actual causes, sources, and conditions of overt change of patterns and structures in society. Conventional wisdom to the contrary in modern social theory, we shall not find the explanation of change in those studies which are abstracted from history: whether these be studies of small groups in the social laboratory, group dynamics generally, staged experiments in social interaction, or mathematical analyses of so-called social systems. Nor will we find the sources of change in contemporary revivals of the Comparative Method with its ascending staircase of cultural similarities and differences plucked from all space and time. For, as we have seen, the Comparative Method has little actual comparison in it and no change whatsoever. Nor will we gain insight into social change by spurious utilization of concepts drawn from contemporary biology—concepts such as differentiation, adaptation, and selection—for whatever may be their explanatory utility in biology they have nothing but further descriptiveness to offer in the social sciences.

Above all, we shall not find the sources of change in society through efforts which seek to deduce it as a fixed property of social structures. Change can no more be deduced from social structure and its processes than these latter can be deduced from the elements of human psychology. Despite the quest for a unified theory of change that has been going on for some twenty-five hundred years now in Western thought—which Professor Parsons has succinctly described as a quest for a theory *"equally* applicable to the problems of change and to those of process within a stabilized system"[54]—it appears to be, on the evidence, as vain as the quest for perpetual youth or for the means of transmuting base metals into gold. Between the study of *change*—in stark contrast to the mere motions, movements, actions, and interactions which are so commonly confused with change—and *history* there is quite evidently an unbreakable relationship, when we come down from the empyrean heights of abstractions, wholes, and universals. True, history means *events* such as the Conquest, *dates* such as 1066, *individuals* such as William, and *areas* such as England. And these are not likely to be assimilated into the categories of a social theory seeking to derive change from social structures and their uniform processes. The language of history admittedly is not to be converted into the language of developmentalism with its hoary concepts and premises of immanence, continuity, directionality, necessity, and uniformitarianism.[55]

Generalization is beyond question what we seek from the empirical and concrete. But it is generalization *from* the empirical, the concrete, and the historical; not generalization achieved through their dismissal; not generalization drawn from metaphor and analogy. Whatever the demands of a social theory, the first demands to be served are those of the social reality we find alone in the historical record. All else is surely secondary.

NOTES AND REFERENCES

INTRODUCTION

1. *Metaphor and Reality* (Bloomington: Indiana University Press, 1962), p. 71. The quotation from Stevens is in this work.
2. *English Prose Style* (New York: Pantheon Books, 1952), p. 23.
3. *The Tacit Dimension* (New York: Doubleday, 1966).

CHAPTER 1. THE GREEKS

1. *The University of California Chronicle*, Vol. 16, No. 4.
2. I have used the Hugh G. Evelyn-White translation in *Homeric Hymns and Homerica* (Cambridge: Harvard University Press, 1914), pp. 289–325.
3. *The Golden Bough*, 1 vol. abridged ed. (New York: The Macmillan Co., 1940), p. 398 and ch. 44, "Demeter and Persephone."
4. W. K. C. Guthrie, *In the Beginning: Some Greek Views on the Origins of Life and the Early State of Man* (Ithaca: Cornell University Press, 1957), pp. 15, 16.
5. S. Sambursky, *Physical World of the Greeks*, tr. by Merton Dagut (New York: Macmillan, 1956), pp. 241–2.
6. F. M. Cornford, *Principium Sapientiae: The Origins of Greek Philosophical Thought* (Cambridge: Cambridge University Press, 1952), pp. 179–81 *passim*. "If we would understand the sixth-century philosophers," Cornford writes, "we must disabuse our minds of the atomistic conception of dead matter in mechanical motion and of the Cartesian dualism of matter and mind." *Physis*, Cornford emphasizes, was the transition between motion conceived primitively as sexual generation and motion conceived as growth.
7. "The Background of Greek Science," as cited, p. 17.
8. *Ibid.*
9. *Aristotle's Metaphysics*, Translated with Commentaries and Glossaries by Hippocrates G. Apostle (Bloomington: Indiana University Press, 1966), p. 77.
10. *Aristotle's Politics*, tr. by Benjamin Jowett (Oxford: At the Clarendon Press, 1923), Bk. 1 *passim*.
11. A. E. Taylor, *Elements of Metaphysics* (London: Methuen & Co., 1903), p. 266.

12. Theodor Gomperz, *Greek Thinkers, A History of Ancient Philosophers* (London: John Murray, 1901), I, 141.

13. For one fascinating account of these influences, see Mircea Eliade, *Cosmos and History: The Myth of the Eternal Return* (Harper Torchbooks, The Bollingen Library, 1954). See especially chs. 2 and 3. See also Guthrie, as cited, ch. 4.

14. I draw this distinction between history and development from Frederick J. Teggart, *Theory of History* (New Haven: Yale University Press, 1925). Application of the distinction to the specific theory of classical cycles is, however, mine alone. See also Arnaldo Momigliano, "Time in Ancient Historiography" in *History and the Concept of Time* (Wesleyan University Press, 1966), pp. 1–23. Although Dr. Momigliano does not deal with the distinction I am here making, he does reinforce the view that the doctrine of cycles in Greek thought had nothing to do with historiography.

15. *The History of the Peloponnesian War*, I, 22.

16. Quoted in Gomperz, as cited, p. 140.

17. My discussion and the specific quotations are drawn from W. R. Paton's translation in The Loeb Classical Library edition (London, 1923) of Polybius's *Histories*.

18. *Works and Days* in *Homeric Hymns and Homerica*, as cited, pp. 3–65. Hesiod's account of the five ages or races is contained in lines 110–200. The quotation immediately following, in which Hesiod expresses his wish to have been born earlier or later, is to be found in lines 175–80 in Hesiod's text.

19. *The Dialogues of Plato*, tr. by Benjamin Jowett, 4th ed. (Oxford: At the Clarendon Press, 1953), III, 480–81, ll. 269, c and d.

20. *Ibid.* For *The Statesman* see III, 482–3, ll. 271–2 of text; for *The Laws* see IV, 245–6, ll. 678 ff. of text.

21. Aristotle, *De Caelo*, tr. by J. L. Stocks (Oxford: At the Clarendon Press, 1922), I, 10.

22. *De Generatione et Corruptione*, tr. by H. H. Joachim (Oxford: At the Clarendon Press, 1922), II, 11.

23. *Metaphysics*, as cited, p. 187 (Bk. K, 8 in text).

24. *De Caelo*, as cited, I, 3.

25. *Politics*, as cited, III, 15, 11. Also Book V, especially the opening paragraph where Aristotle announces his treatment of "what elements work ruin in particular states, and out of what, and into what they mostly change."

26. *Meteorologica*, tr. by E. W. Webster (Oxford: At the Clarendon Press, 1923), I, 14.

27. *Meteorologica*, as cited, I, 14.

28. I have used the Cyril Bailey translation of *De Rerum Natura* (Oxford: At the Clarendon Press, 1929). All quotations which follow are taken from it.

29. Lucretius, as cited, Bk. V, ll. 800–836.

30. Lucretius, Bk. I, ll. 208–37.

31. Lucretius, Bk. V, ll. 326–55.

32. Lucretius, Bk. II, ll. 1135–65.

33. *Virgil's Works, The Aeneid, Eclogues, Georgics*, tr. by J. W. Mackail (New York: Random House, 1934), pp. 274.

34. Seneca, *Epistulae Morales*, tr. by Richard M. Gummere (London: The Loeb Classical Library, 1920), sec. 71.

35. *Ibid.*, 71.

36. Seneca, *Quaestiones Naturales*, tr. by John Clark (London: Macmillan, 1910), sec. 29.

37. *The English Language*. Cited by John Lukacs in "The Changing Face of Progress," *The Texas Quarterly*, Winter 1966, p. 8.

38. John Bagnell Bury, *The Idea of Progress* (New York: The Macmillan Company, 1932), p. 19.

39. Hesiod, *Works and Days*, as cited, ll. 110–20.

40. *Ibid.*, ll. 45–55; the companion myth of Pandora is told in ll. 90–105.

41. Plato, *The Laws*, as cited, IV, 246–7, ll. 679 b, c, d, e.

42. *Metamorphoses*, tr. by Frank J. Miller (London: The Loeb Classical Library, 1916), Bk. 1, p. 9, ll. 90–110.

43. I have used Edith Hamilton's beautiful translation in her *Three Greek Plays* (New York: W. W. Norton & Company, 1937), p. 105.

44. *Ibid.*, pp. 115 f.

45. *Works and Days*, as cited, ll. 110–200.

46. *Ibid.*, ll. 175–80. Hesiod tells us that in the very final stage of the race of Iron, within which he himself lives, the race will so degenerate in its senescence that each new-born child will show the marks of old-age. Even today, as I note in Chapter 7, there are writers who, in dealing with ancient ages of decline and decadence, as for example in the final century or two of Rome, imply strongly that Roman physical stock had become as "enfeebled" as Rome's institutions are declared to have been. From Hesiod to the present day, there is a certain fascination with physical as well as social and cultural stigmata of decay in the so-called declining ages of civilizations.

47. Guthrie, as cited, p. 80.

48. *Sophocles: The Seven Plays in English Verse*, tr. by Lewis Camp-

bell (London: Oxford University Press, 1906), pp. 13–14, ll. 332–76.

49. Francis M. Cornford, *Plato's Cosmology* (London: Routledge & Kegan Paul, 1937), p. 24. Plato himself—despite all the modern treatments of Greek thought which declare that Plato's world was a timeless and changeless one—specifically declared that *only* the divine is changeless; that the world of man and society is in incessant process of development and of becoming. I am inclined to agree with the late Arthur O. Lovejoy that more nonsense has been written on Plato, as the result of misunderstanding and misapplication of his theory of ideas, than on any other classical figure. Plato did indeed believe in a realm of timeless essences. Call this his religion or metaphysics. But he was also a sociologist and developmentalist.

50. *The Laws*, as cited, p. 247, l. 680. Most of Book III is taken up with the development of human society from its primitive seed-like beginnings. See also his *Statesman*, as cited, III, 483, ll. 271 and 272. Also *Protagoras*, as cited, I, 145 ff. where, admittedly, much more is given by Plato to the gods and their helpful interventions.

51. Lucretius, as cited, Bk. V, ll. 1412–42; also l. 1453 where he writes that "the experience of the eager mind taught them little by little, as they went forward step by step." The words are Lucretius' but it is impossible to find any Greek or Roman writer on the development of human society who did not see it as a long, slow, and gradual process.

52. See for instance Bk. I, ll. 208–37, 237–66, 296–326; and Bk. V, ll. 837–67. Broadly speaking Lucretius' anthropology is contained in Book V, but anthropology and cosmology interweave throughout, given their unity by Lucretius' developmentalism.

53. Bk. V, ll. 896–925. See also 856 ff.

54. Bk. V, ll. 1165–96.

55. The first quotation is from Bk. V, ll. 1412–42; the second is from ll. 1448–57.

CHAPTER 2. THE CHRISTIANS

1. *The City of God*, tr. by Marcus Dods, with an Introduction by Thomas Merton (The Modern Library, New York: Random House, 1950), Bk. X, 14. Except as otherwise noted, all citations from *The City of God* will be from this edition.

2. Florus, *Epitome Rerum Romanarum*, cited by Frederick J.

Teggart in *The Idea of Progress* (Berkeley: University of California Press, 1929), p. 50.

3. Charles Norris Cochrane, *Christianity and Classical Culture* (Galaxy Book, New York: Oxford University Press, 1957), p. 154.

4. *Ad Demetr. Apol.*, ch. 3. Quoted by Cochrane, as cited, p. 155.

5. *The City of God*, XII, 14.

6. Cited by Herbert A. Deane in *The Political and Social Ideas of St. Augustine* (New York: Columbia University Press, 1963), p. 75.

7. Seneca, *Quaestiones Naturales*, as cited, III, 29.

8. Cited by Deane, *op. cit.*, p. 75.

9. Robert Flint, *The Philosophy of History in Europe* (London: William Blackwood & Sons, 1874), p. 12. See also the distinguished essay "Jerusalem and Athens" by Leo Strauss in *Commentary*, June 1967.

10. "The drowning of the first world, and the repairing that again; the burning of this world, and establishing another in heaven, do not so much strain a man's Reason, as the Creation, a Creation of all out of Nothing" (Sermon XXV). *The Complete Poetry and Selected Prose of John Donne* (The Modern Library, New York: Random House, 1941), p. 471.

11. *The City of God*, XII, 10.

12. *Ibid.*, XII, 12.

13. *Ibid.*, XII, 12.

14. *Ibid.*, XII, 12.

15. *Ibid.*, XII, 13. The quotations immediately following in the text on cycles are all from this section in Augustine.

16. Isaiah Berlin, *Historical Inevitability* (London: Oxford University Press, 1954), p. 14.

17. *The History of Herodotus*, tr. by George Rawlinson (New York: Tudor Publishing Co., 1928), p. 1.

18. Thucydides, as cited, I, 1.

19. Flint, as cited, p. 12.

20. Leo Strauss, "Jerusalem and Athens," as cited, p. 47.

21. *The City of God*, XII, 27. This section begins with the words: "That the *whole plenitude of the human race was embraced in the first man*, and that God there saw the portion of it which was to be honored and rewarded, and that which was to be condemned and punished." (Italics added.)

22. *The City of God*, XII, 14.

23. *The City of God*, Bks. XV–XIX, deals with the events and per-

sonages of mankind's history which Augustine fits into these stages or epochs. The clearest statement of the rationale of his philosophy of history is to be found in an earlier work, *De Genesi contra Manichaeos*, i, 23. See Flint, as cited, p. 20, and Deane, as cited, p. 71.

24. Cochrane, as cited, pp. 479 and 485.
25. Thomas Merton, in his Introduction to *The City of God*, as cited, p. xii.
26. *The City of God*, XV, 1.
27. *Ibid.*, XV, 2.
28. *Ibid.*, XV, 4.
29. *Ibid.*, XV, 5.
30. Thomas Merton, as cited, p. xiii.
31. *The City of God*, XIV, 28.
32. *Ibid.*, XII, 21.
33. *Ibid.*, XII, 21.
34. *Ibid.*, XII, 27.
35. *Ibid.*, XXII, 24.
36. *Ibid.*
37. *Ibid.*
38. *Ibid.*
39. *Ibid.* Lucretius wrote: "Sweet it is, when on the great sea the winds are buffeting the waters, to gaze from the land on another's great struggles; not because it is pleasure or joy that any one should be distressed, but because it is sweet to perceive from what misfortune you yourself are free." Lucretius, as cited, II, ll. 1–5.
40. Quoted by Deane, as cited, pp. 75, 73–74.
41. Deane, p. 71.
42. *The City of God*, XX, 16. That St. Augustine believed the end of the world to be near hardly permits doubt. He was, however, much too shrewd to assign a precise date. "In vain, then, do we attempt to compute definitely the years that may remain to this world, when we may hear from the mouth of the Truth that it is not for us to know. Yet some have said that four hundred, some five hundred, others a thousand years, may be completed from the Ascension of the Lord up to his final coming. . . . But on this subject He puts aside the figures of the calculators, and orders silence, who says, 'It is not for you to know the times, which the Father hath put in His own power'" (XVIII, 53).

43. A. L. Rowse, *The England of Elizabeth: The Structure of Society* (London: The Macmillan Company, 1951).

44. See Richard F. Jones, *Ancients and Moderns: A Study of the Rise of the Scientific Movement in Seventeenth Century England*, 2nd ed. (Berkeley and Los Angeles: The University of California Press, 1961), p. 23.

45. *Ibid.*, p. 22.

46. *Ibid.*, p. 25.

47. *Ibid.*, p. 25.

48. *Ibid.*, p. 26.

49. *Novum Organum*, tr. by R. Ellis and James Spedding (London: George Routledge and Sons, The New Universal Library), pp. 106–8 (Section LXXXIV).

50. *The Essays, Or Counsels, Civil and Moral* (The Home Library, New York: A. L. Burt Company), Essay LVIII, p. 277.

CHAPTER 3. THE MODERNS

1. See Richard F. Jones, *Ancients and Moderns*, as cited, *passim*. See also J. B. Bury, *The Idea of Progress*, as cited, especially chs. 4 and 5. Despite the fact that I have differed in almost every essential way from Bury's main argument with respect to the modern idea of progress, I admire his book. In the half-century since its first publication in England it has probably done more than any other single work to stimulate interest not only in the history of the idea of progress but in the history of ideas generally. For millions of readers Bury's book *is* the idea of progress. And for this it must be honored.

2. Robert K. Merton, *On the Shoulders of Giants* (New York: The Free Press, 1965) deals with this metaphor learnedly and charmingly.

3. Pascal's essay, tr. by Leona Fassett (Neuhaus), may be found in F. J. Teggart, *The Idea of Progress*, as cited above, pp. 105–10.

4. *Ibid.*

5. Fontenelle, "On the Ancients and Moderns," tr. by Leona Fassett (Neuhaus) in Teggart, as cited, p. 117.

6. *Ibid.*, p. 124.

7. Charles Perrault, "A Comparison of the Ancients and Moderns," tr. by Leona Fassett (Neuhaus), in Teggart, as cited, p. 130.

8. Leibniz, *The Monadology and Other Philosophical Writings*, tr. by Robert Latta (Oxford: Oxford University Press, 1898), pp. 350–51.

9. See Bertrand Russell, *A Critical Exposition of the Philosophy of Leibniz* (London: George Allen & Unwin, 1900), p. 222. Also *The Monadology*, as cited, p. 376.

10. *The Monadology*, as cited, p. 419. In his *General Principles* Leibniz wrote: "When I speak of the force and action of created beings, I mean that each created being is pregnant with its future state, and that *it naturally follows a certain course if nothing hinders it.*" (Italics added.) *The Monadology*, p. 44, n. 1. Leibniz, in this passage, seems to have biological organisms alone in mind, but there was nothing to prevent others from applying that powerful thought to *social* organisms, and this in fact is precisely what happened during the next two centuries. The conception of the science of social change as one directed to the study of the course of change that *naturally* occurs in a given entity, when there are no interferences or hindrances, is the conception which underlay not only the philosophy of social progress but the eighteenth century's theory of natural history and the nineteenth century's theory of social evolution. See Chapters 4 and 5 below. It is this perception, perhaps above any other, that highlights Teggart's *Theory of History*. See especially pp. 85 ff.

11. Quoted in Teggart, *The Idea of Progress*, p. 224.

12. *On History*, ed. with an introduction by Lewis White Beck (The Library of Liberal Arts, Indianapolis: Bobbs-Merrill Company, 1963), pp. 11, 21.

13. *Ibid.*, pp. 12–13.

14. *Ibid.*, p. 60.

15. Condorcet, *Sketch for a Historical Picture of the Progress of the Human Mind*, tr. by June Barraclough (London: Weidenfeld and Nicolson, 1955), p. 4.

16. *Ibid.*, p. 9. In the final pages of his book Condorcet writes: "All the causes that contribute to the perfection of the human race, all the means that ensure it must by their very nature exercise a perpetual influence and always increase their sphere of action. The proofs of this we have given and in the great work they will derive additional force from elaboration. We may conclude then that the perfectibility of man is indefinite" (p. 199).

17. Cited in Teggart, *The Idea of Progress*, p. 227.

18. Hegel, *Lectures on the Philosophy of History*, tr. by J. Sibree (London: George Bell and Sons, 1894), p. 82.

19. Comte, *The Positive Philosophy*, tr. by Harriet Martineau (London: George Bell and Sons, 1896), II, 232.

20. Darwin, *The Origin of the Species* (The Modern Library, New York: Random House), pp. 160, 235.

21. Spencer, *Essays Scientific, Political, and Speculative* (New York: D. Appleton and Company, 1891), pp. 60, 9. See also Spencer's *Social Statics*, especially Chapter 2 "The Evanescence of Evil." There he writes: "Progress, therefore, is not an accident, but a necessity. Instead of civilization being artificial, it is a part of nature; all of a piece with the development of the embryo or the unfolding of a flower . . . As surely as the tree becomes bulky when it stands alone, and slender if one of a group . . . so surely must the human faculties be moulded into complete fitness for the social state; so surely must the things we call evil and immorality disappear; so surely must man become perfect."

22. Spencer, *Essays*, as cited, p. 10.

23. Adam Ferguson, *An Essay on the History of Civil Society*, ed. with an Introduction by Duncan Forbes (Edinburgh: University of Edinburgh Press, 1966), pp. 105–6.

24. *Ibid.*, pp. 208–9.

25. See Hume's essay "Of the Populousness of Ancient Nations" in *Essays Moral, Political, and Literary* (London: Ward, Lock, and Tyler, Warwick House, 1870), pp. 222–3.

26. *Ibid.*

27. Cited in Henry Vyverberg, *Historical Pessimism in the French Enlightenment* (Cambridge: Harvard University Press, 1958), p. 181.

28. Constantin François Volney, *The Ruins, or a Survey of the Revolutions of Empires*, 5th ed. (London: Thomas Tegg, 1811), pp. 6–8.

29. On this literature of exoticism, see Hoxie N. Fairchild, *The Noble Savage: A Study in Romantic Naturalism* (New York: Columbia University Press, 1928). Also Gilbert Chinard, *L'Exotisme Américain dans la Littérature Française au XVIe Siècle* (Paris: Hachette et Cie, 1911).

30. See my *The Sociological Tradition* (New York: Basic Books, 1967), especially ch. 7.

31. Cited in *Catholic Political Thought, 1789–1848*, ed. by Bela Menczer (London: Burns Oates, 1952), p. 81.

32. *Ibid.*, p. 82.
33. *The Recollections of Alexis de Tocqueville*, tr. by Alexander Teixeira de Mattos, ed. by J. P. Mayer (London: The Harvill Press, 1948), p. 73.
34. See the forthcoming translation of Sorel's important work by John Stanley (University of California Press, 1969).
35. Timothy Paul Donovan, *Henry Adams and Brooks Adams: The Education of Two American Historians* (Norman: University of Oklahoma Press, 1961), p. 131.
36. *Ibid.*, p. 135.

CHAPTER 4. THE THEORY OF NATURAL HISTORY

1. On this distinctive mode of inquiry see Teggart, *Theory of History*, as cited, pp. 87–90; also Ernest Lee Tuveson, *Millennium and Utopia: A Study in the Background of the Idea of Progress* (Berkeley: University of California Press, 1949), ch. 5; also Gladys Bryson, *Man and Society: The Scottish Inquiry of the Eighteenth Century* (Princeton: Princeton University Press, 1945), *passim.*
2. See John Linton Myres, "The Background of Greek Science," as cited, pp. 22–33. Also Ernest Barker, *Greek Political Theory: Plato and His Predecessors* (London: Methuen & Co., 1918), pp. 53 f.
3. Rousseau, *The Social Contract and Discourses*, tr. with an introduction by G. D. H. Cole (New York: E. P. Dutton and Company, 1950), p. 198.
4. *Ibid.*, p. 198; also 195.
5. *Ibid.*, p. 189.
6. Arthur O. Lovejoy, "The Supposed Primitivism of Rousseau's Discourse on Inequality," *Modern Philology*, XXI, 165–86.
7. Rousseau, as cited, p. 208.
8. *Ibid.*, p. 233. Despite the title, it is really a natural or conjectural history of *equality* that Rousseau wrote. The eruptions of circumstance which in time produced artificial inequality are the "accidents" which all the natural historians of the eighteenth century were only too well aware of.
9. *Ibid.*, pp. 233–4.
10. *Ibid.*, pp. 234–5.
11. *Ibid.*, p. 243.
12. *Ibid.*, p. 244.
13. Adam Smith, *An Inquiry into the Nature and Causes of the*

Wealth of Nations, ed. with an Introduction by Edwin Cannan (The Modern Library, New York: Random House, 1937), p. lvii.

14. *Ibid.,* pp. 13 ff.

15. *Ibid.,* p. 357.

16. *Ibid.,* p. 360.

17. *Ibid.,* p. 360.

18. Adam Ferguson, as cited, p. 81. See W. C. Lehmann, *Adam Ferguson and the Beginnings of Modern Sociology* (New York: Columbia University Press, 1930), especially Chapter 4, "Social Change and Social Continuity." One other work should be mentioned here, also done by one of the Scottish moral philosophers to have great influence on the study of social evolution in the nineteenth century. I refer to John A. Millar, *The Origin of the Distinction of Ranks; or an Inquiry into the Circumstances which Give Rise to Influence and Authority in the Different Members of Society.* It was published in 1771 and may be regarded properly as the first systematic evolutionary study of social stratification. Whereas, as I noted above, Rousseau's second Discourse turns out to be in fact a natural history of *equality,* despite its title, Millar's study is indeed a natural history of social ranks and classes.

19. Quoted in Teggart, *The Idea of Progress,* as cited, p. 205.

20. *Ibid.,* p. 207.

21. *Ibid.,* p. 208. It would be difficult to find anywhere a more penetrating and concise account of eighteenth-century natural history, as a method of studying human behavior, than Dugald Stewart's. It is, equally, a vantage point for surveying the nineteenth century's theory of social evolution.

CHAPTER 5. THE THEORY OF SOCIAL EVOLUTION

1. See the illuminating article by Kenneth E. Bock, "Darwin and Social Theory," *Philosophy of Science,* XXII (1955). Also Donald G. MacRae, *Ideology and Society: Papers in Sociology and Politics* (London: Heinemann, 1961), with its excellent treatment of the relation of Darwinism to social evolution (chs. 11 and 12).

2. Ernst Mayr, *Animal Species and Evolution* (Cambridge: The Belknap Press, Harvard University Press, 1963), pp. 5–6.

3. Spencer, *Essays,* as cited, pp. 9–10.

4. Comte, *Positive Philosophy,* as cited, Bk. VI, ch. 3, especially

pp. 218–28. I should like to pay my respect here to Kenneth E. Bock, *The Acceptance of Histories: Toward a Perspective for Social Science* (Berkeley: University of California Press, 1956) for its penetrating insights into social evolution as an idea-system. See also his article, "Evolution, Function, and Change" in *American Sociological Review*, 28, 2 (April 1963), 229–337.

5. I base this definition of social change on the treatment of change to be found in A. E. Taylor, *Elements of Metaphysics* (London: Methuen & Co., 1903). See Chapter 5 on change and causality.

6. See my "The Year 2000 and All That" in *Commentary*, 45, 6 (June 1968), 60–66. It is the assumption of linear directionality in historical change that lies behind efforts to predict the future—efforts which are rife at the present time, but which, as I emphasize in this article, have ever been an aspect of the Western philosophy of history or of development.

7. Durkheim abandoned his "panoramic" approach to social evolution with the completion of this book; he did not, however, abandon the cardinal elements of developmentalism in his subsequent works. He merely narrowed the focus. See Chapter 7 below.

8. It is worth recalling here that from Aristotle through Augustine and down to the modern exponents of the idea of progress, the essence of the theory of change set forth by each was its internal character; that is, its emergence from fixed and lasting forces contained *within* the entity under observation—whether this was the *polis*, mankind as a whole, or human knowledge. It is the assumption of internal sources of change that is, above anything else, the link between nineteenth-century social evolutionism and contemporary functionalism, a point I discuss in some detail in Chapters 7 and 8.

9. Leibniz, *The Monadology*, as cited, p. 44, n. 1.

10. Marx, *A Contribution to the Critique of Political Economy*, tr. from the 2nd German ed. by N. I. Stone (Chicago: Charles H. Kerr and Company, 1904), p. 13.

11. Comte, *The Positive Philosophy*, II, 299.

12. John Henry Newman, *An Essay on the Development of Christian Doctrine* (London: James Toovey, 1845), pp. 58, 63–64.

13. Darwin, *The Origin of the Species*, as cited, p. 361; see also p. 152.

14. *Ibid.*, p. 235.

15. *Ibid.*, p. 249. As I have stressed in several places in the book, Darwin's degree of adamancy on the principles of continuity and

uniform causation went beyond what even his most devoted supporters felt they could endorse. See on this Gertrude Himmelfarb, *Darwin and the Darwinian Revolution* (Anchor Books, New York: Doubleday & Company, 1962), especially ch. 4.

16. Comte, *The Positive Philosophy*, as cited, II, 228–9. Comte's approving quotation of Leibniz comes just before this passage.

17. *Ibid.*, III, 3.

18. Marx's words are to be found in the Preface to the first edition of *Capital*, I. Translation is by Moore and Aveling.

19. *Ibid.* "My standpoint, from which the evolution of the economic formation of society is viewed as a process of natural history. . . ."

20. Marx, *Critique of Political Economy*, as cited, p. 13.

21. Hegel, *Philosophy of History*, as cited, p. 57.

22. Darwin, *The Origin of the Species*, as cited, p. 93.

23. From the beginning, Marx's critics were aware of this aspect of his work despite all his protestations that he had dealt with the problem in strictly "material" terms. See, for example, Marx's not very successful replies to some of these criticisms in the Preface to the second edition of *Capital*. Turning Hegel right side up, as Marx described his use of the Hegelian dialectic, still leaves the substance essentially unchanged. For Marx, as I argue below, capitalism is a social system in pretty much the same sense that is today used by functionalists. Hence Marx's candid admission that human behavior is dealt with solely insofar as it is a reflection of *economic categories*. See the Preface to the first edition of *Capital*.

24. Marx, in the Preface to the first edition of *Capital*, as cited.

25. Tocqueville, *The Old Regime and the French Revolution*, tr. by Stuart Gilbert (Doubleday Anchor Books, New York: Doubleday and Company, 1955), p. 20.

26. See Teggart's treatment of this, *Theory of History*, as cited, pp. 127–9. Also Gertrude Himmelfarb, as cited, ch. 4. Hutton we think of as a "geologist"; but he was first and last a natural historian in precisely the sense that Rousseau, Ferguson, Adam Smith, and scores of others in the eighteenth century were. The earth, rather than equality, civil society, or economy, was the subject of his natural history.

27. Kant, *Idea for a Universal History*, as cited, p. 15.

28. Hence Rousseau's emphasis on avarice and ambition as persisting causes of the growth of the arts and sciences; hence Mandeville's thesis that in the evolution of mankind "private vices" are the lasting causes of "public benefits"; and hence too Adam Smith's

reliance upon the "instinct to truck and barter" as the uniform cause of growth of affluence, Ferguson's emphasis on conflict in individual personality and among social institutions, and so on in both the eighteenth and nineteenth centuries. In the theory of natural history and of social evolution alike the search for a uniform cause of development through time was hardly more than search for what Aristotle had called the "efficient" or "motor" cause.

29. Hegel, *Philosophy of History*, as cited, p. 57. Conflict is, of course, what the Hegelian dialectic is all about.

30. Comte, *The Positive Philosophy*, as cited, II, 227.

CHAPTER 6. THE COMPARATIVE METHOD

1. No one was more explicit on this point than Comte. "It is the selectest part, the vanguard of the human race, that we have to study: the greater part of the white race, or the European na- tions,—even restricting ourselves, at least in regard to modern times, to the nations of Western Europe. When we descend into the remoter past, it will be in search of the political ancestors of these peoples, whatever their country may be." *Positive Phi- losophy*, III, 1–2. What Comte wrote would have been found utterly acceptable by Hegel, Marx, Spencer, Morgan, Tylor, and the other social evolutionists of the century. What they thought of as "comparative" in their method was solely designed to rein- force the authenticity of the developmental series which had the modern West as the vanguard of the march of mankind.

2. John Linton Myres, "The Background of Greek Science," as cited, p. 18. See also Myres's *The Influence of Anthropology on the Course of Political Science* (Berkeley: University of Cali- fornia Press, 1916), *passim*.

3. Myres, *The Influence of Anthropology*, as cited, pp. 22–33. In Hobbes's day there were abundant reports coming in of the matriarchal institutions of Southern India, Negro Africa, and North America, and, as Myres notes, these reports certainly helped Hobbes to his anti-Aristotelian position that matriarchal dominion precedes patriarchal. Locke was well acquainted with the hunting and berry-eating Indians of North America but not the settled, agricultural Indian communities of the southeastern part. Hence he was spared a good deal of ethnological data which would have run strongly counter to his highly individualistic state of nature.

4. Turgot, "On the Successive Advances of the Human Mind" (Discourse at the Sorbonne, December 11, 1750), tr. by Leona Fassett (Neuhaus) in Teggart, *The Idea of Progress*, as cited, pp. 173–89. The quoted passage is on p. 174.

5. I would like to express my indebtedness here to Margaret T. Hodgen, *Early Anthropology in the Sixteenth and Seventeenth Centuries* (Philadelphia: University of Pennsylvania Press, 1964), and also to Katherine B. Oakes, "Social Theory in the Early Literature of Voyage and Exploration in Africa" (unpubl. Ph. D. diss., University of California, Berkeley Library, 1944), and Kenneth E. Bock, *The Acceptance of Histories*, as cited. See also Teggart, *Theory of History*, as cited. All of these deal accurately and authoritatively with the nature of the Comparative Method.

6. Comte, *The Positive Philosophy*, as cited, II, 250. "By this method," writes Comte (again for all the social evolutionists), "the different stages of evolution may all be observed at once" (*ibid.*, p. 249).

7. Edward B. Tylor, "On a Method of Investigating the Development of Institutions: Applied to Laws of Marriage and Descent," *Journal of the Royal Anthropological Institute*, XVIII (1889), 269.

8. Tylor, *Anthropology: An Introduction to the Study of Man and Civilization* (London, 1881; New York: J. A. Hill & Company, 1904), p. 19.

9. Margaret T. Hodgen, *The Doctrine of Survivals* (London: Allenson and Company, 1936). See also her *Early Anthropology*, as cited, especially ch. 11.

10. Talcott Parsons, *Societies: Evolutionary and Comparative Perspectives* (Englewood Cliffs: Prentice-Hall, 1966).

11. Gerhard Lenski, *Power and Privilege* (New York: McGraw-Hill, 1966).

CHAPTER 7. THE PERSISTENCE OF METAPHOR

1. Oswald Spengler, *The Decline of the West*, tr. by Charles F. Atkinson (New York: Alfred A. Knopf, 1926), I, 104 f.

2. Toynbee, "History" in *The Legacy of Greece*, ed. by R. W. Livingstone (Oxford: At the Clarendon Press, 1921), p. 290. See Toynbee, *A Study of History*, especially Volumes 1 through 5. I have used D. C. Somervell's abridgment (New York: Oxford University Press, 1947, 1957).

3. Nicolas Berdyaev, *The Meaning of History*, tr. by George Reavey (London: Geoffrey Bles, 1936), p. 194.

4. *Ibid.*, p. 194.

5. *Ibid.*, p. 121. "History is in truth the path to another world. It is in this sense that its content is religious. But the perfect state is impossible within history itself; it can only be realized outside its framework" (p. 197). Berdyaev's words are pure Augustine.

6. Reinhold Niebuhr, *The Nature and Destiny of Man: A Christian Interpretation* (Gifford Lectures, New York: Charles Scribner's Sons, 1943), II, 306.

7. *Ibid.*, p. 307.

8. Reinhold Niebuhr, *Faith and History* (New York: Charles Scribner's Sons, 1951), p. 233.

9. *Ibid.*, p. 233.

10. *Ibid.*, pp. 233–4.

11. *Ibid.*, p. 110.

12. *Ibid.*, p. 107.

13. V. Gordon Childe, *What Happened in History* (New York: Penguin Books, 1946), p. 275. "How has Man progressed during the several hundred thousand years of his existence on the Earth? That is the question to which this book offers an answer . . ." (Preface). This, of course, was the prime question of the eighteenth century.

14. Charles Galton Darwin, *The Next Million Years* (Dolphin Books, New York: Doubleday & Company, 1952), p. 149. Not that Sir Charles thought that it will all be free of interruptions, or that each and every nation will so progress. But then neither did Condorcet or Comte.

15. Pierre Teilhard de Chardin, *The Phenomenon of Man* (New York: Harper and Bros., 1959), pp. 112, 232.

16. *The Communist Blueprint for the Future: The Complete Text of All Four Communist Manifestos, 1848–1961* (New York: E. P. Dutton and Company, 1962), pp. 107, 118, 160.

17. Quoted by Leslie A. White, Foreword to *Evolution and Culture*, ed. by Marshall D. Sahlins and Elman R. Service (Ann Arbor: The University of Michigan Press, 1960).

18. Robert H. Lowie, *The Origin of the State* (New York: Harcourt, Brace & Co., 1927). See the Preface.

19. *Evolution and Culture*, as cited, pp. 23–4.

20. Parsons, *Societies: Evolutionary and Comparative Perspectives*, as cited. See ch. 1 *passim*.

21. Émile Durkheim, *The Rules of Sociological Method*, tr. by Sarah

A. Solovay and John H. Mueller and ed. by George E. G. Catlin (Glencoe, Ill.: The Free Press, 1950), p. 113.

22. Durkheim, *The Elementary Forms of the Religious Life,* tr. by Joseph Ward Swain (Glencoe, Ill.: The Free Press, 1947), p. 3.

23. Talcott Parsons, *The Social System* (Glencoe, Ill.: The Free Press, 1951), p. 535. In his very recent *Societies: Evolutionary and Comparative Perspectives,* Parsons writes: "At the most general theoretical levels, there is no difference between processes which serve to maintain a system and those which serve to change it" (p. 21).

24. A. R. Radcliffe-Brown, *A Natural Science of Society* (Glencoe, Ill.: The Free Press, 1957). See especially pp. 71–89.

25. Robert K. Merton, *Social Theory and Social Structure,* rev. and enl. ed. (Glencoe, Ill.: The Free Press, 1964), p. 40.

26. Talcott Parsons, "A Functional Theory of Change," in *Social Change: Sources, Patterns, and Consequences,* ed. by Amitai Etzioni and Eva Etzioni (New York: Basic Books, 1964), pp. 87 f.

27. Wilbert Moore, *Social Change* (Englewood Cliffs, N.J.: Prentice-Hall, 1963), pp. 18–21. I know of no one in modern sociology who has so ably set forth the key factors involved in any *systematic* theory of change. Like the others I have mentioned who are in the forefront of modern sociological theory, Professor Moore is well aware of history and the problems it presents to the study of change. This does not prevent him, any more than other theorists, from turning, however, to the premises of a non-historical developmentalism for the elements of his theory of change. Matters are no different, in short, from what they were in Comte's and Spencer's day.

28. Raymond Firth, *Elements of Social Organization* (Josiah Mason Lectures, University of Birmingham, Boston: Beacon Press, 1963), p. 83.

29. *Ibid.,* p. 82.

30. *Ibid.,* p. 86.

31. George P. Murdock, *Social Structure* (New York: The Macmillan Company, 1949), p. 199.

32. *Ibid.,* p. 198.

33. I refer to his *Societies: Evolutionary and Comparative Perspectives* (1966) as cited; also to such an article as "Evolutionary Universals in Society," *American Sociological Review,* XXIX, 3 (June 1964), 339–57. See also in the same issue Robert Bellah, "Religious Evolution," pp. 358–74. There is little question, it

seems to me, but that contemporary social science is undergoing a renascence of classical evolutionism at the present time.

CHAPTER 8. REFLECTIONS ON A METAPHOR

1. Lynn Thorndike, A Short History of Civilization (New York: Crofts and Company, 1963). What I have written of Thorndike's single-volume work holds equally for the massive, and eminently readable, The Story of Civilization by Will and Ariel Durant, which bids fair to be the most popular and widely read history of civilization ever written. Whether in one volume or ten, the so-called history of civilization tends invariably to reflect the same kind of ethnocentrism we found above to be inherent in the Comparative Method of the social evolutionists.

2. I have in mind the kind of heated, often bitter, and profoundly black-nationalist reaction precipitated by William Styron's brilliant novel, The Confessions of Nat Turner (New York: Random House, 1966). White historians are currently pleading with black historians to be objective, dispassionate, and sub specie aeternitatis, as they presumably hold themselves to be. They are not likely to have any more success, however, than critics ever have when a new nationalist historiography is emerging. Black historians are perfectly correct when they refer to the white nationalist foundations of most histories of the United States that are extant. Wherever there is historiography there is, by the nature of this enterprise, a set of preconceptions, and, given the immense influence of nationalism in the modern world—nationalism of whatever color or type—it would be strange if American history-writing were free of it, or could be.

3. W. W. Rostow, The Stages of Economic Growth: A Non-Communist Manifesto (Cambridge: Cambridge University Press, 1960), passim.

4. Marion Levy, The Family Revolution in Modern China (Cambridge: Harvard University Press, 1949).

5. Ibid., p. 86. My treatment of functionalism here is a revised and expanded version of my article "Social Structure and Social Change" in Research Studies of the State College of Washington, XX (June 1952).

6. Neil J. Smelser, Social Change in the Industrial Revolution: An Application of Theory to the British Cotton Industry (Chicago: The University of Chicago Press, 1959).

7. *Ibid.*, p. 3.
8. *Ibid.*, pp. 3–4.
9. *Ibid.*, p. 402.
10. *Ibid.*, p. 402. As I say, there is a great deal to be learned in this book about (1) modern functionalist theory and (2) social change in the cotton industry in a seventy-year period in England. With all respect to Professor Smelser I have to say, however, that any relation between (1) and (2) is purely Procrustean.
11. Parsons, as cited. Professor Parsons tells us that in his study he is guided by "both an evolutionary and comparative perspective," that "socio-cultural evolution, like organic evolution, has proceeded by variation and differentiation from simple to progressively more complex forms," that "we must be concerned with the evolutionary development of societies, both as wholes and in their principal parts," and that in his book he presents "a very broad—and tentative—schema that divides the evolution of societies (so far) into three stages: primitive, intermediate, and modern." For all the qualification implied by the words "tentative" and "so far" in the last, it is hard to see how there could ever be any need to replace the names he gives to his three great stages. They would appear to be unassailable within the limits of social evolutionary theory. How capacious his stages are can be gathered from the fact that within the second, "intermediate," he has societies as disparate and far flung in space and time as the Chinese imperial empire, the Indian caste system, the Islamic empires, and the Roman empire, among others.
12. *Ibid.*, p. 42.
13. *Ibid.*, pp. 47 f.
14. *Ibid.*, p. 23.
15. *Ibid.*, p. 111.
16. *Ibid.*, p. 111.
17. F. W. Maitland, "The Body Politic" in *Collected Papers*, ed. by H. A. L. Fisher (Cambridge: Cambridge University Press, 1911), III, 294 f. This is an appropriate note in which to express my profound admiration of, and indebtedness to, the work of George Caspar Homans who is a consummate historian and at the same time a sociologist who has ignored systems in favor of the concrete and finite study of social behavior. See *inter alia* his *English Villagers of the Thirteenth Century, Social Behavior,* and his most recent seminal little volume *The Nature of Social Science.*

18. There is no need to specify any of these works. Their number is legion, their variety nearly infinite. They are to be found in history, anthropology, sociology, geography, and also in the humanities. The identifying character of such studies is concern *in time and place* with some recognizable and persisting pattern of human thought or behavior, be it an idea, an idea-system, a custom, tradition, institution, social group, or social organization. Such studies are concerned with what actually happens in time and place rather than with justifications or illustrations of what would happen, or should happen, or might happen, or normally does happen, accidents and interferences set aside. Suffice it to say that in *none* of these empirical studies is the assumption ever made that, in Professor Parsons' words, "there is no difference between processes which serve to maintain a system and those which serve to change it" (*Societies*, as cited, p. 21).

19. Wilbert Moore's wise insistence on this point is one of the several distinguished features of his *Social Change*, as cited, pp. 28 f. See all of ch. 2, "The Qualities of Change." Professor Moore's study is a rarity in contemporary social theory in that it also emphasizes the vital difference between change and mere activity, motion, and interaction.

20. None more vividly, more overwhelmingly indeed, than the idea-system that is the subject of this book: the metaphor of growth and development. There is literally nothing in contemporary functionalism that Aristotle (and before him Heraclitus) could not feel perfectly at home with, perfectly responsible for.

21. John Livingston Lowes, *Convention and Revolt in Poetry* (London: Constable and Co., 1919). See especially pp. 34 f.

22. This is the distinctive feature of the brilliant and also profound study by Thomas S. Kuhn, *The Structure of Scientific Revolutions* (Phoenix Books, Chicago: The University of Chicago Press, 1962). Here is an excellent example of the contrast between what actual, thoughtful investigation of persistence and change leads to in the way of generalization and the kind of conventional wisdom in our social theory that relies simply upon the metaphor-derived concepts of growth, differentiation, endemic motivation, etc., and which seeks to derive crucial properties of change from properties of social structure.

23. Teggart, *Theory of History*, as cited, p. 148.

24. Max Weber, *The Protestant Ethic and the Spirit of Capitalism*, tr. by Talcott Parsons (New York: Charles Scribner's Sons, 1958).

25. Marx, *Capital*, as cited, Preface to first edition.

26. Weber's monumental studies in the comparative history of religion are the primary setting for this investigation.

27. Radcliffe-Brown, *A Natural Science of Society*, as cited, p. 87.

28. See the introductory pages of Ernst Mayr's great work, *Animal Species and Evolution*, as cited.

29. See, for example, the all-too-deadly criticisms of Toynbee's *A Study of History*, among them, and at their best and most relevant, that of Pieter Geyl, the distinguished Dutch historian. See also Teggart's removal of the problem of the so-called decline and fall of Rome from metaphoric process to actual correlations of events involving peoples remote from the borders of the Roman empire: *Rome and China: A Study of Correlations in Historical Events* (Berkeley: University of California Press, 1939).

30. See Teggart, *The Processes of History* (New Haven: Yale University Press, 1918), especially chs. 2 and 3, for an early and systematic emphasis on this. The whole, vast literature on contacts of peoples, on migrations, and on cultural impact is, of course, filled with evidences of what I am here stressing.

31. See Teggart, *The Processes of History*, as cited, ch. 3.

32. Gustave Glotz, *The Greek City*, tr. by N. Mallinson (New York: Alfred A. Knopf, 1930). Also John Linton Myres, *The Political Ideas of the Greeks* (New York: Methodist Book Concern, 1927). Both of these books offer fine insight into the processes of cultural change involved.

33. See Turgot's *Researches into the Causes of the Progress and Decline of the Sciences and Arts* and also his *Plan for a Work on Political Geography*. See Hume's essay "Rise and Progress of the Arts and Sciences" and Teggart's commentary on both writers in his *Theory of History*, as cited, Chapter 15.

34. Contrast the kind of conventional wisdom regarding change in kinship that comes from the whole social evolutionary tradition —Morgan, Engels, Spencer, down to the latest functionalist study of kinship—with the kind of genuine insight that is gained from such a *historical* study as George E. Howard, *A History of Matrimonial Institutions* (Chicago: University of Chicago Press, 1904). See also my "Kinship and Political Power in First Century Rome" in *Sociology and History*, ed. by Werner J. Cahnman and Alvin Boskoff (Glencoe, Ill.: The Free Press, 1964), pp. 257–71.

The way in which the glaring contrast between social evolutionary vacuities regarding change and the concrete insights of the historical tradition of study is commonly handled by functional theorists is to refer to the former as "general" theory and the latter as "particular." This would be fine if only there were the slightest relation between the central elements of the one and the other. But there isn't. It is like trying to derive grapes from oranges.

35. This classic has so often been dealt with in terms of the categories of social organization and of social deviance that its profound relevance to the study of social change tends to be overlooked. Even with due regard for the criticisms of the book made by Herbert Blumer, *The Polish Peasant* remains, without any question, I believe, the greatest single study done thus far by an American sociologist. Had American sociology somehow managed to follow the lines of guidance contained in this remarkable work, it would not be so largely lost today in its tortuous and too often vapid categories and concepts relating to social systems and their asserted properties.

36. William Graham Sumer's *Folkways* is another classic that might well be dusted off for use in courses in *social change* rather than for the familiar and tedious purpose of exemplifying "obstacles to change."

37. See my "Social Structure and Social Change" in *Research Studies of the State College of Washington*, XX (June 1952). Also "History and Sociology" in the volume of my essays, *Tradition and Revolt* (New York: Random House, 1968). The latter essay was first published in 1957 in the *Bucknell Review*. By "functionalist studies of cultures, groups, and customs" I am referring most especially to the vital literature in British social anthropology, especially relating to East Africa and South Africa, that emanated so largely from the influences of Malinowski and Radcliffe-Brown and that was highlighted by its explicit studies of the impact of European on African native.

38. Cited by Geoffrey Barraclough, *History in a Changing World* (Oxford: Basil Blackwell, 1956), pp. 222–3. Fisher's words are from the Preface of his great *History of Europe*.

39. Talcott Parsons, *Societies*, as cited, where everything that is held to be distinctively Western is also held to be, in the evolutionary sense, "modern" and thus to characterize a mode of development characteristic of mankind—apart only, of course, from the interferences, stagnations, and deflections which may be categorically swept into that all-important bin known to social evolutionists as "divergence."

40. See my *The Sociological Tradition* (New York: Basic Books, Inc., 1967) where I have dealt with the principal perspectives of contemporary sociology as products of a century's obsessive concern with this particular direction.

41. Parsons, *Societies*, as cited, p. 42, n. 33.

42. Siegfried Kracauer, "Time and History" in *History and the Concept of Time*, as cited, pp. 66, 68.

43. Durkheim, *The Rules of Sociological Method*, as cited, pp. 116 f.

44. *Ibid.*, p. 117.

45. *Ibid.*, p. 117.

46. Siegfried Kracauer, as cited, p. 66.

47. Geoffrey Barraclough, as cited, pp. 4–5.

48. J. H. Hexter, "The Rhetoric of History" in *International Encyclopedia of the Social Sciences* (New York: Macmillan, 1968), XI, 368–94, especially pp. 374–80.

49. *Uniformity and Simplicity: A Symposium on the Principle of the Uniformity of Nature*, ed. by Claude C. Albritton, Jr. (Geological Society of America, New York, 1967). I know of nothing within many years that has so ably explored the issues involved in the study of change in time which stem from uniformitarianism.

50. Raymond Firth, *Elements of Social Organization*, as cited, pp. 39–40.

51. *Ibid.*, p. 82.

52. *Ibid.*, p. 83.

53. George P. Murdock, *Social Structure*, as cited, p. 199.

54. Parsons, *The Social System*, as cited, p. 535. And, since *The Social System* was published twenty years ago, it is well to cite again Professor Parsons' very recent statement in his *Societies* . . . , p. 21: "At the most general theoretical levels, *there is no difference between processes which serve to maintain a social system and those which serve to change it.*" (Italics added.) From the mighty Greek concept of *physis*, drawn by the pre-Socratics from metaphor and myth and rationalized by Plato and Aristotle into the foundation of the science of society, through St. Augustine's momentous fusion of the Greek and Hebrew traditions, down through Leibniz, Condorcet, Comte, Spencer, and Marx, all the way to the conventional wisdom of current social theory, especially in its functionalist forms, this has been the sovereign goal of the study of human society: to find in one and the same set of properties the crucial attributes of stability and change alike.

55. Which does not mean, of course, that the language of history is incompatible with the language of science: that is, with a *scientific and comparative study of social change*, its sources, mechanisms, patterns, and impacts. Such a science of social change will have little if any dependence, however, upon the metaphor-based concepts of social developmentalism and upon the second-hand, overhauled terms borrowed loosely from biology.

INDEX

Adam, as seed of human race, 80-87, 90-91
Adams, Brooks, 134-36
Adams, Henry, 134-36
Adams, John Quincy, 134
Adonis, seed-myth of, 18
Aeschylus, 48, 52-55, 107, 110
Alaric and sack of Rome, 63
Albritton, Claude, 327
Analogy of life cycle, 8-11; in Christian thought, 62, 66-70; in contemporary thought, 211-23; in Greek thought, 17-24; in modern thought, 104-14
Apostle, Hippocrates G., 305
Aristotle, 8, 9, 15, 16, 24-29, 30, 31, 35, 37, 38-41, 48, 54, 63, 107, 110, 116, 136, 143, 157, 184, 192, 193, 212, 213, 214, 220, 223, 268, 275, 279, 284, 288
Atkinson, Charles F., 319
Augustine, Saint, 8, 10, 29, 50, 62-103, 105, 106, 107, 113, 114, 118, 125, 130, 136, 149, 172, 173, 180, 184, 211, 213, 217, 218, 219, 220, 223, 251

Bacon, Francis, 8, 98, 99, 101-3, 113
Bacon, Roger, 98, 99
Bagehot, Walter, 280
Bailey, Cyril, 307
Barker, Ernest, 314
Barraclough, Geoffrey, 292-93, 326
Barraclough, June, 312
Beck, Lewis White, 312
Becoming, genetic idea of: Augustinian-Christian, 63-70, 76-85; among Greeks, 15-29; in idea of progress, 104-25; in theory of social evolution, 166-88
Bellah, Robert, 321
Berdyaev, Nicholas, 8, 77, 217-18
Berlin, Isaiah, 76-77
Black nationalism, 250
Blumer, Herbert, 326

Boas, Franz, 224, 228
Bock, Kenneth, 315, 316, 319
Bodin, Jean, 99
Boileau, Etienne, 107
Bonald, Louis de, 126, 131-32
Boskoff, Alvin, 325
Bossuet, Jacques-Bénigne, 66, 67
Briffault, Robert, 232
Bryson, Gladys, 314
Buckle, Henry T., 135
Burckhardt, Jacob, 126, 133-34
Bury, J. B., 46-47, 106, 311

Cahnman, Werner, 325
Campbell, Lewis, 307-8
Cannan, Edwin, 315
Cartesianism, 108-10
Carthage, 35
Catlin, George E. G., 321
Cause, doctrine of: in theory of change, Aristotelian, 25, 27-29; Augustinian, 85-90; in theory of social development, 182-88
Change: and continuity, 287-94; and crisis, 282-83; defined, 168; and development, 166-88, 223-39, Chs. 1-5, *passim*; and directionality, 284-87; and events, 275-82; and fixity, 270-74, 283-84; and functionalism, 228-39, 256-57; as growth, 7-11, 15-16, Chs. 1-5 *passim*; and history, 268ff.; and immanence, 276-82; and natural history, 139-58; and social behavior, 268-70; and social systems, 228-29
Chaucer, 302
Childe, V. Gordon, 220
Chinard, Gilbert, 313
Chomsky, Noam, 301
Christ and doctrine of cycles, 62, 72, 75
Christian epic, as philosophy of history and development: Augustinian, 62-103; contemporary, 217-20

329